CULTURE SHOCK!

A Survival Guide to Customs and Etiquette

MALAYSIA

Kate Mayberry

T0294102

Marshall Cavendish
Editions

Published by Marshall Cavendish Editions
An imprint of Marshall Cavendish International

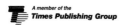

A member of the
Times Publishing Group

Other Marshall Cavendish Offices:
Marshall Cavendish Corporation, 99 White Plains Road, Tarrytown NY 10591-9001, USA • Marshall Cavendish International (Thailand) Co Ltd, 253 Asoke, 12th Flr, Sukhumvit 21 Road, Klongtoey Nua, Wattana, Bangkok 10110, Thailand • Marshall Cavendish (Malaysia) Sdn Bhd, Times Subang, Lot 46, Subang Hi-Tech Industrial Park, Batu Tiga, 40000 Shah Alam, Selangor Darul Ehsan, Malaysia.

Marshall Cavendish is a registered trademark of Times Publishing Limited

National Library Board, Singapore Cataloguing-in-Publication Data

Name(s): Mayberry, Kate.
Title: CultureShock! Malaysia : a survival guide to customs and etiquette / Kate Mayberry.
Other title(s): Malaysia: a survival guide to customs and etiquette. | Culture shock Malaysia. | Series: Culture shock!
Description: Singapore : Marshall Cavendish Editions, 2019.
Identifier(s): OCN 1102616165 | ISBN 978-981-47-9451-0 (paperback)
Subject(s): LCSH: Etiquette--Malaysia. | Malaysia--Social life and customs. | Malaysia--Description and travel.
Classification: DDC 959.5 --dc23

Printed in Singapore

Photo Credits:
All photos by the author except pages viii (Omar Elsharawy on unsplash.com); xi (Izuddin Helmi Adnan on unsplash.com); and 217 (Joshua Anand on unsplash.com). Cover photo by Jegathisan Manoharan (pexels.com)

All illustrations by TRIGG

ABOUT THE SERIES

Culture shock is a state of disorientation that can come over anyone who has been thrust into unknown surroundings, away from one's comfort zone. *CultureShock!* is a series of trusted and reputed guides which has, for decades, been helping expatriates and long-term visitors to cushion the impact of culture shock whenever they move to a new country.

Written by people who have lived in the country and experienced culture shock themselves, the authors share all the information necessary for anyone to cope with these feelings of disorientation more effectively. The guides are written in a style that is easy to read and covers a range of topics that will arm readers with enough advice, hints and tips to make their lives as normal as possible again.

Each book is structured in the same manner. It begins with the first impressions that visitors will have of that city or country. To understand a culture, one must first understand the people—where they came from, who they are, the values and traditions they live by, as well as their customs and etiquette. This is covered in the first half of the book.

Then on with the practical aspects—how to settle in with the greatest of ease. Authors walk readers through how to find accommodation, get the utilities and telecommunications up and running, enrol the children in school and keep in the pink of health. But that's not all. Once the essentials are out of the way, venture out and try the food, enjoy more of the culture and travel to other areas. Then be immersed in the language of the country before discovering more about the business side of things.

To round off, snippets of information are offered before readers are 'tested' on customs and etiquette. Useful words and phrases, a comprehensive resource guide and list of books for further research are also included for easy reference.

CONTENTS

ACKNOWLEDGEMENTS

In the course of my work as a journalist I have met all kinds of Malaysians, from prime ministers to eager schoolboy footballers, transgender activists, market stallholders and high-flying bankers, and travelled to every state of the country (with the glaring exception of Perlis).

Those experiences inform the heart of this book, which I hope provides a flavour of what it is like to live in Malaysia today and answers at least some of the many questions you may have about this fascinating, but all too frequently overlooked country.

Help and advice came from far too many people for me to name them individually, but special mentions must go to my wonderful husband and daughter who put up with endless questions, gave valuable insight—particularly on food—and provided necessary encouragement.

Researching and writing this book has given me another excuse to read and the opportunity to revisit old classics like Rehman Rashid's *A Malaysian Journey,* which was one of the first books I read when I decided to move to Malaysia and convinced me I had made the right choice.

While much of my working life has tended to involve late night discussions over glasses of tea lamenting the state of Malaysia with despondent activists, the historic change of government in May 2018 has triggered a renewed sense of optimism.

This is truly an exciting time to be in Malaysia. Make the most of it.

Just another day in Malaysia's busy capital city.

PREFACE

My first home in Kuala Lumpur was a post-independence two-bedroom flat with parquet floors and an expansive balcony in the city's eastern hills, surrounded by tropical gardens and forest, and home to wild boar, monkeys and native birds. I expect there were snakes there too, but I never saw them.

The road to the apartment block took me along tree-shaded roads past 1950s-style terraced houses, sprawling mansions and patches of jungle. After it rained, mist would settle over the tarmac. All this only seven kilometres from the Twin Towers.

I had moved from Singapore, where I'd arrived a few years before with only a rucksack, packing my now rather more extensive possessions into the back of a locally-hired truck and hoping that customs would allow the consignment through and that nothing would be broken on the 350-kilometre journey north. As it happened, the border proved relatively smooth and the only casualty was a riotously coloured fruit bowl that I didn't even realise had gone missing until a few months later.

The apartment was a retreat from the frenetic activity of the city and the endless traffic jams—I soon learned that I had to leave for work at 6.45am if I wanted to have a stress-free start to the working day; if I left just five minutes later the traffic would be bumper-to-bumper and the space between each lane of cars filled by an apparently endless stream of moped riders.

The area itself was a sharp contrast with Singapore, where, although we'd also lived in a walk-up apartment, everything seemed more carefully manicured and the city appeared to be engaged in a constant battle for control—of nature, people, climate. In KL and its suburbs, people seemed more willing to let things be. Beyond a strange predilection for topiary, particularly in the city centre, trees grew wild, bougainvillea spilled from houses, road verges were left untended for months, and kerbstones, where they existed, were painted only rarely. And while the Malaysian capital was less wealthy than Singapore, it had a spirit that often seemed lacking in its more prosperous southern neighbour.

At that time, Malaysia was still emerging from the Asian Financial Crisis that had brought years of rapid economic growth to an end. My four-storey block, with just two flats on each floor, had few residents. Sometimes the water that spluttered out of the tap was brown with sediment. Every few months the power disappeared. Even the phone line was unreliable, although we later discovered that was the fault of the resident macaques who liked to while away the afternoons playing with the junction box.

From the balcony, we looked out towards the Twin Towers, a symbol of the country's meteoric rise. Emerging from the grounds of an old race course, the towers dominate a skyline dotted with the half-finished visions of buildings that had been brought to a premature end with the recession.

The pool at our apartment block was renowned for the packs of monkeys that had made their home there. According to urban myth, they had stolen numerous outfits from unsuspecting residents, raided fridges and destroyed apartments. I had pooh-poohed such stories, but when I went to the pool one morning came across a group of them lounging about at the top of the steps, picking out fleas from each other's fur. There were a couple of babies clinging to their mothers and some big monkeys too. I thought they would move. They thought I would. We stared at each other for a while. I took a step forward. They carried on sitting. The large males looked decidedly hostile. Teeth were bared. I realised this wasn't a stand-off I was going to win and retreated back to my apartment.

Sparkling, modern, iconic—the Petronas Twin Towers designed by Cesar Pelli are still the tallest twin towers in the world today.

> When my daughter was about three we decided to splurge on a weekend break at The Datai in Langkawi. The resort is one of the region's most stunning, built within an ancient rainforest with views across the emerald waters of the Andaman Sea to Thailand. One morning, when the light was particularly beautiful, I stepped out onto the balcony to take a photo of the scene. Heeding the warnings pasted to the windows about marauding troops of macaques waiting for their moment to sneak into the rooms of unsuspecting guests, I made sure to close the door behind me, but was astonished when I turned around to see a hairy grey monkey about the same height as my daughter standing in front of her, eyeing the cookie she was just about to put in her mouth. The scene played out in slow motion, as we grabbed the cushions from the sofa and threw them at the intruder and the monkey grabbed the cookie from my shocked daughter's hands, turned on its heels and rushed out of the door.

Malaysians themselves were bruised but unbowed. Mahathir Mohamad, then nearing the end of his first term in office (although no one yet knew that) had boosted morale with a year-long tax holiday even as his decision to fire his former deputy Anwar Ibrahim and put him on trial for corruption and sodomy undermined his hold on power.

The process of change was underway, although few could have imagined that two decades later, the two men would reunite in a successful election bid that would end the political dominance of the United Malays National Organisation (UMNO) and its Barisan Nasional (National Front) coalition after the incumbent prime minister became embroiled in a multi-billion dollar fraud scandal described by the US Department of Justice as one of the worst cases of kleptocracy it had ever known.

Even before moving to the country, I had always found Malaysia an easier place to work as a journalist than Singapore—the government might have been semi-autocratic but people were more open, and more willing to share an opinion even if it ran contrary to the official view.

Indeed, sitting in the local coffee shop, a cup of milky tea or coffee in hand, discussing the latest political gossip seemed almost a national pastime.

Over the years, of course, I have come to understand that beyond that somewhat superficial 'first impression' there are many layers to Malaysia's political and cultural discourse and that race and religion, all too frequently exploited by political leaders, continue to cast a long shadow over Malaysian life much as they have since the British adopted a policy of 'divide and rule' to better maintain their control of the Southeast Asian territory.

When I introduce myself to a Malaysian and the conversation comes around to the fact that I am married to a local, the first question is always about race. "Is he Malay, Chinese or Indian?" they ask, in that order and never any other. In 20 years and numerous encounters, only one Malaysian has not asked the question. The question, I suppose, helps that particular Malaysian decide how best to deal with me. But the order of the question is revealing too: Is it that Western women who are married to locals are more likely to be married to Malays—hence putting Malay first—or is it indicative of a kind of national pecking order, an order of supposed importance?

What it means to be Malaysian, and how to keep such a diverse group of peoples together, is a question the country has been struggling with since even before independence in 1957. Some six decades later, it seems it is no closer to finding an answer.

MAP OF MALAYSIA

CHAPTER 1

FIRST IMPRESSIONS

‘We are all Malaysians. This is the bond that unites us.’

**— Tunku Abdul Rahman,
first prime minister of Malaysia**

What you'll notice first:

1. **The humidity**. It's inescapable, and the first thing that will hit you, particularly if you are used to a temperate climate, when you emerge from the the air-conditioned comfort of the airport. Humidity also means plenty of rain and combined with the heat (see point 2), regular and spectacular thunderstorms.

2. **The heat**. Also inescapable. When the temperature falls to 22 degrees Celsius, as it sometimes does, Malaysians put on sweaters and complain about how cold it is.

3. **Greenery**. The lush landscape comes with the year-round humidity. The orderly lines of palm oil and rubber plantations start at the boundary fence of Kuala Lumpur International Airport, and cover much of the peninsula (and an increasing area of the Borneo states of Sabah and Sarawak). In between, the more chaotic landscape of the millennia-old tropical rainforest survives. Cities like Kuala Lumpur are developing fast—buildings replaced, highways expanded—but trees are, for now, still more common than in many other Asian metropolises. Some of the oldest and most beautiful raintrees, their branches reaching out into a canopy across the car park and manicured lawns, can be found within the grounds of the Royal Selangor Golf Club in the heart of Kuala Lumpur. The Forest Reserve Institute of Malaysia, just 20 kilometres from the city centre, offers a more rustic jungle experience for urban residents.

4. A majority of Malaysia's 32 million people are Muslim and, for the most part, both men and women **dress conservatively**. This does not mean women are required to cover their heads, although many Muslim women choose to do so, but when visiting government offices it is advisable to dress appropriately: shirts, trousers and proper shoes for men (no flip-flops or sandals), covered shoulders and a longer skirt or trousers for women.

5. Malaysia is one of the world's most **ethnically diverse** countries. The trading routes that put Malaysia on the map brought people to the country from all over the globe, some of whom married and stayed, creating unique blended cultures with their own traditions, foods and dress. These days, the majority of the country's people are known as *bumiputra* (sons of the soil), a designation that includes the majority ethnic Malays who are Muslim, as well as some indigenous people. Together, they make up about 68.8 per cent of the population

The ornate, 19th-century home of the Chans, a wealthy Peranakan family in Melaka. The house became a museum in the 1980s.

and are entitled to special treatment in getting loans, buying property and securing places at local universities. There are also large numbers of ethnic Chinese (23 per cent), whose ancestors started coming to Southeast Asia as early as the 15th century, as well as citizens of Indian ancestry (7 per cent). In Melaka, Penang and Singapore, the earliest Chinese settlers married local Malay women and together created the Peranakan (or Nyonya) culture with its distinctive food, fashion and culture. The orang asal, the original inhabitants of the peninsular, continue to live in the forest, but face growing pressure from logging companies and their political supporters. The country's enormous diversity also means you'll hear Malaysians switching easily between different languages. From the official national language of Bahasa Malaysia/Bahasa Melayu to English, Mandarin, Tamil, indigenous languages such as Iban and Kadazandusun, and a wealth of other dialects (even for Malay). According to the CIA World Factbook, Malaysia has 134 living languages.

6. **Incredible food**. A result of the country's ethnic mix, which means spicy curries laced with coconut milk,

freshly grilled satays, noodle soups of everything from curry to prawns to fish balls and pork, and laksas unique to almost every state. And that's just for starters. It is impossible to tire of the food in Malaysia. No wonder Bahasa Malaysia has so many words for delicious.

Hawker food remains hugely popular throughout Malaysia and the best stalls may have been in families for generations.

7. **Religion**. Malaysians, particularly the ethnic Malays who are Muslim by birth, take their faith seriously. Under the constitution, Islam is the country's official religion, but followers of other faiths are guaranteed the right to profess and practice their religion. There are mosques in every town and suburb (smaller places of worship are known as *surau*) with prayer rooms in shopping malls, offices and even airports and railway stations. There are also numerous Chinese temples (usually Buddhist or

Taoist), Hindu places of worship and Sikh *gurdwaras*. Most churches were built during colonial times, but these days there are also Evangelical Christian congregations holding services in converted shops and cavernous former factories.

Lanterns decorating the courtyard at the Cheng Hoon Teng temple.

8. **Acronyms**. Malaysians love them. Almost as much as Singaporeans. Kuala Lumpur is KL (kay-el), Petaling Jaya is PJ (pee-jay). Then there's the LDP (Lebuhraya Damansara Puchong—a highway), the MRT (Mass Rapid Transit), LRT (Light Rail Transit), KLIA (Kuala Lumpur International Airport), ERL (Express Rail Link), MAS (Malaysia Airlines) … And every town seems to have the name of success—Jaya.

9. **Traffic**. LOTS of it. Not on the scale of Jakarta, Bangkok or Manila, but KL still has lots of cars. Even with the arrival of a new metro line, congestion remains a problem and journeys to and from the city centre are usually a crawl at peak times; on occasion it can take as long as two hours to cover the ten kilometres between the city and the inner suburbs in the west popular with foreign residents. Friday nights can be gridlock, especially when it rains. During holiday seasons, everyone takes to the roads, bringing the main North-South highway and the Karak highway, which connects the east and west coasts, to a halt. Be prepared to spend a lot of time stuck in traffic. Charge up the phone, get some snacks and make sure you have been to the toilet before you embark on your journey. The sheer volume of cars also means that parking is a nightmare. Malaysians think nothing of double or even triple parking. Most of the time, the culprit will leave a note on your windscreen, but if they have not and a car

is blocking your exit, the custom is to press your horn continuously until the driver comes out and moves their vehicle.

10. **Shopping malls**. Malaysians love shopping malls—by the end of 2019 there are expected to be nearly 700 across the country—but not necessarily because they love to shop (although it seems they do). In such a hot, humid and occasionally oppressive climate, an air-conditioned shopping mall is a great place to cool down, and it is not too expensive either—if you can avoid the lure of the shops and cafés and just wander the marble walkways.

CHAPTER 2

GEOGRAPHY AND HISTORY

*There were days of cloudless skies and
unforgiving heat, but the one impression
that remains now is of rain, falling from a bank of
low floating clouds, smearing the landscape
into a Chinese brush painting.*

— Tan Twan Eng, *The Gift of Rain*

Malaysia is made up of two parts—west and east—covering a total land area of 328,657 square kilometres separated by the expanse of the South China Sea. West Malaysia, otherwise known as Peninsular Malaysia, extends for more than 1,000 kilometres from Thailand's southern border down to Cape Piai, the most southerly point of the Asian continent, which lies just north of the equator.

The so-called main range, or Titiwangsa range, is the mountainous and forested spine that runs almost the length of the peninsula (rising as high as 2,134 metres) and remains a distinct barrier between its east and west coasts, as it has done since the first explorers fought their way into the interior. The highest peak on the peninsula is Gunung Tahan at 2,207 metres, in the central part of the country.

A highway across the mountains was finished in the 1970s, and now runs as far as Kuala Terengganu on the east coast, significantly reducing the time it takes to drive across the country. Political manoeuvring and the Asian Financial Crisis stretched construction to two decades with the final stretches opening only in 2015, and the road is still in the process of being extended further north. It will eventually end in the northeastern state of Kelantan.

Although the project has been the subject of much controversy, mainland Chinese companies are also building a railway that will skirt the mountains and provide another way for people and cargo to travel between the east and west. The existing railway line to the northeast was completed between 1910 and 1930 and takes between nine and ten hours to cut through the country's forested heart.

Despite the pressures of development, the mountainous jungle terrain remains a haven for endangered wildlife including tigers and elephants. The mountains are also the source of many of the rivers that run to the Strait of Malacca in the west or South China Sea in the east and provide much of the country's drinking water.

The peninsula has 11 states, from the agricultural 'rice bowl' of the northwest—Perlis and Kedah—to the more laid-back and conservative east coast—Kelantan and Terengganu—where life continues to move to the rhythm of the climate even with recent (often controversial) efforts to develop more industry in the area.

Rice remains a staple of Malaysian cooking. It is typically grown in the states of the northwest.

The central state of Pahang, the biggest in the peninsula, includes the ancient rainforests of Taman Negara, Malaysia's national park, but stretches as far as the South China Sea, while Selangor, which hugs the west coast on one side and Kuala Lumpur on the other, is the richest part of the country.

Johor takes up most of the southern part of the peninsula. In between are the smaller states of Penang, Perak, Melaka and the so-called Federal Territories of Kuala Lumpur and Putrajaya, the administrative centre that was built at the end of the 1990s.

Originally the home of the most senior colonial official, Carcosa Seri Negara in KL later became a government guest house, then luxury hotel. It was used as the location for Nick's family home in *Crazy Rich Asians*.

Tin ore and natural resources were what helped make the city of Kuala Lumpur, and the states of Perak and Selangor wealthy, leaving behind an architectural legacy of ornate mansions and homes that still survive—despite the march of development—in smaller cities like Ipoh and George Town, and in isolated enclaves around the parts of Kuala Lumpur that have managed to avoid the clutches of the developers.

East Malaysia is a two-hour flight away from Kuala Lumpur and is made up of the two Borneo states of Sabah and Sarawak, which agreed to join Singapore and the states of the Malayan peninsula in 1963 to create the country known as Malaysia.

In size and scale, both Sabah and Sarawak dwarf all of the peninsula states—Sabah covers 73,631 square kilometres and Sarawak a colossal 124,450 square kilometres. Borneo as a whole is the world's third-largest island. Sabah is the location of Mount Kinabalu (at 4,095 metres the highest peak in Malaysia and one of the tallest mountains in Southeast Asia) and also boasts some of the world's most stunning dive sites. The two Malaysian states share a border with Indonesia (the province is known as Kalimantan) and Brunei, where the Sultan remains an absolute monarch.

Adding to the sense of separation, the two states have jurisdiction over their own immigration. Malaysians from the peninsula are not allowed to work in Borneo without a permit and can be, and have been, barred from entry. Foreign visitors, even though they might have 'arrived' in Malaysia when they showed their passports to immigration officers at KLIA, will need to go through the whole process again once they arrive in the Borneo states.

THE CLIMATE

There is nothing quite like a tropical downpour: the rain comes in sheets, cascading off roof tops, the sound of falling raindrops drowning out everything else.

Traditionally, Malaysia has two seasons a year—the wet (monsoon) season and the not-so-wet season—but the weather has become more unpredictable in recent years and now it is not unusual for there to be rain when it is supposed to be dry and dry when it should be raining. In the past, most beach resorts on the east coast would close for the monsoon season, but these days many stay open and some even offer refunds if it rains for more than a certain number of hours in the day.

The timing of the monsoon depends on whether you're on the west or east coast of the peninsula, or in Borneo. The monsoon on the east coast tends to start around October and continue until the end of February, bringing spectacular storms, rough seas and the risk of flooding. At the end of 2014, towns and villages across the east and south of the country were inundated and at least 21 people lost their lives. Some parts of the highway connecting the two sides of the peninsula were also submerged beneath the flood waters.

On the west coast, the monsoon lasts from the end of May to the beginning of October manifesting itself in thunderstorms in the late afternoon and early evening.

Usually, it is hottest around August and September: the time of year which has been plagued by the so-called 'haze' from the burning of forest owned by plantation companies in Indonesia, and sometimes Malaysia itself. Some laugh wryly that thanks to the haze pollution the country now has three seasons, but some years have been so bad that schools have been forced to close and people urged to stay indoors.

Even outside the monsoon season, humidity in Malaysia remains extraordinarily high; the thick, sticky air wraps itself around your face every time you step outside, glasses mist up, and condensation forms not on the inside of the car windscreen (as in cold climates), but on the outside. Given the country's position just north of the equator the humidity is not at all surprising, but for people used to more temperate climates it does take a while to get used to. A check on any weather app at any time during the year will usually show the temperature in Kuala Lumpur between 25 and 35 degrees Celsius with humidity upwards of 80 per cent, and regular downpours.

The only places where it is cool on the peninsula are the hill resorts—Cameron Highlands, Genting Highlands, Fraser's and Maxwell Hill—where temperatures can drop to about 15 degrees Celsius at night. It is not unusual in these areas to see people wrapped up in winter jackets and wearing woolly hats once the sun has gone down.

Tea bushes on the valleys of Cameron Highlands. Tea was first grown here by the Russell family, founders of Boh Tea.

Given its elevation, temperatures drop sharply at night on Kinabalu, as well. Of course, the other places where it is decidedly chilly are offices and shopping malls. Most people bring sweaters to work to beat off the air-conditioning.

HISTORY

The nation of Malaysia as we know it today is actually relatively new—created in 1963 when the Borneo states of Sabah (then a British colony known as North Borneo) and Sarawak (also a British colony, but before that a private fiefdom of the Brooke family) decided to join Malaya to form a new federated nation. Singapore was also part of the initial Malaysia Agreement, but the island went its own way just two years later as political tensions between the country's constituent parts increased. Singapore's departure left Malaysia with 13 states, and a multicultural population majority Malay but with significant minorities of Chinese, Indians and indigenous people.

Homo sapiens, modern human beings, have been living in the parts of Southeast Asia now known as Malaysia for millennia.

In Sarawak's Niah Caves, British palaeontologists unearthed a fossilised skull thought to be as many as 35,000 years old back in 1958, while evidence of early human settlement has also been found in Perak on the peninsula where archaeologists in the Lenggong Valley unearthed 'Perak Man' in 1991, the skeleton of a Stone Age man, which is now preserved in a museum close to the cave where it was found.

About an hour north of Penang, in the Bujang Valley, archaeologists have also discovered the remains of what they think may be the country's oldest settlement. The Kedah Tua (Old Kedah) Kingdom is thought to be about 1,900 years old, which makes it older than the empires of the Majapahit (AD1200) and Sri Vijaya (AD700), and the first Malay Hindu-Buddhist kingdom in the Malaysian peninsular.

Mokhtar Saidi, an Associate Professor at Penang's Universiti Sains Malaysia who led the dig, says he believes Kedah Tua was both a centre of iron ore manufacture and an early port city—a convenient place for traders to rest as they travelled from west to east and back again. Archaeological digs have unearthed the remains of a jetty, iron-ore smelters, kilns and temple, probably of Indian/Hindu origin—complexes that suggest the Bujang Valley was more than a simple trading port and a site not only of commercial importance, but also of cultural significance.

After Kedah Tua fell into decline, Malaysia continued to benefit from its strategic location, as the ports along the peninsula's west coast provided a safe place for both Arab and Chinese traders to rest.

While early populations were animist—the country's earliest inhabitants were the peoples now known as orang asal (original people), a collective term for about 150,000 people from at least 18 different ethnic groups—trade exposed the people of the peninsula to new ways of thinking.

The Javanese, who were then Hindu, occupied the peninsula around 1330–1350 and gradually Hinduism and Buddhism began to put down roots.

Melaka was the place it all began for modern Malaysia, after Srivijaya prince Parameswara, who had been forced out of Singapore (then known as Temasek) by the Siamese, sailed north in search of a refuge and established a small settlement, nothing more than a fishing village, on the west coast in around 1400. Fortuitously for Melaka, China decided to resume trade with Southeast Asia and the Ming Emperor despatched Admiral Cheng Ho to the region. For some 200 years, with China's protection

A young man performing the Kuda Kepang, a dance that was brought by settlers from Java.

helping keep the Siamese armies at bay, Melaka flourished attracting traders from far and wide.

It was around this time that Islam also became established in the peninsula, starting in Melaka with (it is said, although debated) Parameswara himself. The gradual inter-mingling of religions and cultures is still evident today. Traditional Malay performances are often inspired by Hindu epics such as the Mahabharata while Malay weddings include many customs that predate Islam's arrival in the peninsula.

In the years that followed, as European nations scoured the globe for spices and other exotic goods, Melaka became a wealthy and strategically important port. But the city's success and its position on such a crucially important sea route meant it was coveted by others. In 1511, the Portuguese seized control of Melaka, building the A Famosa fortress—the ruins of which can still be seen today—and, on the hill behind where the Sultan's palace had once stood,

St. Paul's Church. But even as Melaka boomed, punitive taxes began to undermine its success and the ascendant Dutch were able to wrest control of the city after securing the support of both the Acehnese and the Sultan of Johor.

The British, meanwhile, and the East India Company, which had already established itself in parts of Sumatra, were also circling. In 1786, the company convinced the Sultan of Kedah to give them Penang, which they renamed Prince of Wales Island and turned into a duty-free port. Ten years later, the British took Melaka.

Throughout the 19th century, the British were able to gradually extend their influence across the peninsula, signing successive treaties with the nine Malay sultanates. Melaka, Penang and Singapore were ruled directly from London as the Straits Settlements, and in 1896 the Federated Malay States were formed, including Selangor, Negri Sembilan, Perak and Pahang, with Kuala Lumpur as the capital. In Borneo, Sarawak, Sabah and Brunei became British protectorates.

The British interest in Malaysia was far from altruistic. Starting with the East India Company, colonisation was largely about money and resources. By the turn of the 20th century, the Malay peninsula was no longer just a trading post, it was an engine of Empire and a source of vital commodities. The prospect of striking it lucky in the tin mines brought waves of Chinese to colonial Malaya while the British brought people from India to work on the rubber plantations that were spreading across the land, replacing the lush jungles that had once cloaked the interior.

The first Japanese troops landed on the beaches of Kota Bharu on 8 December 1941 and quickly overran the peninsula, capturing Penang in ten days and Kuala Lumpur by the middle of January. By the end of the month, the last allied forces had retreated to Singapore, destroying the causeway that connected the island to the mainland as they went, but they were powerless to stop the Japanese advance. On 15 February 1942, Singapore surrendered.

The British had been building up land and sea defences ever since the end of the First World War—the naval base at Sembawang on Singapore's northern coast, boasted the world's largest dry dock when it opened in 1938—but the British had failed to ensure they had enough troops to confront the Japanese when the attack came. In *The Battle for Singapore*, Peter Thompson called the fall of Singapore the "greatest catastrophe of World War Two".

The Japanese occupation of Malaya was brutal, characterised by violence and deprivation. Food was scarce, and rationed, and many Malaysians survived off a meagre diet of tapioca and other root vegetables. A new currency—the Japanese dollar—was introduced, Japanese became the language of instruction in schools and newspapers became mouthpieces of the new regime.

It was the job of the Kempetai—the Japanese military

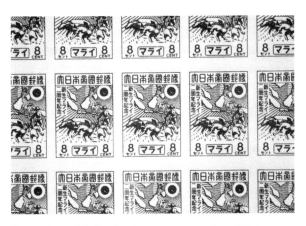

Stamps issued during the Japanese occupation of Malaya.

police—to gather intelligence, keep order and stamp out even the tiniest glimmers of dissent. People were often detained on the flimsiest of excuses, and those who rebelled could expect a harsh response from the Japanese—those suspected of helping the resistance were killed and their heads displayed on spikes as a warning to others. Still, some refused to be cowed.

There had been rumblings of discontent against British rule since 1915, when a week-long mutiny among Indian soldiers (known as Sepoys) in Singapore led to the deaths of 31 people, including British, Malay and Chinese civilians.

The Malayan Communist Party was established in 1931, drawing support mainly from the ethnic Chinese who were horrified by the Japanese invasion and occupation of Manchuria, and the deepening conflict between China and Japan. Malays were also chafing against colonial rule and becoming more assertive. Some joined the MCP, but Malay nationalist movements secured a broader following within the community. The war temporarily changed the focus of the struggle, but its ultimate goal—independence—remained the same.

The Malayan People's Anti-Japanese Army, which took to the jungles during the war to wage an insurgency against the occupying forces was backed by both the British and the MCP with the Communists providing the recruits and the British the guerrilla training (hasty and scrappy as it was). By the end of 1944, the MPAJA had grown to some 7,000 fighters, and the insurgency had established the credentials of the party's next generation of leaders, including Ong Boon Hua, who would become better known, infamous even, by his alias, Chin Peng.

The conflict and the Japanese occupation were a turning

point for the country. The British might have been welcomed back after the war ended, but it was a qualified welcome and it would not last. The people of Malaya now knew the British were not infallible, and the dream of independence was stirring.

Chin Peng and the Malayan Emergency

With the Japanese surrender and the return of the British, the Communists hid their weapons in the jungle and shifted their attention to politics, building support within Chinese-language schools and increasing their strength within the union movement to advance the goal of Malaya's independence.

But the disappearance of party leader Lai Teck in March 1947 proved critical. Revealed as a double, even triple, agent spying for both the British and the Japanese, party members grew suspicious of Lai Teck's political strategy , a scepticism that was reinforced as the British cracked down on the trade union movement that was the foundation of the Communists' support.

In their 4th plenary session, with Chin Peng now party leader, delegates agreed to prepare for more radical action against the colonial government: armed struggle. In June 1948, three European planters were found murdered. Chin Peng denied any knowledge of the killings, but the authorities blamed the Communists and banned the party.

It was the start of a 12-year insurgency—described as an 'emergency' to allow plantation owners and mining companies to claim compensation from insurers who would not have paid if the conflict had been designated a 'war'—against the backdrop of deepening distrust between the United States and the Soviet Union and their allies.

The state of Emergency also gave the British the power to detain people without trial and hundreds of suspected

Communists or sympathisers were jailed. It also fed into the colonial government's propaganda efforts, which included referring to the Communists as terrorists and criminals and deploying the local police rather than the British army to lead the campaign against the insurgents.

Whether terrorists, criminals or guerrilla fighters, the Communists proved a formidable opponent, and Chin Peng an astute leader. Born in Perak in 1924 as Ong Boon Hua, Chin Peng grew up with his father who had arrived in Malaya from southern China and ran a bicycle shop. As a teenager, Chin Peng found himself drawn to Communist ideas and he decided to join the party's youth wing when he was just 15, with the goal of advocating for the rights of the thousands of Chinese who had settled in Malaya.

The war against the Japanese gave the young revolutionary a chance to show his mettle, and as the resistance intensified he became the main liaison for the British, even being awarded an OBE for his services to Queen and country. The exposure of Lai Teck propelled Chin Peng to the leadership when he was still only 24. But with the declaration of the emergency a reward of $250,000 was offered to anyone who could provide information leading to his capture.

"I suppose I am the last of the region's old revolutionary leaders," Chin wrote in his memoir, *My Side of History*, which was published in 2003. "It was my choice to lead from the shadows, away from the limelight."

Under Chin Peng's command, an estimated 10,000 Communist guerrillas made the jungle their home. The dense undergrowth provided much needed cover, but it was a difficult and unforgiving place to live. Chinese communities who had settled on the fringes of the forest channelled food, medical supplies and information to the fighters, and not always because they supported the Communists' cause. Instead, it was done, according to Barbara and Leonard Andaya in *A History of Malaysia*, in a "mixture of gratitude and fear."

The gratitude stemmed from the help the Communists had provided in the settlers' continuing struggle to secure rights over the land; the fear reflected the fact that they knew the fighters would have no qualms about using violence against them if they did not co-operate.

In 1951, the highest-ranking British official in Malaya, high commissioner Henry Gurney, was on a weekend trip with his wife to the secluded highland resort of Fraser's Hill. The couple was in the rear of a black Rolls Royce, a Union Jack pennant fluttering on the bonnet, Gurney's aide seated next to the chauffeur in the front seat. A military Land Rover was in front, and an armoured car behind, but as the motorcade rounded a bend on the narrow and winding road up the mountain, it was ambushed by a group of fighters.

The Rolls was hit by a wave of machine gun fire, and the chauffeur was killed almost instantly. Gurney's wife and his aide crouched down behind the seats, shaking with fear as the fighters unleased their weapons. Gurney opened the door and got out, drawing fire away from the others. Moments later, he was dead, collapsing into a shallow ditch by the side of the road. Investigators later found nearly 40 bullet holes pockmarked across the body of the car.

Newspaper reports from the time suggest the guerrillas had been in position for two days. Needing to replenish their cache of weapons, they were planning to attack a military convoy that they had been told would be on the road, but as Gurney's motorcade appeared around the corner and with no new intelligence on the army vehicles they changed their target. As Chin Peng later put it, the team just "got lucky".

The killing of the most senior British official in Malaya, whether by luck or design, was a wake-up call to the territory's colonial rulers. The British responded with military might—deploying thousands of troops to Malaya—but Gerald Templer, who took over from Gurney, also stepped up efforts to win 'hearts and minds', enlisting more of the local population into the campaign, and holding out the promise of independence once the insurgency came to an end.

He also intensified efforts to separate the Communists from their local support networks. Having persuaded the Malay rulers to give up land for new settlements, hundreds of thousands of Chinese were moved into what the British called 'new villages' (most of which still exist today).

"The answer lies not in pouring more soldiers into the jungle, but in the hearts and minds of the Malayan people…" Templer said. "The shooting side of this business is only 25 per cent of the trouble and the other 75 lies in getting the people of this country behind us."

In the newly built villages, people had proper homes with running water and other modern amenities. There were schools and medical centres too. But the settlements— numbering some 500 by the end of 1951—were surrounded by barbed wire, and the residents' movements restricted so the authorities could further isolate the fighters in the jungle.

Supported by the surge in troop numbers, Templer focussed on 'clearing' the guerrillas, creating what he called 'White Areas' where restrictions on the local communities could be lifted—an additional incentive for them to avoid co-operating with the Communists.

In 1955, the authorities offered an amnesty to the fighting and, slowly, exhausted by years of jungle living, the insurgency began to lose its momentum. Two years later, the Commuist campaign suffered another blow when Malaya got its independence and in July 1960, the state of Emergency was finally declared to be over. More than 500 soldiers and 1,300 police had lost their lives over the 12 years of unrest, while at least 6,000 Communist guerrillas were thought to have been killed.

The remaining fighters retreated further into the jungle, taking refuge in southern Thailand from where they were able to mount sporadic attacks on Malaysian targets. Chin Peng was heard in the occasional broadcast on the underground radio network Malaysian Revolution Radio, before he slipped away—first to China and finally to join his comrades in Southern Thailand.

It was only in 1989 that a final peace agreement was signed. It included a commitment for Chin and his remaining comrades to return home, but the deal was never honoured. Despite numerous appeals to be allowed back into Malaysia, Chin died in exile in 2013. He was 88.

"I make no apologies for seeking to replace such an odious system with a form of Marxist socialism," Chin wrote as he looked back on his life. "Colonial exploitation, irrespective of who were the masters, Japanese or British, was morally wrong."

Malayan Independence

The archive photograph of Tunku Abdul Rahman holding his hands aloft to proclaim "Merdeka" seven times is one of the most famous in Malaysia. The Cambridge-educated prince from Kedah, stood on a stage in the specially constructed Medeka Stadium wearing traditional dress, his ceremonial kris tucked into the *samping songket* folded at his waist, and spoke of his dreams for the newly independent country.

Ramon Navaratnam, now one of Malaysia's most respected intellectuals, was in the crowd. Then a 22-year-old student, he had begged his parents to be allowed to go to the stadium and remembers the day as one of pride and hope.

"Whenever I hear Tunku Abdul Rahman shouting 'Merdeka!' as he did seven times on that historic day, tears well in my eyes," he said in an interview with a Malaysian website. "Because that encapsulated for me the whole ethos and quintessence of Merdeka, of freedom, and what it really meant to me at that time, and the prospects it held out for me as a young man of 22."

The agreement that secured independence—a testament to the political skills of those who negotiated the deal—ensured Malaya's ethnic minorities were given citizenship in the nation their ancestors had done so much to build, while the Malays' special position in the country was recognised in the Constitution.

In September 1963, Malaya became Malaysia as Singapore, Sabah and Sarawak, territories that were controlled by the British and the Brooke family, joined the federation despite vociferous objections from the Philippines, which had long maintained a claim over Sabah, as well as left-leaning Indonesia, which was hostile to the idea of the union and had embarked on a policy of 'Konfrontasi' or Confrontation.

Singapore had long been viewed with unease by the politicians in the peninsula. Not only was the country predominantly Chinese, which they worried might undermine the new nation's carefully constructed racial balance, its politics was decidedly more left wing.

Tunku Abdul Rahman hoped that without Singapore's destabilising presence, Malaysia would be able to focus on developing "goodwill and understanding" among the country's different ethnic groups, but amid disagreements over issues such as education and language, communal discontent festered, threatening to undermine the lofty ideals of the country's founding leaders.

In May 1969, following elections in which the ruling coalition lost the popular vote, and opposition parties did particularly well, ethnic differences exploded into the open. Opposition supporters took to the streets of Kuala Lumpur to celebrate, taunting ethnic Malays and predicting further political success.

The next day, May 13, a rally by UMNO supporters descended into violence, as rioters torched houses, businesses and cars in a four-day orgy of violence and looting. "Malaysia's proud experience in constructing a multiracial society exploded in the streets of Kuala Lumpur last week," *Time* magazine noted on May 23 of that year.

Officially, 196 people died in the unrest, but many analysts suggest as many as 1,000 people lost their lives, many of them ethnic Chinese. The shock of the riots triggered a sea change in Malaysian politics and gave new momentum to identity politics and Malay nationalism.

The government declared a state of emergency and parliament was suspended. The New Economic Policy was introduced to boost the Malays' economic income and rectify the economic disparities that were thought to have contributed to the resentments that triggered the rioting. Gradually, the country began to recover but the clashes were rarely discussed.

In 2018, a local newspaper discovered a series of graves

for people who appeared to have been victims of the violence in Sungai Buloh, an area now almost consumed by Kuala Lumpur. When the 50th anniversary of the unrest took place, local media were full of special reports and videos on what happened. Young people, it seems, are more interested in what happened than many thought.

In the 1980s, the country began to move away from its traditional focus on agriculture and resources to focus its economy on manufacturing and exports. New prime minister Mahathir Mohamad, who had taken the job in 1981, was a man determined to make his country one of Asia's economic powerhouses. A powerful streak of nationalism underpinned his policies as he stepped up efforts to take control of Malaysia's major companies and he gained a reputation internationally as voice for the developing world.

Penang was the first to experiment with export-driven manufacturing and as the island prospered, Mahathir decided that Malaysia would roll out the welcome mat to multinationals that were then beginning to set up factories in competitively-priced locations. At first, most of the businesses were simple assembly lines, but Mahathir had bigger ambitions. He wanted technology transfer; for Malaysians to learn from foreign investors and their expertise and to have some input into their own economic development. Malaysia boomed. Between 1987 and 1997, the economy grew an average 8 per cent a year, according to the OECD.

It all came to a crashing halt with the Asian Financial Crisis, which started in Thailand and swept through Asia. In Malaysia, as elsewhere in the region, the crisis was not only economic, but also political as Mahathir's differences with his younger and charismatic deputy, Anwar Ibrahim, were exposed in the most dramatic fashion. In September

1998, Mahathir fired Anwar and accused him of sodomy—a criminal offence in Malaysia—and abuse of power. Tens of thousands of people flooded onto the streets of KL in Anwar's support, hopeful that this moment would be the catalyst to reform in Malaysia.

It was not to be. Despite outrage both at home and overseas, and the widespread revulsion that greeted Anwar's appearance in court with a black eye following a beating from the then police chief, the former deputy prime minister and finance minister was convicted and jailed. It was not until 2004 that he was freed, a year after Mahathir had left office.

MAHATHIR MOHAMAD

In June 2002, Mahathir Mohamad walked across the stage of the cavernous Putra World Trade Centre in Kuala Lumpur to deliver the closing speech at his party's annual meeting. Delegates shifted in their chairs and made themselves comfortable. At the local television stations, crews prepared to broadcast the prime minister's address live to the nation.

Mahathir, the softly-spoken son of a school teacher from Kedah, had been in power since 1981. Over a period of more than two decades he had transformed Malaysia into an economic powerhouse—an 'Asian tiger'—but he had also presided over a deterioration in the country's democratic institutions, cracking down on his critics and sending former deputy, Anwar Ibrahim, to jail on charges of sodomy and abuse of power that had drawn international condemnation.

Few expected anything groundbreaking from the speech. The 76-year-old took his place at the podium, dressed as was customary at the party's biggest events, in *baju melayu* and *songkok*. Mahathir had chosen mauve for the occasion. He gazed out across the room and talked of economic recovery, the benefits of meritocracy and his aversion to the strict religious laws being pushed by the opposition Islamic party.

But after an hour and a half the tenor of his speech began to change. The prime minister gulped at the water placed in the corner of the lectern. "I have an important announcement to make," he said, as tears welled in his eyes. He had decided to resign from his party posts. He would also resign from his position at the head of the ruling coalition, he added.

Most people in the hall were too stunned to do anything. But some of those who were sitting behind him on the stage and had been by Mahathir's side throughout his administration rushed to the lectern, pleading with him to change his mind. Rafidah Aziz, his long-serving Minister of International Trade and Industry, and then head of the party's women's wing was first. Then Hishammuddin Hussein, the leader of the youth section. They clustered around the veteran leader, now crumpled and in tears, asking him why he was resigning, and begging him to stay. But Mahathir insisted he had made up his mind "long ago". Delegates urged him to withdraw his resignation. "Long live Mahathir!" they shouted. In the event, party colleagues persuaded Mahathir to stay on. But it was only temporary. Four days later, the government announced that Mahathir would leave office in October 2003, after 22 years in power.

Mahathir was born in July 1925 to an ordinary family in the northern town of Alor Setar. In his memoir, *A Doctor in the House*, Mahathir described the family home as little more than 'a slum' that was at risk of flooding during the rainy season. A studious boy whose father was a teacher, Mahathir earned a place to study medicine in Singapore where he met the woman who would become his wife, Siti Hasmah Mohd Ali.

After marrying Siti Hasmah and qualifying as a doctor,

Mahathir returned home and opened his own clinic in 1957, the same year that the couple's first child, a daughter they called Marina, was born. The young doctor quickly built a thriving private practice—the first in Alor Star—and, aided by some successful business ventures, was soon able to buy himself a blue Pontiac at a time when most residents walked or cycled.

Even with his success in medicine, Mahathir flirted with politics. He joined the United Malays National Organization (UMNO), the party that helped lead the push for independence from Britain and would go on to dominate the country's politics for the next six decades, establishing himself as an outspoken Malay nationalist.

He got his first taste of parliament in 1964, but then lost his seat in the tumultuous polls that took place five years later. It was not long, however, before the young politician was back in the public eye. Even now the racial riots that rocked Kuala Lumpur in May 1969 continue to cast a shadow over Malaysia. But Mahathir, displaying the ruthlessness that helped him become Malaysia's longest-serving prime minister—and kept him there—used the instability triggered by the violence as an opportunity to attack the leadership of then Prime Minister Tunku Abdul Rahman.

While Malays are generally known for being solicitous and polite, Mahathir "hammered out the most notorious letter in Malaysian politics," according to biographer Barry Wain in *Malaysian Maverick : Mahathir Mohamad in Turbulent Times*. It was direct to the point of rudeness.

Mahathir accused the Tunku of being out of touch with the Malays, who "hated him", and claimed the fun-loving prince had been playing poker as Kuala Lumpur burned, too much in thrall to his "Chinese friends". Within two months, Mahathir had been expelled from UMNO's Supreme Council, and two months later the party itself.

But the trauma helped transform Mahathir into a hero of Malay nationalism. As he returned to medical practice, he also had more time to write, and in 1970 he published *The Malay Dilemma*, the book that would come to define Mahathir and his politics. The book, which focussed on the economic disparities between Malaysia's different ethnic groups and claimed the majority Malays were held back by feudalism, content to sit back and let others take the initiative, helped cement Mahathir's notoriety and also his reputation.

The government, long dominated by the elite, could no longer ignore the firebrand outsider and soon Mahathir was restored to the party and politics. Moreover, UMNO began to adopt his ideas. Malay "rights" dominated decision-making and Malays were given special access to education, government jobs and cheap loans.

By 1981, Mahathir was leading the party and the country and quickly set about implementing his vision for Malaysia. He ripped up the rulebook on business in post-colonial Malaysia, staging a notorious 'dawn' raid on the London Stock Exchange to wrest control of Guthrie, a plantations conglomerate, and launching a 'national car' (with the help of the Japanese) that he hoped would compete with the best in the world to fuel the country's industrialisation. And then there were the massive infrastructure projects. Highways, bridges, mega dams, a new airport, the world's tallest twin towers, and a sprawling new city for officials and civil servants that he named Putrajaya.

Through it all, Mahathir showed he was unafraid to take on the establishment or dispense with those he believed were impeding his plans or no longer loyal. An independent media, the judicial system, numerous opposition politicians and critics, and a succession of deputies—most notoriously of all, Anwar—were left trailing in the wake of Mahathirism. So, it would seem odd that in 2018, at the age of 93, he rode back into power.

When Mahathir left office shortly after the arrival of the new millennium, few Malaysians had known any other leader. While his leadership had transformed the country economically, a younger generation emboldened in the mass demonstrations that followed Anwar's sudden ouster and inspired by the changes taking place in Indonesia, was impatient for political reform.

For the next 15 years, reformers and conservatives would tussle for power, but it took a multi-billion-dollar scandal at state fund 1MDB and Mahathir's 'star power' to make political change a reality.

Even after 2003, he had never really retired. He installed himself in his own foundation on the shores of the lake at Putrajaya, the administrative city he had carved out of an oil palm plantation only a few years before. From there he wrote his memoirs, kept a close eye on political developments and took calculated pot-shots at his successors—first Abdullah Badawi and later, Najib Razak—who had taken up office in the grandiose-looking building housing the Prime Minister's Office further along the shore.

But it took the enormity of 1MDB to propel Mahathir back into frontline politics. With the US Department of Justice reporting as much as $4.5 billion had been stolen to fund the lavish lifestyle of fugitive financier Jho Low, Najib, his wife, and his stepson, and Najib then undermining any domestic investigation by firing those in charge, Mahathir felt compelled to take action. He quit UMNO a final time, appeared among the crowds at a rally in support of democracy and against corruption and announced he was setting up his own party.

It was only a matter of time before he and the opposition found common cause, but even after Mahathir had been named the person who would become Prime Minister in the event the opposition won, few actually believed Malaysians would be able to dislodge the coalition that had governed the country almost since independence.

Mahathir himself left little to chance. Defying his years, the veteran politician campaigned frantically ahead of the May 2018 poll, criss-crossing the country to speak at rallies in towns big and small, drawing huge crowds wherever he went. Mahathir knew how to appeal to the people like no other politician. The message was simple—Najib was a thief. And he was stealing money from 1MDB.

Mahathir won his Langkawi seat with a massive majority and used the political nous he had developed over his decades in politics to ensure that the change in power that the people had voted for was respected. A few days later, Anwar—jailed a second time for sodomy—was released from prison. The two men responsible for Malaysia's emergence as an 'Asian tiger' were once again back in power.

Prime minister for a second time, Mahathir appears to have learned some of the lessons of the past. While still forthright, he appears more willing to listen to others and to compromise. His age and experience afford him the kind of respect that few other politicians enjoy, and as unlikely as it might seem, the man who was once feared for his authoritarian tendencies is the one now at the helm of what has been dubbed 'new Malaysia'.

ANWAR IBRAHIM

Anwar Ibrahim speaks to a crowd in Port Dickson in his successful campaign to re-enter parliament in October 2018.

Ambitious. Firebrand. Reformist. Islamic. Democratic. Poised once again to take over from Mahathir, Anwar Ibrahim is frequently criticised for trying to please everyone, a man who inspires devotion and disgust among Malaysians in apparently equal measure.

Born on 10 August 1947, it was as a student at the University of Malaya that Anwar first got involved in politics, grabbing nationwide attention in the 1970s as the leader of a series of spirited protests against poverty and deprivation that landed him in jail. The young Anwar underlined his reputation as a religious conservative as the founder of the Islamic youth movement ABIM. Most expected that if he entered politics, he would do so with the Islamic party, but in 1982 Mahathir convinced him to join UMNO. By the mid-90s, Anwar's political skills and powerful oratory had propelled him rapidly up the ranks to become the party's deputy president and the country's finance minister; a bona-fide political star.

But behind the apparent bonhomie between the two men there were tensions, in particular a feeling that Anwar was too ambitious and too impatient, and the differences were dramatically exposed with the Asian Financial Crisis. Mahathir, ever the maverick, had his own ideas about how Malaysia should respond to the country's deepening economic problems. Anwar was more minded to follow the IMF's suggestions.

In September 1998, Anwar was sacked from the government and, sensationally for such a conservative society, accused of sodomy. Thousands of people spilled onto the streets of Kuala Lumpur in defiance of strict rules on public gatherings in what were the biggest protests the country had ever seen. Inspired by the mass rallies in Indonesia that had forced Suharto to resign, young Malaysians thought that this might be their opportunity for change, and that sustained pressure would force Mahathir, whose rule had become increasingly autocratic, to step down.

As the protests gathered momentum, Anwar was arrested by armed police in the middle of a press conference at his then Bukit Damansara home and held under the Internal Security Act, a colonial-era law that allowed for detention without trial. With Mahathir publicly accusing his former protege of sodomy, and claiming a black eye was "self-inflicted" (the then police chief was later convicted of the attack), Anwar was found guilty in a lurid trial—a stained mattress that was said to be the scene of the tryst was hauled in and out of the courtroom—that was widely criticised as unfair and politically motivated.

There was not only the matter of Mahathir's public comments about Anwar's supposed homosexuality that were reported in excruciating detail in the local media, but that under the original charge the condominium building where the offence had supposedly taken place had yet to be completed. The prosecution simply changed the date.

At the time he was imprisoned, Anwar, a self-styled Asian Renaissance man with five young children, was seen as the man who would have presided over a more democratic and open Malaysia. His wife, Wan Azizah Wan Ismail, set up a new party to campaign for his release and champion the ideals of justice and democracy—its symbol was a stylised eye, a symbol of Anwar's beating.

Anwar was released in 2004, five years to the day of his arrest, when the country's highest court overturned his conviction. Crowds of supporters welcomed him back home, but the jail term meant that he was barred from politics. Anwar moved into academia, lecturing at Georgetown University in the US, touring Western capitals and thanking those in the region and beyond who had stood by him throughout his ordeal.

But behind the scenes he also began piecing together a coalition that could take on the formidable power of Barisan Nasional, which had held power since independence. In 2008, defying all expectations, the opposition coalition— grouping together Anwar's party, the mainly Chinese but multiracial Democratic Action Party and the Islamic party—won control of five states in the peninsula and deprived BN of its long-cherished two-thirds majority in parliament, a margin that had enabled it to make changes to the Constitution.

Shortly afterwards, new sodomy rumours surfaced, once again plunging Anwar into an X-rated high-stakes legal drama that the government-backed media was only too happy to detail on the front pages and national television. Anwar denied all charges, saying the case was politically motivated. In 2012, the High Court said there was not enough evidence to convict the politician and he was acquitted.

The Anwar-led opposition then turned in another stunning electoral performance, holding onto states like Penang and Selangor, and winning the popular vote. BN, under Najib Razak who had taken office in the wake of 2008's poor showing, had started out with promises of political and economic reform, but the continued erosion of support five years later heralded a tougher line. Reform went out the window and a higher court overturned Anwar's acquittal. The opposition leader was once again back in jail.

While Anwar had been confident his coalition would hold together even in his absence, Najib had begun to make overtures towards the Islamic party—even touting the possibility of introducing harsh new punishments for religious offences—and succeeded in splitting the opposition. But he had not anticipated the depth of anger about the corruption at state fund 1MDB. The multibillion dollar scandal described by investigators in the United States as one of the worst cases of kleptocracy it had ever known—succeeded in the unthinkable—reuniting Mahathir and Anwar in the face of a common enemy—and forcing BN from power for the first time in six decades. A week after the opposition coalition's victory, the king pardoned Anwar of all crimes and he walked out of the hospital where he had been undergoing treatment a free man.

History appears to have come full circle.

"There is a new dawn for Malaysia," Anwar told the media on his release. "The entire spectrum of Malaysians, regardless of race or religion, have stood by the principles of democracy and freedom. They demand change."

CITY PORTRAITS
Kuala Lumpur, Selangor

The capital of Malaysia, the Kuala Lumpur of the 21st century, is a sprawling city of high-rise towers and suburban housing estates, bound together in an ever-expanding network of highways. It is a city pockmarked with billboards and alive with neon light, populated by office workers, Malay women with or without brightly-coloured head scarves, tourists from across the globe, business tycoons in chauffeur-driven Mercedes and Alphards and legions of workers from Indonesia and Bangladesh labouring, barely acknowledged, as construction workers, waiters, cooks and cleaners. Without them, the city of four million would grind to a halt.

It is hard to imagine its humble beginnings, but KL, as the city is popularly known, would probably not have existed without the discovery of tin. It all started in the 1850s, when the ruler of Klang sent a group of Chinese men inland from the port city to explore for new deposits of the lucrative ore. Tired from the journey, the weary explorers decided to take a rest at the point where the Klang and Gombak rivers met, and it was at this 'muddy confluence' where Kuala Lumpur began.

Today, the rivers are hemmed in by the Masjid Jamek mosque, and run behind the stately brick buildings that were designed to house the administration during colonial times, as well as newer office blocks that began to appear in the area from the middle of the 20th century. With their concrete walls to address flooding, the rivers themselves now look more like drains despite recent rehabilitation efforts.

The early settlement was far from genteel—more like a wild, frontier town, heaving with men—mostly Chinese migrants—with only a single purpose in mind: making their fortune in the mining industry. The work was tough and dangerous, the climate oppressive, and the settlers risked not only outbreaks of life-threatening tropical diseases, but frequent floods and fires that destroyed their simple, wooden houses. Many sought escape during the little spare time they had at the brothels and opium dens that sprung up around the settlement.

It was Yap Ah Loy, the third Kapitan Cina (a position that carried significant power within the colonial administration), who brought some semblance of order to what had become a rather riotous town, and earned himself the reputation as the founder of Kuala Lumpur. By 1880, thanks to his efforts, KL had become the administrative centre of Selangor state while Klang remained the home of the Sultan and the royal city.

Strict new rules on construction requiring all new structures to be built in brick and tile were introduced after devastating floods just a year later. Roads were also widened as KL began to take the form of a more orderly city. By 1939, it was the largest town on the peninsula with 120,000 residents.

The city was also divided into areas for each of the ethnicities who had come to Malaya in search of their fortunes, a system of organisation that is today reflected in the fact that the city still has a Chinatown and a Little India. Malays were carved out a district known as Kampung Baru (new village) that these days is squeezed in by a wall of high rise office blocks and developers who covet the now prime city centre location.

As property prices have risen, the owners of the few traditional Malay houses that are left, their titles recorded by hand in now-yellowing journals, are struggling to hold off the development that is encroaching into their neighbourhood. Traditional inheritance laws provide some measure of protection, not least because some properties have been divided between multiple generations making it difficult for everyone to agree on what to do with the property. There are some plots with more than 100 owners.

The British, meanwhile, based themselves around the 'muddy confluence', establishing their administration around the Padang—the field where they liked to play cricket—overlooked by a club (entry only to colonial men) designed in Tudor-style with an expansive veranda. Here, they could relax with a drink, and play cricket when they felt like it. Next door was St. Mary's, an Anglican church.

Many of these colonial buildings remain today, albeit in varying states of decay, and still overlook the field that has now been renamed Dataran Merdeka (Independence Square). Women are still excluded from the club.

The Sultan Abdul Samad Building with its Moorish domes, elegantly arched colonnades and 140-foot copper-domed clock tower was built between 1894 and 1897 to house the colonial administration. After independence it was used as

The Sultan Abdul Samad building overlooks what was once known as the Padang, and is now known as Dataran Merdeka. The road is closed to traffic on Sundays.

the High Court and the Supreme Court and is now home to the Ministry of Culture and Tourism.

Next door, the distinctive red and white striped building that houses the Textile Museum was designed by A.B. Hubback, one of the most talented architects of the colonial period, as the headquarters of the railway company.

Other buildings, despite being listed as national heritage, have been empty for years. Only the homeless, and the occasional curious photographer, now walk the corridors of the old law courts, built originally to house the survey office of the Federated Malay States. Some of the domes have collapsed and plants are pushing their way through the brickwork as the authorities dither over restoration.

Still, in recent years, the city authorities have been paying more attention to conserving Kuala Lumpur's heritage and older city centre buildings that might once have been demolished are being restored. ThinkCity, a government-linked agency, is a crucial part of the process and is working not only to regenerate Malaysia's cities, but also to raise public awareness about old buildings and how the architecture of the past can help tell the story of the present and the future.

KL's historic heart is now recovering some of its élan after being overshadowed (literally) by the Cesar Pelli-designed Twin Towers and other less stylistically-pleasing skyscrapers. Murals have replaced the mouldy, peeling paint on the walls of older shop-houses, the river has been cleaned up and pavements improved to encourage people to walk instead of drive.

While traffic remains a daily challenge and trees are too frequently cut down to make way for roads, the MRT or simply another building, Kuala Lumpur is one of Southeast Asia's

The Istana Negara at dusk with the Twin Towers in the background.

greener cities. Around Dataran Merdeka and the river, huge old raintrees have survived the pressures of development and are lit up with twinkly white lights once the sun goes down.

The Twin Towers, and a cluster of surrounding skyscrapers, are built around what was once the city's main horse racing track, which has been transformed into a popular park with shady, manicured lawns, a running circuit, musical fountain and giant paddling pool that is crowded with children at the weekend.

Further away from the centre, the Lake Gardens are a popular place for a stroll especially in the early morning or late afternoon and there are newly opened nature walks through the native forest in nearby Tugu Park. In the east, residents like to head up into the hills around Ampang—watch out for troops of marauding macaques grown lazy (and fat) from people feeding them—while in the west

hikers and mountain-bikers head for Bukit Gasing and the Kiara Park.

Further still, while the canopy walkway has been closed, the Forest Reserve Institute of Malaysia, better known as FRIM, offers KL residents an opportunity few other city-dwellers anywhere in the world enjoy—the chance to experience 545 hectares of tropical rainforest on the edge of a vibrant city.

The canopy walk at the Forest Research Institute of Malaysia on the outskirts of Kuala Lumpur.

George Town, Penang

A wall mural that was created by Penang-based Lithuanian artist Ernest Zacharevic for the city's annual arts festival and is now a popular tourist attraction.

The main city on the island of Penang, George Town dates from the 18th century when the Sultan of Kedah agreed a deal with Captain Francis Light to cede the island to the East India Company in exchange for British protection from the threatening armies of Burma and Siam.

Light was not so much interested in Penang's potential as a military base, but as a hub for trade. He wanted a port that could provide assistance and protection to British ships making their way through the Strait of Malacca, but his decision to make the first British possession in Southeast Asia a 'free port' also created a vibrant competitor to Malacca, which was then controlled by the Dutch.

As a free port Penang, which the British called Prince of Wales Island, thrived and by 1800 the population had ballooned to 10,000 people. The main city with its bustling docks and jetties was named after George IV and became part of the Straits Settlements—with Singapore and Malacca—In 1826. The discovery of enormous tin deposits, coupled with the demand for rubber fed the Penang boom, and even more people came to settle in George Town. The wealthiest built ornate mansions overlooking the sea.

George Town was designated a World Heritage site in 2007, which has helped protect the heart of the city from unsuitable development—on the fringes there are plenty of towers and architecturally-questionable buildings—although the city faces a continuing battle to preserve the traditional trades and crafts that were once ubiquitous along the narrow streets and are being slowly crowded out by cafés and souvenir shops.

A man carves a wooden sign board outside his shop in Penang.

Whatever the pressures of tourism, George Town remains a charming place to visit and offers plenty of rewards for those willing simply to wander its streets, from the numerous temples, mosques and churches to sampling the food from street hawkers and traditional kopitiams, some of which have barely changed in decades.

Traditional craftsmen and businesses, like this sign maker (left) and rattan weaver (right), are increasingly rare in George Town, Penang.

The Blue Mansion, which dates from the late 19th century, took conservationists six years to restore using only traditional methods and materials, and reusing timber, tiles and other original fixtures. The building stands out not only for its distinctive cobalt blue exterior, but the exquisite detailing. Cheong Fatt Tze, the tycoon who owned the mansion, was determined to create an elegant and refined home that was befitting of his wealth and status. He brought in craftsmen from China to work on the building and sourced only the very best materials—some from as far away as Scotland.

In its heyday the mansion, with its five courtyards, was a centre for Cheong's businesses and even housed the Chinese Vice-Consulate. Favourite members of the family, including his cherished seventh wife, lived in a more secluded central part of the house while those who were out of favour found themselves banished to one of the mansion's far wings. These days, like many old buildings, the Cheong Fatt Tze Mansion is a boutique hotel. It is also a popular location for films, including *Crazy Rich Asians*.

Penang is not only about George Town. The beach at Batu Ferringhi underwent major development in the 1970s and is now home to a string of family-orientated resorts including two properties belonging to the Shangri-La group and Lone Pine, a hotel originally built in the 1950s but updated, modernised and expanded by E&O, the owner of the colonial-era hotel of the same name in the city proper.

Then, there is the island's nature.

The British discovered Penang Hill, also known as Bukit Bendera (Flagstaff Hill), in the 18th century and began exploring the highest slopes as a way to escape the heat, getting to the top on sedan chairs that were attached to bamboo poles and had to be carried by as many as eight men, or on hardy Sumatran ponies.

The view from the top of Penang Hill over George Town.

As the colonial rulers solidified their hold over the island they began to build properties on the hill—houses where they could retreat for calm and relaxation in a more forgiving climate than the lowlands. One of the most spectacular was Bel Retiro, built in 1789 for the island's governor and still a government retreat. Others include Convalescent Bungalow, which was completed in 1803.

The funicular railway to Penang Hill first began operations in the 1920s.

The funicular railway was completed in 1924, and the near two-kilometre track was completely overhauled in 2011. Today's Swiss-engineered system takes just five minutes to transport visitors to the summit some 800 metres above sea level.

Most visitors do not stray far beyond the museums, souvenir shops and cafés that cluster around the funicular's upper station—there are spectacular views over George Town and the peninsula, after all—but away from here there are plenty of paths to explore and the peace that first entranced the island's colonial rulers.

A privately-operated nature reserve known as The Habitat opened on the edge of the tropical forest that envelopes the hill's highest peak in 2016, offering the chance to spot rare flora and fauna including the dusky leaf monkey with its distinctive white 'spectacles' on guided walks through the property. There are giant swings on platforms between the trees for those who want to take in the beauty of the forest and the views across to the Andaman Sea, and a spectacular canopy walkway.

Melaka, Malacca

A street in Melaka's World Heritage zone.

We hear them before we see them: the tinny blast of K-Pop muscling its way into our conversation. Then, from around the corner a convoy of trishaws appear, some pink, some electric blue, festooned in fake flowers and pictures of Hello Kitty or Elsa from *Frozen*, Korean tourists on the back seats taking pictures and giggling among themselves while the sinewy drivers propel the garish three-wheeler forwards.

Welcome to Melaka in the 21st century; an amalgamation of ancient and new overlaid with the cute and the kitsch. The top of St Paul's Hill, just ten minutes up the steps behind the burgundy-red walls of the Dutch-era Stadthuys, provides a visual perspective on the city's history.

Filtered through a canopy of giant rain trees, the modest terracotta orange roofs of the old city are dotted with the ornate sculptures of Chinese temples, the minarets of mosques and the occasional church spire, the river winding its way towards the Strait of Malacca past rows of more modern terraced houses, warehouses, shabby apartments and still-to-be-completed condominium blocks whose hoardings promise luxury lifestyles.

Along the shoreline, office towers and monolithic shopping malls rise up from land that was once the sea, while dredgers and cranes are still hard at work expanding the city ever further into the Strait of Malacca.

St. Paul's itself was originally a modest chapel, built in 1521 by a Portuguese seafarer to thank the Virgin Mary for helping him find shelter in Malacca. It is not only the oldest church in Malaysia, but the whole of Southeast Asia.

Out of this polyglot city arose new cultures and traditions— among them: the Peranakan or Straits Chinese (the Chinese who married local Malays and merged their traditions to create a distinct culture of their own), and the Kristang (Malaysians descended from the Portuguese).

Having made their fortune in the rubber trade, wealthy Peranakan families built grandiose townhouses along Heeren Street (now Jalan Tun Tan Cheng Lock) filling their homes with the best European furniture and artefacts.

Number 48 was the home of Chan Cheng Siew who first arrived in Malaysia from Fujian in the early 19th century and

The Chinese nationalist Sun Yat Sen had close ties with Penang and it was while living in George Town that he made preparations for his eventual overthrow of the Qing Dynsty in China. The house where he lived is now a musuem.

the house remained in the hands of the Chan family until the 1980s when it was turned into a museum.

Visitors enter into a somewhat austere reception room furnished in traditional Chinese-style with mother-of-pearl and marble inlaid blackwood chairs placed at the edges of the room, watched over by formal portraits of the family's ancestors.

Only men were allowed into the reception hall—women spent most of their time in the kitchen or the private areas of the home hidden behind the ornately carved wooden screens that separated the reception area from the rest of the house.

A few doors down the street towards the river, the painstakingly-restored building at number 8 is a window onto a more modest way of life. The somewhat austere house is thought to have been built in the middle of the 18th century and was home, stable and shop rolled into one.

A short walk away, beyond the tourist trap of Jonkers Street, Jalan Tokong is a living, thriving showcase of

The restored home in Melaka of an ordinary merchant is a marked contrast to the lavish decoration of the Peranakan mansions further along the street.

the multiracial past. Within a short stroll is the country's oldest Chinese temple—built in the 17th century—Cheng Hoon Teng, its oldest Hindu temple Sri Poyyatha Vinayaga Moorthy, which dates from the 18th century and the Kampung Kling Mosque, which was established in 1784 but rebuilt in its current form in the19th century. Squeezed In between, are shops and stalls catering to the needs of the faithful whether specialising in paper effigies for Chinese to burn as offerings or colourful flower garlands for Hindu deities.

The Cheng Hoon Teng temple is said to be the oldest in Malaysia and was built in the 17th century.

When night comes, the trishaws are once again back on the city's streets. They are no less garish, now ferrying tourists in a whirligig of flashing lights and thumping beats around the base of St. Paul's.

Kuching, Sarawak

Kuching is one of Malaysia's most charming towns; a multi-cultural and sophisticated place where largely intact 19th century shophouses line a gentle promenade along the banks of the Sarawak River, a few kilometres upstream from the South China Sea.

While the word 'kucing' means cat in Malay, and there is an enormous sculpture of a cat at one end of the city, it is more likely that Kuching got its name from the Chinese 'kochin' or 'harbour' or even—as one story claims—that it was named after the cat's eye—mata kucing—a fruit that is popular in the area.

The city was nothing more than a small fishing village of palm-roofed houses when James Brooke wrested control of southern Borneo from the Dutch in 1838 and was given the territory of Sarawak by the grateful Sultan of Brunei. Brooke sailed upstream to the modest settlement and decided that this was where he wanted to build his capital city. He went on to establish a private fiefdom in the state that would endure for three generations and lead the Brookes to be called 'The White Rajahs'.

Many of the Brookes' historic buildings remain despite the encroachment of skyscrapers into the historic centre. A short sampan ride across the river from the Main Bazaar, Fort Margherita was built in 1879 to provide protection against marauding pirates. Charles Brooke named the white-washed turreted building on the top of the hill after his wife, Ranee Margaret, and it now stands in marked contrast to the nearby spacecraft-like form of the state assembly, which was designed by Malaysian architect Hijjas Kasturi and opened in 2009.

Back on the other side of the river, the Old Court House was once—as its name suggests—home to the law courts and doubled as the administrative centre for the state. Dating from 1871, its high-ceilinged rooms with their elegant colonnades are now occupied by stylish restaurants and cafés.

A few hundred metres further inland is the Sarawak Museum. It might sound dull, but the 19th century institution is an ideal place to learn about the lives of Sarawak's indigenous people at a time when many of their traditions are under threat. A new, expanded museum is due to open in 2020.

Like many other Malaysian cities, nature is never far away. The beach at Santubong and the nearby Bako National Park are half an hour's drive away and the area is also the setting for the hugely popular Rainforest Word Music Festival which takes place every July. A new arts festival—a measure of Kuching's increasingly arty vibe—has also been established in the city, conceived by Joe Sidek, the man behind the George Town Festival, an event that has done so much to put George Town on the map.

Kota Kinabalu, Sabah

KK, as Kota Kinabalu is affectionately known, is not in the same historical league as places like Penang and Melaka because nearly the entire city was destroyed in allied bombing raids in the Second World War—reports say just three buildings were left standing—but what it lacks in architectural heritage it more than makes up for with its location between sea and mountain, and its multi-cultural population.

The city grew out of a fishing village and natural port known as Api Api that was settled by the British North Borneo Company in 1898 and renamed Jesselton after the firm's then manager Charles Jessel. Rival Sultanates in Brunei and what is now the Philippines had long fought for control over the territory, and the British wanted it as a sheltered port for vessels carrying goods to, from and between China and India.

The colonial company maintained the state capital in Sandakan on the east coast, but over the next few decades, Jesselton developed into important trading hub for rubber and rattan as well as jungle products like honey.

The Japanese invasion of 1942 proved devastating for the territory and brought serious suffering to the local population.

It also led to the now infamous Sandakan Death Marches in 1945 when the Japanese forced already skeletal Australian and British prisoners of war to walk through challenging jungle terrain from Sandakan to the village of Ranau on the slopes of Mount Kinabalu. The Japanese wanted to use them as labourers in Jesselton, but of the 1,000+ men who made the 250-kilometre march, half died en route, the rest when they got to their destination. Just six survived.

With the war at an end, the British returned to North Borneo which was made a crown colony with Jesselton as its capital. They began to rebuild the devastated town, but it wasn't until 1968 that the city was named Kota Kinabalu, after the mountain that looms over it.

KK in the 21st century is a vibrant, multicultural city made up of indigenous people, as well as a significant population of Filipinos, some of whom have lived in Sabah for years, and Indonesians, many of whom are without documentation.

One of the best ways to get a feel for the rhythms of the state and the city is to visit a *tamu*—the local market. These days they are popular with tourists, but they have not entirely lost their authenticity and it is still possible to get a feel for local life through the range of fruit, vegetables and food on offer, as well as the handicrafts.

Prominent artist collective Pangrok Sulap has put the *tamu* and the community at the heart of its work, often setting up a stall in the market and asking visitors to participate in the development of their woodcut prints.

There are also many sights to enjoy just a short distance from the city—the magical islands of the Tunku Abdul Rahman marine park are only a 10-minute boat ride, while Mount Kinabalu is about an hour's drive away. Be sure to have the necessary permits and accommodation before attempting the climb.

CHAPTER 3

WAYS OF SEEING: THEY AND YOU

> ❝The only thing wrong with Malaysia
> is the way Malaysia sees itself.❞

— **Rehman Rashid, *A Malaysian Journey***

Malaysia is hugely diverse and its minorities make up a significant proportion of the country's 32 million people (in mid-2018). Just over half are ethnic Malays, who are Muslim by birth, while the next biggest group are Chinese, followed by Malaysians of Indian descent, and the myriad indigenous peoples who live across the peninsula and in Borneo. Together, the Malays and indigenous people are known as '*bumiputera*' (often referred to colloquially as '*bumi*'), which translates as 'sons of the soil'.

MALAYSIAN MALAYSIANS

On the face of it, and to the uninitiated, Malaysians are Malaysian. On the sporting field, athletes compete for Malaysia and, if they win, sing the national anthem with pride as the flag is raised into the sky. Ordinary Malaysians of all ethnicities will gather around the television to watch the competitions events, cheering on the national team.

But Malaysia is also a country where race remains a prominent issue, defined on each citizen's national identity card and asked on every official form whether it is an application for a passport, a bank loan or even gym membership, where what might seem like an innocuous idea—a Malaysian Malaysia—is anathema to some.

This hyper-awareness of race and religion can be traced back to the colonial-era when the British governed Malaya through a policy of divide and rule, where British administrators created and defined settlements according to race and looked to certain ethnicities to perform certain roles and do certain jobs.

While the men who negotiated Malaysia's independence scrupulously tried to meet the differing demands of the all the country's inhabitants—under Article 153 of Malaysia's constitution, the Malays and the indigenous people of Sabah and Sarawak were recognised as having a 'special position' within the federation, while the minorities were given citizenship in the new country—underlying resentments continued to fester in the post-independence period.

After the race riots of May 1969, blamed partly on the disparities of wealth among the different communities—the government introduced positive discrimination in favour of the majority Malays to boost incomes and help them secure a greater stake in the country's economy.

The policy was only ever supposed to be a temporary measure, but it has remained in force in one guise or another ever since. Policymakers have proved reluctant to enact reform for fear of angering the Malay voters on whom they depend for support in the country's race-based political system, and the longer the system has endured the more strident its defenders have become. More extreme Malay nationalists are given to claiming they were granted special rights rather than privileges in the Constitution.

Despite this political reality, ethnically-mixed parties are beginning to take a more prominent role in Malaysia. The government that wrested power in May 2018 has appointed non-Malays to senior positions in the finance ministry and attorney general's office, but race remains a significant consideration in all kinds of decision-making and a potent force in the country's politics.

THE MALAY COMMUNITY

According to the Malaysian constitution a Malay is someone who 'speaks the Malay language, professes Islam and habitually follows Malay customs.'

The civil service, which includes some 1.6 million people including doctors and teachers, is almost overwhelmingly Malay so an understanding of both the Malay language and Malay culture can be enormously useful when working with officialdom, whether it is securing approvals for a house renovation, setting up a business or getting a driving licence.

But the decision to appoint an ethnic Chinese Finance Minister (Lim Guan Eng) and an ethnic Indian Attorney General (Tommy Thomas) attracted criticism from some even though the postiions had been held by non-Malays during the post-independence years.

The popular image of the Malay living in a traditional elevated wooden house in a rural village—the kampong—maintains a romantic hold over the public imagination even as more and more Malays move to the cities and live in apartments and terraced houses just like everyone else. Some of the wealthiest live in palatial mansions in some of Kuala Lumpur's swankiest suburbs, driving Audis and BMWs, wearing designer clothes and luxury watches and spending the weekend cycling, doing CrossFit and relaxing in hipster cafés.

Still, whether in the kampung or in the upmarket enclave of Damansara Heights, Malays often live as an extended family. It is not unusual for children—both sons and daughters—to continue to live with their parents well into adulthood and even after they have married. Some wealthier families may even live in a series of houses in the same street, while others may rebuild a family home to accommodate spouses and grandchildren and any family members who may decide to come and visit.

The Traditional Malay House

Almost every state has its own version of the 'Malay house'—a wooden home, lifted above the ground on stilts and designed to ensure it remains breezy and cool even in the heat and humidity.

Traditionally, Malay houses were built in compounds surrounded by gardens of rice fields and fruit orchards and in rural areas there are still plenty of such homes sitting in picturesque gardens.

One of the oldest surviving Malay houses is in the centre of Kuala Lumpur where it is now the headquarters of Badan Warisan Malaysia, the Malaysian Heritage Society, which rescued, relocated and restored the house in the late 1990s. The Rumah Penghulu Abu Seman stood originally in a village in the northern state of Kedah and was built in stages over a period of 20 years, starting in 1910.

Traditionally, such homes were built from local timber, tropical woods like chengal that were hardy enough to withstand the climate and the sometimes ferocious monsoon—turning them into a showcase for traditional craft and construction skills. Wooden walls were interspersed with full-height shutters to create a large and well-ventilated space inside, with elaborately-carved wooden screens above to allow air into the home even with the shutters closed. Usually the roof was thatched from attap (dried palm fronds) while a generous overhang provided protection from the sun and during heavy rain.

Rural Malaysia has picturesque farms, orchards and traditional wooden homes. This one is in Balik Pulau in Penang.

Most importantly, the traditional Malay home was designed for communal living providing spacious rooms (and little in the way of furniture) that could be used for a variety of functions from entertaining to eating and sleeping. As the house of the village headman, the Rumah Penghulu Abu Seman had a large central area known as the *'rumah ibu'*, the highest room in the house and a symbol of its importance.

The *ruman ibu* is the heart of any Malay house; the place for the family to eat, sleep, pray and hold feasts, known as *kenduri*, for special occasions like weddings and rites of passage. In the old days, there would have been little in the way of furniture other than low tables, and people would sit cross-legged on a woven mat on the floor instead.

Traditional houses are also distinguished by the staircase leading up to the covered entrance porch known as the *anjung*. Some stairs are quite simple, while others are almost sweeping, crafted from bricks and cement and painted or tiled.

The *anjung* was where the family could relax and watch the world go by, but it was also the place where guests would enter the home before they were ushered into the *serambi gantung*, an airy anteroom with plenty of windows and views onto the garden.

In a typical house, the kitchen, or *dapur*, was at the back of the dwelling at the lowest level, connected by a veranda to the *rumah ibu*. The cooking was done over a charcoal fire.

A number of resorts have opened in recent years to give visitors the chance to experience life in a traditional Malay home, albeit with the addition of some 21st century comforts. One of the pioneers of the genre is Australian entrepreneur Narelle McMurtrie who bought a number of old Malay houses—including a modest fisherman's hut and the grand home of a village chief—and reassembled them around a coconut grove not far from the beach in Langkawi, naming the resort Bon Ton. She has since added other traditional homes from around the peninsula of both wood and brick to create Temple Trees next door.

Closer to Kuala Lumpur, Rimbun Dahan, the artistic centre that is also home to prominent architect Hijjas Kasturi, has a number of Malay houses dotted around its lush grounds representing the different styles that were once common throughout the peninsula. The homes are usually occupied by guests and resident artists, but others can visit when Rimbun Dahan is open for performances and events.

On the east coast, Terrapuri is a resort of rescued and restored traditional Terengganu-style Malay homes elevated far off the ground with steep, pitched roofs.

Malay Names

As Muslims, Malays often turn to Arabic for inspiration when it comes to naming babies. There are numerous boys named Ibrahim, Mohamed (often spelled Mohamad or Mohammed or shortened to Mat) and Ahmad, and girls called Siti (usually the first part of two names), Aishah and Fatimah. Parents these days often create names themselves, which is acceptable providing it passes muster with the registrar of births.

Many foreigners find Malay names confusing because there are no family names, or surnames. A Malay man might be called Ahmad Zahari, but Zahari is not his family name, it is his father's name (officially, his name is Ahmad bin Zahari (Ahmad son of Zahari). On second reference, he should be called Mr Ahmad (Encik Ahmad).

Women's names are similar so Azlin Ahmad is Azlin binti Ahmad and Ms (Cik or Puan) Azlin on second reference. For these reasons, it is also common for Malaysians to get confused with Western names. Instead of being addressed as Ms Mayberry, I am usually called Ms Kate.

Parents often like to give their children similar names, so it is quite common to find brothers and sisters with names that all start with the same letter or sound.

Religion

Malays are Sunni Muslims and Islam guides every aspect of their lives from birth to death, but it was not always like that. Before the arrival of Islam, the Malays were largely Hindu and many of today's customs and traditions, from language to wedding rituals and performing arts, are rooted in that past.

Words like *asmara* (love) and *kenchana* (gold) came to Malay from Sanskrit. According to local commentator Sabri

Zain, when a Malay says a sentence with ten words, five will have originated from Sanskrit, three from Arabic, and the remainder from English, Chinese, Persian or another foreign language. Whatever the past, however, it is Islam that is now central to Malay existence and identity—to be Malay is to be Muslim.

Every Malay is required to live by Islam's five central pillars—to pray five times a day, fast during the month of Ramadan, complete a pilgrimage to Mecca at least once in a lifetime, give to charity and accept that there is no God but Allah. The five prayer times are at dawn (*subuh*), midday (*zohor*), mid-afternoon (*asar*), sunset (*maghrib*) and *ishak* (about an hour or so after maghrib). The exact times change every day, according to the moon, and are published daily in the media and broadcast on television.

Malays may often go to the mosque to pray (particularly at *zohor* on Friday or at *maghrib*), but they can also do so at home or at office; finding a quiet spot to place their prayer mat if there's no *surau* available.

Sharia laws that apply only to Muslims (including Muslims from overseas who are visiting or living in Malaysia) ensure everyone follows the rules. Eating during Ramadan, pre-marital or extra-marital sex are among the many personal transgressions that can land Muslims in court and even prison if they are found guilty.

Malay children begin to learn the Quran from an early age and when they start school they are required to attend religious classes, known by the Malay name, *agama*, as part of the curriculum. Many parents will also sign their children up for Quran classes at the local mosque, with the local *ustaz* (religious teacher) or simply a knowledgeable and respected elder.

Everyone is encouraged to memorise the Quran, but the young children must first learn the Arabic script (even today, students may simply recite the words without really understanding what they mean) before they can even get to grips with reading the passages laid out on the page.

At the higher levels, Quran recital has evolved into an art form with regular competitions. The national level event is held once a year and broadcast on primetime television and for more than five decades Malaysia has hosted the world's biggest international event for Quran recital—the International Al Quran Recital and Memorisation Assembly.

Tahfiz Schools

Tahfiz, Islamic schools that specialise in teaching the Quran, have become increasingly popular among Malay parents who believe such schools will help their children understand their religious obligations and develop a strong sense of right and wrong.

The first *tahfiz* were established in the 1960s but they mostly remained a niche option until Kelantan's Islamic government started supporting them three decades later. In 2017, for the first time, the national government gave millions of ringgit to support the privately run schools.

Tahfiz often take students as boarders—when they go outside the children can usually be distinguished by their white robes and skull caps—set their own syllabus and are largely unregulated (although a fatal fire at a *tahfiz* in Kuala Lumpur in 2017 and reports of children suffering abuse and violence at the hands of their teachers have fuelled calls for the government to monitor their operations more closely).

Few *tahfiz* give their students the opportunity to follow the typical school curriculum of maths, English and science—

many may not even follow a timetable—and students who want to develop such a mainstream education alongside their religious knowledge often have to take up private tuition classes.

Critics say the focus on religion to the exclusion of all else is also detrimental to Malaysia's future development, creating a cohort of young people qualified only to be religious teachers. Whatever the truth, there is no doubt that *tahfiz* schools have become increasingly attractive to Malay parents. As one parent told Singapore's *Straits Times* in 2017: "Children who go to tahfiz schools are more polite, obedient and fulfil their religious obligations."

Circumcision

For Malay boys, circumcision is one of the defining rites of passage of their childhood and something that happens before they are 12 years old. It is a far from private event. *Berkhatan* or *bersunat* is a mass ritual that usually takes place during the end-of-year school holidays and can involve hundreds of boys at the same time. Sometimes, it is organised by the local neighbourhood committee, with the local MP stopping by to offer their support to the, frequently nervous, youngsters.

Traditionally, the boys would jump into the river for a soak before undergoing the procedure, but these days they are more likely to dress up in their finest clothes including *sarong* and *songkok* and be doused by a hose from the Fire Department in a massive pre-surgery water fight.

In a large hall, where beds are laid out for each of the boys, doctors and nurses are ready to carry out the procedure. Anxious fathers hover by the bedside holding their son's hand and keeping them calm as the doctors move from bed-to-bed. Some boys manage to remain admirably stoic but others, particularly the younger ones, struggle to hold back the tears.

Once the procedure is over, and a dressing has been applied, the boys lie on their beds with their sarongs lifted above their sore spot—a scene affectionately drawn by Lat, Malaysia's most popular cartoonist. At the end of their ordeal it is time to celebrate, and a feast is served.

Traditional Circumcision

Most Malays prefer a trained medic to circumcise their son rather than the healer known as the Tok Mudim, who was called on to do the operation in the past.

Part of a village house would be curtained off for the Tok Mudim to do his work, with each boy going one-by-one into the room and taking their place astride a banana trunk. The Tok Mudim would then use a razor or the blade of a sharp knife to slice off the foreskin, applying a dressing of traditional medicines to the wound.

Those circumcised this way say that while it was quick, there was no anaesthetic, no antiseptic or, it would seem, proper cleaning of the razor used to operate on the boys.

The 'Ritual is Complete'

Female circumcision, or genital mutilation, was rarely talked about in Malaysian society until recently, and many people were shocked to discover that the practice was common within the Malay community.

Although figures are hard to find, a survey of Malay women in 2012 found 93 per cent had been cut. Most were subjected to the procedure as a baby, or before the age of nine. The government has said FGM is part of 'Malay culture', while health officials claimed the procedure was 'harmless'.

Not everyone agrees. An investigation into the practice by local newspaper, *The Star*, found the procedure carried out in private clinics and by traditional midwives. Some admitted using box cutters or stationery blades to do the operation.

"So far, I have not hurt any baby," Azizah Daud, a traditional midwife, told *The Star*. "The danger is minimal. Some blood will come out and I will use a cotton swab. Once there is a blood stain on the cotton, the ritual is complete."

The country's Human Rights Commission has said female circumcision is not part of Malay culture and should be banned, a view shared by international organisations.

Ramadan

Ramadan, or the fasting month, is one of the most holy parts of the year for the Malays; a time when they forego food and drink (even water) and give up vices like smoking during the hours of daylight.

As Malays' interpretation of Islam has become more conservative, Ramadan has become more strictly enforced. Many Malay stalls close and Muslims of any ethnicity can be punished for eating during the day or failing to follow other elements of the fast. Those who 'look' Malay may also face disapproving looks and requests for their ID card to confirm their religion.

During Ramadan, many Malays will opt to change their working hours (starting earlier and leaving earlier) so they can be home in time to break their fast with their family. In the first few days, some people find themselves losing energy around lunchtime, but the fast becomes easier as the month progresses and the body becomes accustomed to the routine.

Not all Muslims will be fasting throughout the month. Women do not need to fast if they are pregnant or having their period, while the elderly and the young are also exempted. Long-distance travellers may also be allowed a break. Adults who miss a day or two for these kinds of reasons will usually try to 'make up' the time later in the year. Most Malay children will start to learn to fast around the age of ten, starting with a few hours each day before building up to the full month.

Although Ramadan is about restraint, it is also a time when many Malay delicacies are served. Traditionally, this would mean a lot more work for women who would have to get up in the early hours of the morning to make sure food was prepared for the dawn meal, and a suitable spread for the evening breaking of fast.

But many families now visit their local Ramadan bazaars, where business usually gets underway about three in the afternoon. Here, Malaysians of all ethnicities come together thanks to their shared passion for food. Malays, Chinese and

Indians will all try to visit a bazaar so they can enjoy special *bubur* (porridge), *kueh* (local cake) and *lemang* (banana leaf wrapped rice cakes cooked inside a bamboo pole over charcoal).

Five-star hotels also offer expansive buffets to mark the 'breaking of fast' seemingly in competition over the quality and quantity of food on offer. Many companies spend a fortune on entertaining during this time, booking tables at hotel buffets for staff and clients.

After roughly 12 hours of fasting, the evening meal is the most important of Ramadan. Most Malays will listen for the call to prayer and break their fast by saying a prayer and then eating a date. Meals at home are likely to be simpler than the lavish spreads laid out at hotels, but many families like to make more of an effort to eat together during the fasting month.

The ninth month of the Islamic calendar, marking the time when the Quran was first revealed to the Prophet Mohammad, is not just about abstinence and food. It is also about developing a deeper spiritual understanding of Islam, to forgive others and ask forgiveness for mistakes of one's own.

Many Malays will take the opportunity to make financial donations to charity (*zakat*) during the month. They may also give food and new clothing to the needy including homes for children and the elderly.

Hari Raya Aidilfitri

Once universally referred to as Hari Raya Aidilfitri (or simply Raya), many Malays now call their biggest holiday of the year Eid, but the festival marking the end of the fasting month remains their most anticipated celebration of the year and the moment when the entire extended family can gather together back 'home'.

The date is usually announced far in advance, but it remains provisional until the last night of the month when religious officials will gather for the sighting of the new moon. If they see the moon, the Keeper of the Sultan's Seal makes an official announcement to the country that the next day will be the first day of Hari Raya. It is rare that the officials do not sight the moon, but if that happens then Muslims will have no choice but to fast for an extra day.

A few days before Eid, the whole family will pile into the car and make their journey back to their village in a mass movement known as '*balik kampung*' in Malay (the term has also been adopted by other Malaysians). It is so ingrained into the Malay psyche that it even has its own song—'Balik Kampung'—which you will hear in every shopping mall in the run-up to the celebration.

Although some Malays also now choose to spend the holiday in Kuala Lumpur (two days are granted as public holidays, but schools usually close for longer and most people take a longer break), grandparents having moved to the city or passed away, it remains one of the few times of the year—the other being Chinese New Year—when the capital is relatively free of traffic. It can seem eerily quiet in streets devoid of cars, but larger shops and restaurants are generally open (some on the first day and most on the second).

Like Ramadan before it, Hari Raya lasts about a month. It is mostly a celebration, but on the morning of the first day, the entire family visits the cemetery to pay their respects to the deceased. Families get new outfits for the festivities—traditional *baju melayu* for the husband and any male children and *baju kurung* or *baju kebaya* for the wife and any daughters—often in matching colours.

Some families will hold 'open houses', laying on a feast for family, friends and neighbours, often including a whole lamb barbecued over charcoal, and popular dishes like satay, rendang and char kuey teow. Inside, guests will find a tempting selection of bite-sized cookies and traditional Malay kueh, as well as western cakes, some of which are probably handmade.

Tens of thousands of people attend the 'national level' open house hosted by the prime minister, but the smaller, more intimate events, are far more pleasant and provide a better insight into Malay traditions.

Depending on the size of their home and whether they are in the city or a village, the family will usually erect a canopy outside with tables and chairs for their guests. Some may cook a few of their favourite dishes, but it is also common to ask caterers to set up stalls in the driveway. Drinks are usually colourful and sweet.

It is not unusual to receive more than one open house invitation so it is wise to eat judiciously, sampling a little of each delicacy to ensure there is plenty of space for the delights on offer at the next function. Some families will have a speciality, Johor laksa, perhaps, a roast lamb even or the inevitable cookies and cakes. Guests are encouraged to sample as much as possible.

Hari Raya is a time when shops are full of new *batiks*, silks and *songket*, making it an ideal opportunity to buy a new outfit off the peg or follow the Malaysian custom of having one made. There are many tailors and dressmakers offering bespoke Malay clothing and many foreigners, especially women, opt to wear traditional dress to open houses.

Giving *duit raya* has become a Hari Raya trend in recent years—influenced by the Chinese tradition of giving red packets or ang pow at Chinese New Year—and the host of the open house (or his eldest son) will usually give a few ringgit in a green packet to any children who come and join the festivities.

Thanks to the Chinese, firecrackers have also become popular at Hari Raya and the festival is greeted in urban neighbourhoods around the country amid a cacophony of bangs and firework smoke.

Festive Songs

Mariah Carey dominates the malls at Christmas in Malaysia, but at Hari Raya and Chinese New Year, the country has its own songs, and they are every bit as catchy and/or annoying.

Balik Kampung, Sudirman

Recorded in 1984, 'Balik Kampung' is the quintessential Hari Raya song, with a chorus that is almost impossible to get out of your head. Pahang-born Sudirman Arshad was one of Malaysia's leading entertainers and died in 1992 when he was only 38.

Selamat Hari Raya, Saloma

Another Hari Raya classic and almost as catchy as 'Balik Kampung'. Saloma was a legendary Malaysian actress and singer who was married to P. Ramlee.

Gong Xi, Gong Xi, composed by Chen Gexin

The most popular Chinese New Year song in the world is heard in every shopping mall in Malaysia throughout the Chinese New Year period. 'Gong Xi, Gong Xi', which means Congratulations, Congratulations in English, wasn't actually written for Chinese New Year though. It was meant to celebrate China's liberation from the Japanese in 1945.

Cai Shen Dao

This ear-worm of a song is all about the arrival of the God of Fortune and is exceedingly popular. You will probably end up humming it whether you want to or not.

Pregnancy and Birth

For Malay people, children are blessings from God and many still choose to have large families—five children are not uncommon even among urban, professional households.

Traditionally, pregnancy was a time when families kept a close eye on the expectant mother both for her health and that of her unborn baby. Taboos were numerous, from not being allowed to look at anything ugly or frightening to avoiding carrying heavy objects. Perhaps they were not altogether surprising at a time when most Malays lived in remote villages and healthcare was often far away.

These days, the vast majority of Malay women give birth in hospital. There are groups across all ethnicities in Malaysia who opt for home births, usually with a medical professional in attendance, but they remain a tiny proportion (five in 1,000, according to local media reports in 2018) and the vast majority of pregnant women will head to the labour ward at their local hospital, returning home with their baby a couple of days later.

While pregnancy and birth was, by custom, a woman's concern, Malay husbands are increasingly likely to stay with their wives, or at least be given the option, in the delivery room. Once the baby arrives, many Malay women, like their compatriots who are Chinese or Indian, will follow a confinement period that is designed to help them recover their strength.

During this time, the newborn might be given the *urut bayi*—a traditional massage of between five and ten minutes—when the child is just a couple of days old—and, at the end of the confinement, the Cukur Rambut, or hair-cutting ceremony. This is the moment when the new arrival is introduced officially to the wider family.

During the event, a passage from the Quran will be read as a blessing for the child and the infant will then be passed around the assembled crowd—from elder to elder—each snipping a lock of the child's hair. At the end of the ceremony, the gathered hair is buried.

Malay Weddings

At the first Malay wedding I went to, we dressed in our best clothes and sat among the guests in the living room of the bride's parents home in Damansara Heights to watch the solemnisation ceremony or Akad Nikah. It is the moment when the couple is officially married, and also one of enormous tension; the occasion when the groom must declare clearly and publicly his intention to marry his bride.

The Akad Nikah usually takes place in the home of the bride's

In a Malay wedding, the groom and bride are king and queen for the day.

family and is a more intimate affair than the wedding dinner that follows (much like the church or registration ceremony in other countries). With mosque officials and his wife-to-be's father looking on, the groom is expected to make his declaration of marriage clearly and without hesitation, but officials often try to trip the groom up, asking him to repeat the declaration again and again in the hope he will make a mistake.

Our friend completed the verses without a hitch, but he later admitted it was the most nerve-wracking moment of his life. He had been so convinced he would forget some of the words or get the sentences twisted around that he was shaking.

Like most people, Malays love a wedding. It is a time when families come together and everyone can wear their best clothes, eat fabulous food and let their hair down, sometimes over a period of days or weeks.

A couple's road to marriage starts with an engagement. These days, the role of the matchmaker is in decline (especially in the cities) and many Malay couples will have met each other at college, through work, shared interests or through an online dating app. The groom (or even bride) will probably pop the question and place a ring on their partner's finger at a specially-chosen romantic location, much like everyone else.

But in Malay culture an engagement is only an engagement once the ceremony known as the Bertunang has been completed. Here the family members from the groom's side will visit the family of the bride bearing gifts and an engagement ring. During the Bertunang the families will discuss the length of the engagement and the question of Duit Hantaran, the groom's payment to the bride's family, an amount that can stretch to thousands of dollars.

The other crucial element of a Malay wedding is the Bersanding, the equivalent of a wedding reception. In the village, the celebration is usually held at the family home beneath a canopy in the garden, but in the cities many families choose to hold the Bersanding at an outside venue—in the ballroom of a glitzy five-star hotel or the function room at the local community centre. Some still have an event at home, but also host a more grandiose dinner in a hotel ballroom so that more guests, particularly business acquaintances, can attend. Most couples hold one Bersanding in the bride's hometown (the one immediately after the Akad Nikah) and another at the groom's home (known as the Bertandang)—usually the following week.

Wherever the Bersanding is held, the space will be lavishly decorated, perhaps in a single colour (I remember one wedding dinner where even the drinks were bright blue), with a flower-filled stage and 'throne' which is the centrepiece of the event and where the couple hold court in all their traditional finery—King and Queen for the day. The dais is also where guests congratulate the couple and pose for photographs.

Most weddings merit a festive feast and dishes usually include *rendang*, and a special celebratory rice (there is always rice) placed in a circular dish in the middle of the table from which the guests can serve themselves. Others might involve a buffet while some couples have food stalls set up around the hall, serving savoury dishes and desserts. Typically, food will be *halal* and there will be no alcohol.

The wedding celebration will take place over a few hours and it is perfectly acceptable to arrive at any time during the period specified on the invitation although most guests will try to attend over lunch or dinner. For more formal dinners in five-star hotels where the guest list might number into the hundreds, it is probably better to arrive on time, especially if the family has chosen to invite VIPs. It is not uncommon for politicians—from the local MP to a senior Cabinet Minister—to be invited to a Malay wedding and sometimes even seem to upstage the couple themselves.

Malay couples do not usually expect gifts from their guests although they are gratefully received—usually whisked away by a family member once they have been passed over. It is also acceptable to give money, slipped inside a green envelope.

The bride and groom exchange presents with each other, known as *hantaran*. Each item is placed on a tray (a *dulang*), elegantly wrapped in cellophane. The gifts range from the simple—favourite foods—to the traditional—wedding ring, prayer mats, Quran—and the extravagant—designer handbags, luxury watches and computers.

Wedding gifts exchanged between the bride and groom.

At the end of the Bersanding, tradition dictates that the couple give each of their guests a hard-boiled egg, a symbol of fertility, but these days couples might give a small slice of cake, some chocolate or a little trinket. Any egg is normally exquisitely presented—coloured, placed in a small basket, wrapped in netting and tied with a bow.

Berinai

When you exchange money in a shop you might sometimes notice that the young Malay woman serving you has brown tips to her fingers or intricately painted patterns of henna on her hands. The staining of henna, known as *berinai*, remains a common practice for brides and a chance for her to get together with her friends and family members before the wedding, rather like a hen's night or a bridal shower. The groom may also have his fingers painted.

Death

According to tradition, a Malay Muslim must be buried within 24 hours of their death and preferably on the same day. There is no cremation. The family will notify the mosque of the person's death and let other relatives know what has happened. Everyone will be expected to do what they can to come and pay their respects to the deceased before the burial. The body will be cleaned, dressed, wrapped and laid out for mourners to pay their respects, with a thin gauze covering the face.

The burial will take place at the nearest Muslim cemetery. In Kuala Lumpur the most well-known are in Bukit Kiara, where many prominent politicians, performers and intellectuals are buried, and just off Jalan Ampang in the heart of the city centre. Many cemeteries are identified by their frangipani trees.

Close relatives will join the mourners as the pallbearers carry the wrapped corpse at shoulder height to the prepared grave, where it is laid on the earth, in the direction of the holy city of Mecca. Those gathered scoop up three handfuls of earth and throw them into the grave as the imam recites the call to prayer for the final time. Mourners then sprinkle the grave with sandalwood and petals. Later it will be marked with a distinctive white stone marker.

THE CHINESE COMMUNITY

Chinese first started arriving in the Malayan peninsula in the 15th century, putting down roots in the thriving port of Melaka and marrying local women to create an entirely new culture of people known as the Peranakans or Straits Chinese.

But the biggest influx probably came in the 19th century when Chinese from the southern provinces of Fujian and Guangdong crossed the sea in droves to work in the tin mines and escape poverty back home. Their lives in the then British colony were tough and the mostly male migrants found their escape in gambling and the opium dens that were appearing all over Kuala Lumpur. Some eventually made enough money to work their way out of the mines to set up their own shops and businesses and contribute to the colony's booming economy.

Nowadays, the Chinese make up the second biggest ethnic group in Malaysia and have lived in the country for generations, mostly in the towns and even in remote communities in Sarawak and Sabah. Many have held onto the beliefs, traditions and languages that their ancestors brought with them when they left the provinces of southern China, even if they now speak Malay or English or have become Christian.

Those miners who made it into business established the kind of shophouse—a shop below and living quarters above—that dominate the central street of every small town across the peninsula and into Borneo. Originally, there would have been a large, hand carved wooden sign hanging at the entrance to the shop with its business carved in Chinese characters on the pillars outside. Outside the main heritage areas, the signs are now brightly-lit plastic, but a few skilled carvers continue to keep the tradition alive.

A traditional shop sign in Melaka.

Chinese Names

Malaysian Chinese generally have three names; the family name comes first, followed by the name that signifies their generation and their first name. Some may also be given a Western name or simply choose one they like when they get older.

A man called Andrew Chan Kuan Hong would be addressed as Mr Chan with his first name Hong unless he prefers to be called Andrew.

A woman named Christina Tan Li Ting would be Ms Tan (or Mrs or even Madam Tan if married) and her first name Ting or Christina. Note that Chinese women do not usually take their husband's name.

In colloquial speech, family and friends might add an 'Ah' in front of the person's given names, although not with a Western name.

Within families most people are addressed according to their position in the family. A little sister is 'mei-mei', for example, and big sister 'jie-jie'.

Many Malaysian Chinese now attend government schools where the teaching is in Malay or private schools where they learn in English so they might not be proficient in writing or reading Mandarin even if they can speak the language fluently. They may also be less knowledgeable about the dialect their family speaks, but Malaysian Chinese are people who remain proud of their culture, and proud of being citizens of Malaysia.

Religion

During the Lunar New Year, Malaysia's Chinese temples throng with the faithful; standing in front of the altar, waving a clutch of gently-smoking sticks of incense and praying for a successful year ahead.

Most Chinese in Malaysia follow a form of Buddhism and Taoism coupled with a Confucian respect for their elders and the generations that went before. Some families might have an altar in their home—a formal photo of their ancestor usually sits at the back with candles on either side and a container to hold burning sticks of incense in front—but they also visit the temple. Most towns have at least one; the oldest still in use is the Cheng Hoon Teng temple in Melaka that dates back to the 17th century.

Chinese temples are easily identified by the colourful, elaborately-carved dragons, birds and flowers that dance along the top of their steep, tiled roofs. Worshippers enter through heavy gates into a courtyard, with the building's layout reflecting the idea of achieving harmony with nature.

The elaborately decorated roof of a Chinese temple in Penang.

With no formal services in the sense of a Christian church or set prayer times as in Islam, the uninitiated might struggle to understand what is going on. Certainly, Chinese temples in Malaysia rarely fit the clichéd stereotypes of calm, inner zen that constitute so many outsiders' perceptions of Buddhism. The smell of incense hangs heavily in the air, temple assistants sweep ash and rubbish into bins, cats lounge in shady corners and worshippers come and go. There is rarely a saffron-robed monk to be seen.

After praying, the Chinese place incense sticks into sand-filled urns, their prayers carried on the wisps of smoke to the gods.

Devotees usually choose for themselves when and how to pray—popular times are on the birthday of that particular temple's resident deity or at various full moons. Taking a handful of incense sticks, which they light from a flame at the entrance to the temple, they position themselves in front of the altar, generally laden with fruit, flowers and food to ensure the god is contented, and chant their prayer, moving the incense sticks gently backwards and forwards. Once the prayer is over—it does not usually take very long—they place the still glowing sticks in the sand-filled containers by the altar, wisps of smoke curling gently up into the air.

Incense can be shaped into cones, or in this case, ingots.

Most Chinese temples in Malaysia are dedicated to the Goddess of Mercy, Guan Yin (also spelt as Kuan Yin), who is revered throughout Buddhism and is considered one of the eight immortals by followers of Taoism.

The 19th century Dharma Sagely Realm Monastery (formerly known as Kum Yam Thong) was one of the first in Kuala Lumpur to be built of bricks and tiles and boasts a large statue of Guan Yin in its main hall. In the heart of the city, next to the Twin Towers and surrounded by construction and office buildings, it also operates a hugely popular vegetarian caféteria.

There are temples devoted to other deities too. At Melaka's Cheng Hoon Teng temple, worshippers can pray to Ma Cha Po, the Goddess of Seafarers and Datuk Hiap Tian Tye Tay, the God of Justice, while some temples have resident mediums who are on hand to tell fortunes, choose auspicious baby names and help believers navigate their way successfully through life.

The most renowned mediums attract hordes of followers. The medium at the Huat Chu Kong temple in Klang, for example, is particularly popular with people looking for success in their business ventures, and appointments to seek his advice have to be made at least two weeks in advance. Dressed in robes, his long, straight hair hanging down across his face, the medium sometimes goes into trance in order to better foresee the prophecy, but he also consults the Chinese Zodiac as he ministers to about 20 people every night.

Some Chinese have become Christians in recent years, most of them joining Evangelical churches set up in shops or, to accommodate the growing congregations, in repurposed factory buildings on industrial estates. It has become quite hard for non-Muslims to build houses of worship in Malaysia, so beyond the Anglican and Catholic churches that were built during colonial times and the early years of independence, those established in the past 30 years or so are more discreet, hidden behind metal shutters or up staircases and heralded not by a cross, but a small sign by the door.

Chinese New Year

The Lunar New Year, also known as the Spring Festival, usually falls around the end of January or early February and is the biggest celebration of the year for Malaysian Chinese. It's also a time when Malaysia as a whole virtually grinds to a halt.

More cultural than religious, although many Chinese will visit the temple at some point during the holiday, Chinese New Year is a time to eat, drink and have fun. Many people will take the week off work, taking advantage of the two-day public holiday and the usually week-long break school break to go back to their hometowns; the Chinese equivalent of the Malays' 'balik kampung'. Even shops close—at least for the first day—and restaurants too, once they have finished catering to diners on the eve; one of their busiest days of the year.

In the days, and even weeks, running up to the festival, families will embark on an aggressive programme of spring-cleaning, sweeping and mopping floors, cleaning away cobwebs and dust and getting rid of possessions that are no longer needed. They will often decorate their houses too—hanging some auspicious calligraphy, red and gold decorations, and vases of pussy willow (its furry buds represent the beginning of spring while its name in Chinese, 'yin liu' sounds similar to 'money running in'). Many will hang large red lanterns outside their home ready to welcome in the new year and any guests who happen to drop by during the festive season.

Reunion Dinner

The eve of Chinese New Year is the most important part of the festivities; the time when the whole family comes back together to celebrate the dawn of the New Year with a mouth-watering banquet.

While some now choose to eat out, many still prefer the comfort and conviviality of home. Wherever the dinner takes place, barbecued duck, a whole steamed fish and Yee Sang, a raw fish salad from Guangdong that was brought to Singapore in the 1940s, are likely to be on the menu, all washed down with beer, wine and a good bottle of brandy.

Yee Sang, a salad that includes raw fish, is a popular dish at Chinese New Year.

The best Yee Sang has top quality salmon, crunchy noodles, radish, peanuts, and a hit of fresh coriander in a salty-sweet dressing, but this is a dish that is more about the experience than the actual taste.

Guests gather around the plate, chopsticks at the ready to toss the ingredients high into the air—the higher the noodles the more luck for the year ahead—calling out auspicious wishes and largely oblivious to any food that ends up on the table. Once the Yee Sang is sufficiently mixed, everyone sits down and the feast begins.

In a restaurant, the dishes will be served one by one, with lotus-wrapped glutinous rice at the end of the meal. At home, the food is laid out on the table for everyone to help themselves. The older members of the family will be served by the younger ones first as a sign of respect.

Come midnight, be prepared for the crackling cacophony of firecrackers as people set off strings of the explosives across town and cities, and make sure your pets are inside. The noise is supposed to frighten away evil spirits and ensure good luck in the year ahead.

Officially, fireworks are illegal, but everyone seems to know where they can buy them and it is rare to see police take any action against anyone using them unless there is an injury. Indeed, Malays and Indians have also developed a passion for firecrackers, and their deafening bangs now welcome not only Chinese New Year, but every other festival too.

After the feasting of the eve, the first day of the New Year is when everyone puts on their new clothes, preferably in red, the colour that symbolises happiness and promise. Some women and children like to wear the traditional cheongsam, a slim-fitting sheath dress with a high mandarin collar and distinctive silk buttons at the shoulder. These days, they come in more contemporary designs and materials including linen and batik as well as the more traditional silks.

Families will visit their grandparents to show respect for their elders, while some may go to a temple to pray. In Kuala Lumpur, the Thean Hou Temple although relatively new attracts throngs of worshippers at Chinese New Year.

Later, young people may go and visit their friends to eat,

drink and relax. Others might like to gamble a little and head up into the hills to the casinos of Genting.

The whole festival lasts a total of 15 days and ends officially on Chap Goh Mei, the 15th night in Hokkien dialect. This is the time when unmarried women write their phone number on an orange and throw it into a lake or the sea in the hope their future husband will fish it out of the water and get in touch, a tradition that originated in Penang.

Angpows

Ask most children what they like about Chinese New Year and the answer is likely to be 'ang pows' or 'hong bao'. The little red envelopes are usually given out for free by banks, supermarkets and department stores so that parents and adults can add money for the children (or young, still single adults) they meet while on festive season visits. Convention requires that the notes be new, or at least crisp, as a symbol of the renewal that accompanies each new year.

Lion Dance

Lion dances have been part of the cultural fabric of Chinese New Year for hundreds of years—the noise is said to chase away bad spirits while the lion itself symbolises power and wisdom—and throughout the celebration shops, restaurants and offices will host regular performances to ensure the coming year is an auspicious one.

Malaysia has some of the world's best lion dancers—young men (almost overwhelmingly) who risk serious injury as they leap across a series of high poles and perform acrobatic stunts—one wearing and manipulating the colourful lion's head complete with shaggy mane and delicately fluttering eyelashes, and the other taking the part of the back legs—to a cacophony of clashing cymbals and drums.

Muar-based Kun Seng Keng Dragon and Lion Dance Association is arguably the best team in the world, taking home the Genting World Championship in 2018 in its 11th win of the past 13 years. The troupe performs throughout the month of the Chinese New Year, drawing huge crowds to watch its signature stunts.

Each lion dance ends with the lion taking a bow and members of the audience reaching out to feed it mandarin oranges and ang pow. The best troupes are booked back-to-back over Chinese New Year so any company that wants a performance needs to choose a date and book early.

Five Chinese New Year Taboos

1. Don't sweep floors on the first day of the New Year to avoid sweeping away all your good fortune.
2. Settle all debts before the eve of the Lunar New Year.
3. Don't borrow or lend money. One will lead to debts and the other turn into losses.
4. Don't fight or argue during New Year or you'll spend the rest of the year doing so.
5. Try not to break or chip anything. It could mean bad luck for the whole year.

Chinese Zodiac

Each year in the Chinese calendar is named after an animal, and those born in that year are said to possess some of the creature's characteristics. Naturally, some signs are more compatible than others, but it is seen as particularly auspicious to be a dragon. Birth rates increase considerably in any dragon year.

Rat
Quick-witted, resourceful and clever, people born in the year of the rat are able to adapt quickly to new environments and take advantage of the opportunities that come their way.

Ox
Anyone who is an ox is said to be dependable, trustworthy and determined.

Tiger
Those born in a tiger year are said to be brave, confident and competitive, but they can also be unpredictable and irritable.

Rabbit
Rabbits are said to be gentle and quiet although they can be overly secretive and stubborn.

Dragon
The dragon is the only mythical creature in the Chinese almanac and is said to be the most powerful—hence the spike in births each dragon year. In terms of personality, dragons are said to be people with courage, intelligence and confidence who are not afraid of challenges.

Snake
Snakes are the people who are probably the hardest to read, guarding their privacy. But they are also said to be among the most thoughtful and wise in the zodiac.

Horse

People born in the year of the horse are active and energetic with a fantastic sense of humour.

Goat

Goats are gentle but tough and have a highly developed sense of right and wrong.

Monkey

Monkeys are said to be sociable, witty and intelligent, but can also be mischievous.

Rooster

There's no avoiding a rooster. People born in the year of the rooster like to be the centre of attention and to regale others with their wit and repartee. On the down side, they can be vain.

Dog

Like man's best friend, people born in the year of the dog are loyal, dependable and honest.

Pig

Pigs are kind, generous and determined—always finishing what they set out to do.

A Word on Education

Education is highly valued among Malaysia's Chinese families who often put enormous pressure on their children to do well, signing them up to regular tuition classes after school and at the weekend, and 'drilling' them in the basics. Children start kindergarten, or pre-school, from the age of two or three (some may start even earlier if their parents work). Usually, there will be a quite significant amount of formal learning with regular updates on the child's progress for the parents in the form of a school report.

Many kindergartens are quite ethnically-diverse, but when it comes to proper school, Malaysia also has a network of Chinese-language schools that focus heavily on highly academic subjects to produce strong results in Maths and the Sciences. These academically-driven environments have also become more popular with Malay families in recent years even though the curriculum is in Mandarin. Parents set great store by top grades, aided and abetted by a local media that reports admiringly on each year's best performers.

In the past, Chinese families would scrimp and save to ensure at least one child would be able to go to university, preferably to study for a 'sensible profession' like medicine, law or accountancy. Nowadays, while an overseas education remains highly valued (the UK, Australia and the US are the most popular destinations), many stay in Malaysia where students attend private universities that have partnership arrangements with international universities, or are the Malaysian campuses of a UK or Australian university (Nottingham and Curtin, for example). Wherever they choose to go, Malaysian Chinese commitment to education remains as strong as ever.

Pregnancy and Birth

Malaysians of all ethnicities love babies and the Chinese are no exception. The arrival of a baby is an event to be celebrated, and one in which the women in a new mother's family, particularly her mother and mother-in-law, will be intimately involved.

Traditionally, Malaysian Chinese women and their babies spend the first month of the newborn's life in 'confinement'. The theory is that the extended rest, and the absence of visitors other than close family, will help the mother recover from the physical and emotional stresses of the birth more quickly, and grasp the rhythms and responsibilities of motherhood.

The new mum's mother and, frequently, her mother-in-law, take the lead in organising the confinement, although some people may hire a caregiver, known as a doula, who will live in the woman's home throughout the month.

New mums are supposed to bathe only in special herbal water after giving birth and avoid washing their hair for the entire month of their confinement. Another no-no is anything 'cool'—whether that's the welcome blast of air-conditioning, a fan or refreshing food.

The older women will cook special dishes for the new mother that are designed to 'warm' the body and will make sure she avoids anything that is remotely cooling like an iced drink, cucumber or watermelon. Fish is supposed to be good for those who are breast-feeding so the typical confinement includes plenty of herbal soups and steamed fish with ginger.

With more women now working, they often find the idea of not leaving the house suffocating and are horrified at the suggestion that they cannot shower or wash their hair after the demands of giving birth so the strictures of confinement are gradually loosening. On the other hand, some women love the idea of being forced to stay at home and be looked after and revel in the seclusion of confinement. In the end, it all comes down to individual preferences.

The good news for many women is that after one month, the confinement comes to end, which means it is time to party. The so-called 'full moon' party is a key milestone in any Malaysian Chinese baby's life, and the time when the child and its mother are welcomed back into the world.

Some people hold the event at home while others take the opportunity to organise a banquet at a hotel. Whatever the location, there will be plates of red-stained eggs—an odd number if it's a boy and even if it's a girl—to be offered to guests. Anyone attending a full moon celebration should bring money, in a red packet naturally, or gifts for the baby. Clothes and toiletries are popular gifts and often packaged together into hampers, although those who relish tradition might bring gold jewellery or coins as a longer-term investment.

Marriage

Matchmakers were once ubiquitous within Chinese society and hired to match eligible men with suitable brides. These days young Malaysian Chinese meet the same way everyone else does—through friends, at a club or bar, online or at work—and decide for themselves if they want to get married.

Some may 'register' their marriage—making them husband and wife in the eyes of the law—well before they host their wedding dinner, inviting close family and a handful of friends to the registery office with a celebratory lunch or dinner afterwards. Those who are Christian might choose to get married in a church with a banquet in the evening, while those who are more traditional might seek out a fortune teller to advise them on the most auspicious date and time for the event.

Most banquets take place at hotels and resorts (hence the sprawling number of function rooms) and while it is possible for the couple to handle the arrangements themselves, many rely on wedding planners to guide them through the process. Whenever and wherever the wedding dinner takes place, it is, almost without exception, an opportunity for a lavish celebration with an eight- or ten-course dinner, fine wines and cognac and a guest list extending into the hundreds and at least two costume changes for the bride.

Even today, physical wedding gifts are rare although not completely unacceptable (it depends how well you know the couple). Most guests bring an ang pow, which they hand over to the ushers on arrival. Notes should be crisp and in even amounts, preferably reflecting the likely cost of the venue (a wedding at the St. Regis in Kuala Lumpur would require a larger amount than one held at an event space in a provincial town) and the number of guests. Many people personalise the envelope with a small note so the couple know who it is from.

Any wedding guest who arrives promptly at the hour specified on the invitation will probably find themselves sitting alone munching peanuts for at least half an hour, but once most tables are filled the lights will drop and the emcee will announce the arrival of the bridal couple—often to the tune of a schmaltzy song—who will walk the red carpet to take their places at the main table, as their guests stand and clap.

The first dish gets a similar entrance—at one wedding I attended the food arrived to clouds of dry ice and the Star Wars theme—as the waiting staff appeared from all corners of the room with silver domed platters, plating the food and serving it up to each individual guest. The other dishes arrive with less pomp, but all form a crucial part of the wedding tradition—a soup (recent publicity over shark's fin means more couples are replacing this particular choice with luxurious seafood like lobster or crab), suckling pig, steamed or fried fish, chicken, a vegetable dish and noodles. All are laden with symbolic meaning to ensure love, longevity and a prosperous life for the newlyweds and will be cooked with the freshest and finest ingredients. Everyone eats a lot, drinks a lot and perhaps enjoys a few hours of karaoke. No one leaves hungry.

In the middle of the meal, the bride may disappear before making a dramatic return in a new gown—a contemporary cheongsam, perhaps, or a Western-style evening dress—to join the groom and visit each table to greet guests, take photos and raise a glass.

The cry is 'yam seng' and the idea, becoming steadily more raucous as the night goes on, is to shout out the word 'yam' for as long as possible—usually until you run out of breath—before shouting 'seng'. The Chinese equivalent of 'Cheers!' actually comes from Cantonese and translates as 'Drink to victory!'

After the toasts have finished, it is acceptable for guests to say their goodbyes and usually the newlyweds and their parents will gather at the door to thank everyone for coming. After that, it's time to count the ang pows.

Tea Ceremony

Traditionally, the bride would serve tea to her parents and in-laws to legalise the marriage. Many couples still perform the tea ceremony on the same day they register their marriage as a sign of respect for their elders.

Wedding Photography

Photos and video are a crucial part of any wedding, but Malaysian Chinese couples do not generally have their formal photos taken on the day of the event, they arrange a shoot months beforehand, trotting around the city's most picturesque locations in wedding suit and bridal dress with a photographer, an assistant and a few friends to dab away the sweat and ensure hair and make-up remain pristine. Sometimes couples adopt a theme—wearing Korean traditional dress for example—but taking the photos early allows them to share the pictures with their guests at the wedding banquet.

Death

A death is a sombre time for any Malaysian Chinese family; an opportunity to show the utmost respect and appreciation to the deceased and recognise the continued bond between the living and the dead.

Generally, the body will be brought to the family home so mourners can come and pay their respects, but it can also be kept at a funeral parlour. Some families alert others to the sad news through modern means like WhatsApp, while others prefer the traditional death notice in the local newspapers

(English language or Chinese) listing all family members and confirming the date and time of the funeral. For prominent figures, it is not unusual to see companies buying full pages of the paper to note the person's contribution to the country and express their condolences.

The body is placed in an open-topped coffin, screened off from the rest of the house, and a portrait of the deceased placed on a stand nearby, surrounded by flowers (usually yellow or white chrysanthemums to symbolise the family's grief and sadness) and candles. More traditional funerals will have some of the person's favourite clothing and possessions laid out to ensure they have everything they need in the afterlife.

The wake, whether at home or at a funeral parlour, is usually spread over about three days and nights with people drinking, chatting and gambling at tables set up around the coffin until the day of the funeral. Even if a wake is longer, which might be the case for someone who was well known, it will only ever take place for an odd number of days as a sign of the "complete cycle of life and the hope of reincarnation."

Mourners are free to attend at any time to pay their respects by bowing at the coffin, expressing their condolences to the family and spending a few hours reminiscing about the deceased over a beer or a cup of Chinese tea. Pregnant women and children are normally not encouraged to attend funerals.

Although some Chinese have become Christian, they continue to incorporate many of the old traditions into the Christian rites, and after the funeral service mourners will be expected to walk past the coffin as a show of respect as they express their condolences to the waiting line of family.

For a Christian funeral, the dress code is similar to Western countries, but for a more traditional Buddhist/Taoist rite, the family will wear rough cream, blue or black shirts depending on their relation to the deceased and take their places behind the hearse, usually a small white van. Other mourners, dressed in sombre colours, walk behind on the final journey to the burial ground.

In cities like Kuala Lumpur where burial grounds and cemeteries are often quite far away, mourners walk only for a few hundred metres before heading off to the graveyard or columbarium in coaches hired by the deceased's family. It is perfectly acceptable—and understood—if someone chooses this moment to go home.

Even though most Chinese consider cemeteries best avoided, they are of huge important to a community that is rooted in its veneration for the generations that went before. As the place where ancestors 'live', the traditional graveyard is the gateway to another realm and endowed with enormous religious significance.

As You Guijun, a writer and researcher on Chinese ghosts, notes: "Chinese do not see cemeteries as repositories of the dead, but as living communities inhabited by sprits capable of both communicating with and giving assistance to their descendants."

Traditionally, as the older sites around KL and Penang attest, hills were the favoured location for a cemetery, with the most sought-after (and expensive) plots towards the summit; the site and layout reflecting the Chinese desire for harmony. That said, cemeteries are places that are said to be high in potentially destabilising energy and beyond burials and Qing Ming (Grave Sweeping Festival), most Chinese prefer to keep their distance.

PERANAKAN OR STRAITS-BORN CHINESE

The Peranakan, sometimes known as Straits Chinese (although that technically refers to Chinese who were born in the Straits Settlements of Malacca, Penang and Singapore that were under the direct rule of the British) are descendants of the earliest Chinese immigrants to the Malay peninsula and the modern-

A room in the Pinang Peranakan Mansion in George Town. It was the home of 19th-century tycoon Chung Keng Quee.

day representatives of a unique culture that started even before the 18th century as Chinese settlers married locally-born women. The word 'peranakan' in Malay simply means locally-born.

The Chinese men, known as Baba, held onto most of their traditions but adopted elements of the local culture as well—the Peranakan dialect, for instance, is a mixture of Hokkien and Malay, while the Nyonya Kebaya, which was what many Peranakan women wore, consisted of a sarong with a fitted top in the style of the Malays of the time. Even Peranakan food was a fusion—a spicy amalgamation of Chinese and Malay tastes.

Peranakans in the 19th and 20th centuries were among the wealthiest people on the peninsula, largely English-educated and with close ties to the British. Even today, Peranakan families remain influential. Nyonya food is hugely popular and the Nyonya Kebaya a stylish addition to many women's wardrobes regardless of ethnicity.

THE INDIAN COMMUNITY

Malaysia's third largest ethnic group are the Indians, making up just over 6 per cent of the population, mostly Tamils from southern India but also other ethnic groups including Telugu or Malayalam.

Mostly they were brought to the peninsula by the British to work as labourers on the colonial government's expanding plantations, but others travelled to Malaya to work for the colonial government as teachers, lawyers, in the police or even on the railways. The result is a vibrant and diverse community—Malaysia's Indians are mostly Hindu, but they are also Christians, Sikhs and Muslims, and speak a huge diversity of languages.

Indian professionals remain highly visible—the country in 2018 appointed Tommy Thomas as Attorney General, the first non-Malay and non-Muslim to hold the position (Thomas is Christian)—and Indians are prominent too in parliament, the legal profession and medicine.

At the other end of the scale, Indians are also among the poorest in Malaysia. Long-running resentments, exacerbated by the demolition of Hindu temples, continuing statelessness and policies that supported conversions to Islam, brought thousands of mainly working-class Indians onto the streets of Kuala Lumpur in 2007 in what was a major wake-up call for the government of the time.

The man who established the Hindu Rights Action Force, better known by its acronym HINDRAF, and led the protests was lawyer P. Waytha Moorthy. He was questioned for sedition, had his passport revoked and spent four years living in exile in the UK. In 2018, following the change in government, he was made a senator and appointed the minister of national unity and social well-being.

Indian Names

Like the Malays, Indians have no family name in the Western tradition; their names are a combination of their given name and their father's name with the term *anak lelaki* (son of) or *anak perempuan* (daughter of) in between, although the terminology a/l and a/p is beginning to be phased out.

Mala Perumal, a woman, would be Mala a/p Perumal while Siva Sivalingam, a man, would be Siva a/l Sivalingam. If Mala were to marry Siva then she could be addressed as Mrs Siva. To complicate matters, some Tamil men—like P. Waytha Moorthy—reduce their father's name to an initial at the beginning of their name. Waytha Moorthy's father was named Ponnusamy.

Malaysia's Sikhs also have different naming conventions with baptised men adding the name Singh and baptised women, Kaur. Traditionally, they do not use the a/l or a/p terms.

There are also Indians with surnames like Rozario or de Silva whose heritage dates back to the time when Melaka was occupied by the Portuguese and Catholicism was the main religion. There are other Indian Catholics who use biblical and saints' names, like John or Abraham.

Clothing

Most Malaysian Indians in the big cities and towns wear Western clothing in their daily life, but traditional outfits remain popular, especially during festivals and special occasions.

Whatever their background women might wear a *sari*—an elegant ensemble made up of a single length of fabric, gathered at the waist and draped around the body and over the shoulder—especially on special occasions where the sari is often made of silk and features delicate embroidery and beading. A short-sleeved crop top, known as the *choli*, is worn underneath.

Salwar kameez, commonly known as 'punjabi suits', are common too, particularly among Punjabi women. Originating from northern India, the *salwar kameez* includes a long tunic—often embroidered—over slim-fitting trousers—and a scarf draped around the shoulders or head. A similar outfit worn by men, the *kurta*, comprises a long sleeved shirt that almost meets the knees over a pair of drawstring trousers.

Some Hindu women might choose to wear the bindi—the spot in the middle of the forehead between the eyes. If they are married it will be red. Otherwise, it is usually black. Indian men are rarely seen in traditional outfits although Sikh men will wear a turban and grow their facial hair. Sikhs also wear a steel bangle known as a *kara*—women on the left wrist and men on their right—as a symbol of their unbreakable commitment to god.

Religion

Hinduism is a belief system that is sometimes referred to as a 'way of life' and has no single founder, scripture or commonly agreed set of teachings. Its influence on Malaysia and the wider region can be traced back hundreds of years—predating the arrival of Islam—but it is now more closely associated with the country's ethnic Indian population who brought one of the world's oldest living religions with them when they settled in their new home.

Put simply, Hindus believe that existence is a cycle of birth, life and death that is governed by karma; that good deeds will be rewarded, bad actions punished and the soul's next incarnation will depend on how the previous life was lived. Followers therefore try to live their lives according to the *dharma*—the duties and virtues that keep the world and its people on the right track.

There are numerous deities within the Hindu pantheon, but the supreme being is Brahman, the creator and the foundation of the universe. The other principal gods are Vishnu, the preserver, and Shiva, the destroyer—in essence representing the different facets of Brahman. Hindu temples can be found throughout Malaysia from small shrines in plantation clearings to walled structures laden with colourful carved figurines of Hindu deities distinguished by towered gateways, known as *gopuram*, in the cities.

Traditionally, temples are built on a grid pattern that is based on the mandala and are designed as places where the boundaries between the human and divine worlds merge, enabling devotees to find the path to truth and knowledge.

Among the most famous is the network of shrines sheltered within the limestone karsts of Batu Caves on the outskirts of Kuala Lumpur, guarded by a towering, gold statue of Lord Murugan, the Hindu god of war. Visitors to the main Temple Cave have not only to walk up 272 steps to get to the site, but to also try and avoid a mugging by the troupes of marauding macaques that have made the caves their home. Batu Caves comes alive during Thaipusam in late January, which is one of the biggest Hindu festivals in Malaysia and is dedicated to Lord Murugan.

Another major temple is the Sri Mahamariamman in KL's Chinatown, which dates from the 19th century and is the oldest in Malaysia. It was originally built as a private shrine by successful businessman and tin miner K. Thamboosamy Pillai who was one of the most prominent people in the city's Tamil community at the end of the 19*th* century. After his death, Sri

Mahamariamman, dedicated to the goddess of fertility, was passed into the hands of trustees and opened to the public.

Thamboosay's original structure was a simple attap building, but by 1887 it had been rebuilt in brick, a testament to the city and the community's growing wealth and status. In 1968, it was demolished and rebuilt again with the *gopuram* added four years later. The monumental tower— more than 20 metres tall and carved with the intricate detail of hundreds of Hindu deities—is now the temple's most famous feature.

The main prayer hall in a Hindu temple is decorated with colourful carved reliefs and occupies the centre of the space, representing the heart of the worshipper. Smaller shrines are positioned around the walled compound. Devotees and visitors must remove their shoes before going inside. In smaller temples, they generally have to be left outside, but bigger temples, like the Sri Mahamariamman, usually have a cloakroom.

During prayers, Hindus usually light a lamp in front of an image or statue of the deity, burning incense and smearing ash on their forehead. They may also leave offerings of food and flowers. It is not always necessary for Hindus to go to a temple to pray, and most have small shrines or images of the deities where they can pray at home.

Sikhs first began settling in Malaysia in the 1870s after a revolt against British rule in India sent them into exile. Later on, Sikhs arrived to join the police as disputes between rival Chinese clans in the rapidly growing tin mining industry threatened to destabilise the colony and have played a prominent role in law enforcement and justice ever since.

There are some 100,000 Sikhs in Malaysia, more than 90 per cent of them from the Punjab. Kuala Lumpur is home to the largest Sikh temple or Gundwara in Southeast Asia. All Sikhs are supposed to follow the five Kakars—leaving their hair uncut (*kesh*), wearing a comb called a *kanga* in their hair and the *kara* (iron bracelet) on their wrists. They are also supposed to wear *kacha* (traditional underpants) and carry the *kirpan* (a sword).

A kolam for Deepavali. The design is carefully constructed from coloured grains of rice.

Indian Festivals

Two Indian festivals are national holidays in Malaysia—Thaipusam and Deepavali (the festival of lights that is known elsewhere as Diwali).

Thaipusam usually falls in late January and is one of Malaysia's most visceral experiences, while Deepavali, which celebrates the triumph of good over evil (light over darkness) is one of the most popular festivals among the broader Indian community and usually celebrated around October and November.

Indian shops and major shopping centres put up Deepavali displays of lights and *kolam*, coloured rice grains laid out on the floor in the form of peacocks, flowers and other symbols of the season.

In individual homes, a more modest *kolam* can be a sign of welcome, but most people opt for a string of festive lights and some may still make use of the traditional oil lamps that cost just one ringgit each from traditional shops.

Like every other community in Malaysia, Indian families

take the opportunity of Deepavali to cook festive foods, give their homes a thorough clean and refresh their wardrobes. Special festive markets are set up around Little India; their tables laden with seasonal specialities. *Murukku* is probably the snack most closely associated with Deepavali in Malaysia—deep fried swirls of spicy ground lentil and rice flour that are dangerously moreish—while *chelebi*, crispy spiral fritters drenched in sweet syrup, and *laddu*, gooey balls moulded from flour and ghee and studded with raisins and nuts, cater to those with a (much) sweeter tooth.

Pongal is a celebration of the rice harvest that lasts four days and is also called the Tamil New Year. It is an increasingly prominent feature of the national calendar and is actually named after the special dish that is cooked as an offering to the Sun God, Surya. Pongal, which means 'boiling over', is a sweetened dish of rice and milk that is cooked in clay pots in the first day of the festival and served as an offering and then to devotees on banana leaves. As it is cooking people gather around the pot to watch the milk bubble over the top, chanting 'Ponggalo, Pongal'.

Thaipusam is one of the most colourful of Malaysia's festivals, a day when Hindus and tourists—together as many as one million people—descend on Batu Caves on the outskirts of Kuala Lumpur; the devotees to honour Lord Murugan, revered as the son of the creator, Lord Shiva, and a symbol of courage and strength, and the tourists simply to experience the spectacle. It is a "bewildering Hindu festival that excites, confuses and tires," according to *Time Out Malaysia*.

For the most devout, preparations for Thaipusam begin two months before the event as they begin the process of cleansing themselves of their sins to develop the spiritual and physical strength to carry the *kavadi*—a cage-like structure loaded with two pots of milk known as *pal kodum*—that will be attached to their bodies with spikes and hooks for the ceremony.

During the cleansing process, the *kavadi*-bearers will refrain from eating meat (some may even fast), sleep on the floor, and forego life's pleasures from smoking to sex. The night before Thaipusam, devotees gather at Chinatown's Sri Mahamariamman Temple to prepare for the 15-kilometre walk to Batu Caves.

At the temple, the bare torsos of the men carrying the *kavadis* are pierced with the steel spikes and hooks necessary to keep the *kavadi*, some of which weigh as much as 30 kilograms, aloft; the weight tugging at their skin. It sounds gruesome and looks painful, but the devotees enter a trance-like state that enables them to overcome the pain. Women also carry the *kavadi*, mostly on a yoke, but some may also pierce their cheeks or tongues with steel spikes. Holy ash is smeared on their faces.

From Sri Mahamariamman, roads around the city centre are closed as the kavadi bearers dance and chant their way to the main temple, accompanied by the throb of drums, and well-wishers who sometimes join in the chant or throw water on the feet of the devotees.

Once they arrive in Batu Caves, the devotees must then climb the 272 steps to the shrine itself before the *kavadi* is finally removed. Miraculously, even the heaviest *kavadis* leave no wounds. Thaipusam is also celebrated in Penang although on a smaller scale than in Batu Caves.

Education
Like the Chinese community, the Indians were allowed to establish native-language schools at the time of Malaysia's

independence. There are now more than 500 government-aided Tamil language schools although they are not as well-resourced as their Chinese counterparts, which benefit from strong alumni networks. Most Indian families will send their children to government schools or to private schools if they have the means.

Births

For Malaysian Indians, as for everybody else, the arrival of a baby is cause for celebration and also a time for a period of 'confinement'. New mothers will spend up to a month hidden away from the world, looked after by a mother or mother-in-law so she can recover her strength after the birth and get to grips with the realities of motherhood. Some may hire a full-time doula for the month.

There is plenty of pampering for both mother and baby with Indian confinement practices rooted in traditional Ayuverdic medicine. The new mother is given herbal baths and scrubs, as well as massages and encouraged to eat nutritious foods, while the newborn gets special baths and oil massages. The special foods are known as *pathiya samayal* and made using a mix of 21 herbs and spices including coriander and cumin that people believe will encourage healing, boost the new mother's immunity and help stimulate the production of breast milk.

After a month away, it is time for mother and baby to make their debut in the real world—visitors are welcome and gifts for the baby gratefully received.

Marriage

In a country where large, extravagant wedding celebrations are the norm—an opportunity to share your good fortune with family, friends and business acquaintances—Indian festivities stand out not only for their tradition and colour but also for their sheer exuberance. A typical Tamil Hindu wedding lasts three days (Indian Catholics, Christians, Sikhs and others have different traditions) and is usually held at the bride's house and the temple.

The first two days are for preparation, and usually only the closest family and friends are invited. Both the bride and groom, fussed over by well-meaning aunties and uncles, are 'cleansed' with turmeric and receive blessings to ensure the success of their married life together. The bride's friends will probably join her for the *mehendi* ceremony when her hands and feet are decorated with intricate patterns of henna—the darker the henna, the deeper the love—in an event, which is similar to a Western-style hen night.

On day three, it is time for the ceremony proper. The bride and groom will dress in their finery—the bride in the *kanjipuram sari* that was said to be a favourite of Lord Vishnu and is made from nine yards (metres) of the finest, lustrous silk embellished with embroidery and beads, and accessorised with gold jewellery, a symbol of her family's wealth and prosperity.

Temple weddings will be officiated by the Hindu priest, guided by the sacred texts known as the Vedas, and include a series of rituals and prayers. The Ganesha Pooja is one of many prayers that are recited throughout the proceedings.

After exchanging flower garlands, the groom will place the *thali*—the Indian equivalent of a ring (although many couples these days will also choose to exchange rings)—around the neck of his new bride to symbolise their everlasting union. As with the exchange of rings in a

Western wedding ceremony, it is the climax of the day, and is accompanied by chants, a rising crescendo of music and flowers thrown by the guests.

Other rituals include the Sapta Padi where the bride and groom—holding hands—circle a ceremonial fire in seven steps proclaiming their vows to each other. It is also auspicious to crack open a coconut—you will often see piles of the husks outside a temple, which are then used to set fires.

Once the ceremony is complete, the wedding couple and their guests sit down to enjoy a feast of curry and other delicacies. They may also choose to have a more Western-style wedding dinner at a hotel or event space. Whichever the couple chooses, and many have both, it is hard not to get drawn into the excitement of the dancing and music.

Most people will dress up in their finest *sari* or, for men, shirt and trousers (some may go for an Indian *kurta* or *jippa*), and vibrant colours, sumptuous silks and decoration are positively encouraged. Just be sure not to wear white or black, which are more associated with mourning, and women should avoid upstaging the bride. If you are attending a temple ceremony, it is best not to wear plunging necklines and to ensure shoulders are covered. A certain amount of practicality might also be necessary since guests may also be required to sit on the floor during some of the temple ceremonies.

Malaysian Indians who are Sikh also dress in their best traditional outfits for a wedding, which normally takes place in the temple. The bride is given away by her father or brothers and after saying their vows, seal the marriage by walking four times around the holy book.

The wedding dinner can be held in the temple—where everyone is likely to have a hand in preparing the feast of vegetarian curries and flat breads—or in a hotel or wedding venue.

Deaths

For Hindus, death is part of the cycle of rebirth with the ultimate aim of achieving *moksha*—a transcendent state of freedom.

Like Malaysia's Muslims, the country's Hindus prefer to hold the funeral within 24 hours of a person's death, believing the soul needs to escape the body as quickly as possible because it is only then that soul can meet the god of death who has the power to decide how it will be reborn.

Traditionally, family members wash the body—making sure the head is facing towards the south, and a lighted oil lamp as well as a picture of the person's favourite deity are placed nearby—before wrapping it in a plain, white sheet. Ash or sandalwood is dabbed on the man's head and turmeric if the deceased is female.

Hindus prefer cremation and while open pyres might have long ago been the norm, nowadays towns and cities throughout Malaysia have crematoria, and the whole process is often handled through a funeral home that can provide a Hindu priest, the flower garlands and even banana trees to decorate the hearse.

At the ceremony, the men (no women take part) recite rituals and mantras, before the body is placed feet first into the incinerator. Later, the ashes are scattered on a river or at sea (traditionally, in the Ganges in India) with friends and family invited to witness the ceremony. White—a symbol of purity—is the appropriate colour if you are invited.

Family and friends will hold memorial prayers on the 8th and 16th days after the funeral, usually in the presence of a Hindu priest. For the ceremonies, a flower garland will be draped on a picture of the deceased and decorated with flowers, while guests will be served with vegetarian food.

ORANG ASLI (ORANG ASAL)

The original inhabitants of the Malay peninsula are among the most marginalised groups in the country, and usually make the news only when they protest against the destruction of their ancestral lands by loggers, plantation owners and developers, or during election times when politicians are stumping for votes. Only in 2019 was the first orang asli elected to parliament—Ramli Mohd Nor, a former policeman, represents the hill station constituency of Cameron Highlands.

The term 'orang asli' is a collective description for about 150,000 people from some 18 ethnic groups who live mostly within the forest, but also in coastal areas. Their knowledge of the natural environment made them highly sought-after as trackers during the Communist insurgency, while today they have been enlisted by the WWF in the fight to protect the country's last remaining tigers from poachers.

About 70 per cent have retained their traditional animist beliefs, according to Minority Rights Group International, although an increasing number have converted to Islam and others have become Christian. Most speak their own languages, as well as some Malay, and have managed to preserve much of their own customs and culture.

Traditional orang asli clothing is fashioned from tree bark, pounded on a hard surface to make it softer and more flexible and made into skirts, vests and hats. Pandanus leaf is woven into skirts and hats. Many orang asli men will make a point of wearing a heat of headdress at an official function even if they are wearing a Western-style outfit.

The Mah Meri, who live on Carey Island about an hour from Kuala Lumpur, are among the most well-known orang asli groups famed for their wood carving and the annual Hari Moyang or Ancestors' Day celebrations, which take place around February or March each year, and draw an increasing number of tourists.

The orang asli of Carey Island are renowned for their woodcarving skills and create highly expressive masks that are worn during traditional ceremonies and festivals.

Orang asli villages—typically a series of bamboo huts with attap roofs—also appear sporadically along the road from Tapah to Tanah Rata in the Cameron Highlands. Some families set up stalls to sell forest produce like plants and jungle honey, or their own crafts including blowpipes, animal or fish traps and products woven from pandanus (screwpine).

Like Rosli, many of the orang asli in the highlands are of Semai or Temiar descent. The Temiar are the second biggest group among the orang asli. Their villages are mainly in the upland areas of Perak and Kelantan living in forested areas and working on the land either using the traditional method of shifting cultivation or on their own smallholding.

INDIGENOUS PEOPLE IN SARAWAK AND SABAH

About 20 per cent of Malaysia's population lives in the Borneo states of Sabah and Sarawak and most of them are indigenous people, although Sarawak has a large population of Chinese and Sabah a huge number of Filipino migrants, many of whom are undocumented.

The indigenous people are often referred to collectively as Dayaks, a term devised by colonial bureaucrats, but some groups like to assert their tribal identity, particularly the Iban, who were once among the island's proudest warriors with a fearsome reputation as headhunters. It is also worth noting that Sabah's indigenous communities are rarely referred to as Dayak.

The rural areas of Sarawak, some accessible only by boat or helicopter, are populated by numerous different indigenous groups who live in longhouses—the Sarawak equivalent of a row of terraced houses, a different family living in each, although in this case the terrace is (usually) lifted from the ground and comes with its own shady veranda for communal events.

The Iban, who make up about 30 per cent of Sarawak's population, are thought to have settled in Sarawak as many as 800 years ago after following the river through the jungle from what is now Kalimantan. The next biggest group, the Bidayuh, also have their roots in Kalimantan, but now live among the gentle hills and valleys that lie about 90 minutes drive from Kuching.

Other tribes—sometimes referred to as 'orang ulu' or upriver people—live further into the interior including the Kelabit, Kenyah and Kayan. All have different customs and traditions based on their 'adat' or native culture.

In the past, indigenous people survived through traditional shifting agriculture and foraging from the forest, and some were able to live a nomadic or semi-nomadic existence. These traditional lifestyles have come under enormous pressure from rapid development, particularly in the past two decades during which great swathes of forest have been converted into plantation, while major rivers have been dammed submerging longhouses and ancestral lands.

However, Iban and other tribes continue to live in longhouses, mostly built along the banks of the rivers that are a crucial link between the interior and the main towns and cities on the coast.

Religion

For Borneo's indigenous tribes the spirits are all around—whether in the towering rainforest trees, the bugs beneath fallen leaves, the monkeys leaping from branch-to-branch, the rivers, water sources or sky. Ancestors too are revered and traditional burial grounds sacred spaces.

Together, that reverence for nature and respect for ancestors formed part of a spiritual world view known as Kaharingan, and while many Dayaks are now Christian (often Evangelical, but also Anglican and Catholic), that has tended to overlay rather than supplant their traditional culture.

The entrance to each longhouse is guarded by a wooden statue or totem to protect its residents and ward off evil spirits. Other sculptures aim to soothe the souls of unhappy spirits or attract good fortune. Even the wooden baby carriers that are decorated with the indigenous people's traditional beadwork, feature patterns that are designed to protect the youngster within.

The hornbill, whose call echoes across the forest, is one of the Iban's most revered spirits, acting as an intermediary between the earthly world and Singalong Burong, the powerful god of war. The bird is incorporated into numerous objects and its likeness is frequently the centrepiece of traditional ceremonies. The bird's feathers are also prized and used in the outfits of male dancers and warriors.

The colour black is thought to possess important protective qualities and is used in numerous traditional motifs including the tattoos that were a crucial element of the Dayaks' headhunting past.

Headhunting itself was said to be guided by the spirits who would reward those who returned with a head by showing them the way to more fertile lands, ensuring an abundant rice crop for the community. Headhunting is firmly in the past in Sarawak, but the occasional skull can still be seen, obscured by dust and cobwebs, tucked away in the rafters of some of the older longhouses.

Tattoos, which were once an indication of achievement—for both men and women—or a form of protection—remain common and have even been adopted among young people from other countries. The *bunga terung*, drawn on the shoulders just below the collarbone, is given to young men ahead of their 'coming of age' ceremony known as *bejalai*.

Hari Gawai/Pesta Kaamatan

Hari Gawai, or Harvest Festival, is the most important celebration of the year for the Iban and Bidayuh people of Sarawak and is marked each year on June 1.

Gawai used to take place whenever the rice harvest had been completed, but a fixed date makes it easier for those who have settled in other parts of the country to make their way back to their childhood longhouse for the two days of festive merrymaking and plentiful drinking that mark the festival.

Communities start preparing for the festivities at least a month beforehand, ordering and preparing food and drink and brewing the *tuak* (a milky-white rice wine) that is essential to the celebration. A small glass might look quite harmless, but once fermented the mix of glutinous rice and homemade yeast packs quite a punch.

Although Christianity has spread through many indigenous communities, Iban people will mark the eve with ceremonies to honour the spirits and their ancestors, inviting them to join in the fun of the coming days.

On Gawai itself, which means 'merrymaking' in Iban, everyone tucks into a feast of dishes sourced largely from the jungle and cooked over an open fire. There are myriad types of ferns, vegetables like aubergine, herbed, seasoned meats stuffed inside bamboo and even pig's head. Rice too is cooked in bamboo over the fire (much like the Malay *lemang*). All of it is washed down with plenty of *tuak*. After that, it's time for traditional dances and songs—and even more *tuak*—with the party continuing well into the night.

Over in Sabah, the celebration is known as Pesta Kaamatan in the Kadazan-Dusun language, and usually takes place at the end of May or beginning of June.

As in Sarawak, there is plenty of food and drink (the home-brewed rice wine in Sabah is called *tapai* and *lihing*) with the special festive dishes including a marinated raw fish dish known as *hunava*.

Traditional dance is also a crucial part of the celebrations with the Sumazau, inspired by eagles flying above farmers' fields during the harvest, and Magunatip, where dancers dance over fast-moving bamboo poles, among the most popular.

The Longhouse

Longhouses are a communal style of living unique to Sarawak (in Sabah most people live in single houses) and the physical embodiment of the Dayak communities' way of life and strong tribal bond.

Traditionally, a longhouse is built on the banks of the river (for easy access), perched high on stilts above the ground with a shared veranda at the front, known as the *ruai* by the Iban, and a communal space at the rear known as the *tanju*.

Each family has a private apartment with a kitchen and bathroom that is accessed from the veranda and is where they sleep, keep their clothing and store their possessions. The more families that live in the longhouse, the more apartments, sometimes identified as 'doors', and the longer the longhouse. The biggest have 200 doors or more and are said to be nearly a kilometre in length. Most average about 250 metres.

The Dayaks who first built longhouses were mostly rice farmers or tended small plots of rubber, pepper and other crops. The longhouses were made from materials that were easily available in the jungle—floors and walls crafted from slats of bamboo, the roof from palm fronds and the stilts and beams of the main structure from sturdy trunks of ironwood.

Even the stairs up to the *ruai* were carved out of a single tree trunk, decorated with motifs of guardian spirits.

The veranda has long played a central role in keeping the community together. With the men away in the fields, the *ruai* was a place for the women of the tribe to cook, weave and chat, while keeping an eye on the children.

"The ruai served as a covered play area, where children played hide-and-seek and chased each other under the benign watch of grandparents who tended to chores such as weaving mats, repairing old baskets or tending to the drying padi," former Cabinet minister Leo Moggie recalled of his childhood in a recent memoir.

Nowadays, many younger generations have moved to the towns and cities for work returning to the longhouse only a few times a year, and the very real danger of fire—the local media has regular reports on longhouses being razed to the ground—mean they are increasingly being built from modern materials like concrete and on the ground rather than elevated above it.

Every longhouse has a chief—the *tuai rumah*—and a deputy. It is their job to arbitrate disputes between families and with neighbouring longhouses, deal with government officials and welcome visitors to the village; Iban tradition requires that anyone who shows up at a longhouse must be welcomed and offered accommodation. These days, however, most foreigners visit longhouses as part of small groups or with Malaysian friends who know some of the community's residents.

It is polite to remove shoes before stepping onto the *ruai*, especially those made from bamboo (in newer longhouses built on the ground this might not be necessary, but always check first). The guide will normally make the introductions for those in a group, and the headman will acknowledge his guests. Mingling is important and the Iban like to welcome visitors with a glass of *tuak*. It is considered impolite to refuse although a medical excuse might pass muster. A longhouse stay is also an opportunity to sample traditional food, which is usually eaten while sitting on the floor of the veranda.

Residents will often stage traditional dances, inviting their guests to join in like an indigenous equivalent of team-building 'ice breaker' sessions, but considerably more fun. It does not matter if the guest appears ridiculous, as long as everyone is laughing and smiling the dance can be considered a success.

Of course, a few rounds of *tuak* from the ceremonial shot glass help everyone relax. The *tuak* may also help once everyone turns in for the night. The communal nature of the longhouse can make it difficult for those unaccustomed to such a way of life to sleep, especially when it is hot (few longhouses in remote places have mains electricity and the generators operate only for a few hours in the evening and morning), and the thin wooden walls mean every noise can be heard.

MALAYSIA'S MIGRANTS

When you go to the checkout to pay for your weekly shop or order food at a local restaurant, it is likely that the person who serves you will not be a Malaysian, but someone who has travelled from one of the region's poorer countries with the hope of earning—and saving—enough money to give their family a better life.

It is not just supermarkets and restaurants, either. Malaysia's migrant population, both men and women, come to do the jobs Malaysians do not want to do, whether that is working on construction sites and plantations, on local market stalls, collecting rubbish or cleaning.

Certain nationalities—the Nepalese—are allowed to work as security guards while women from Indonesia are often found in Malaysian homes, doing domestic chores, but young women are recruited from all around the region earning just a few hundred ringgit a month, and rarely getting time off.

Altogether about two million migrants are on work permits, but even more—estimates reach as high as five million—have no documentation, which leaves them vulnerable to exploitation by employers and regular crackdowns by the authorities, the most recent of which took place in mid-2018.

As well as migrants, Malaysia also has nearly 156,000 refugees and asylum seekers who live among the community, mostly in KL and Penang, although there are also growing numbers living in the Cameron Highlands where they can find itinerant work on the farms.

A learning centre for refugee children in Klang.

In a country where their status is not recognised because the government is not a signatory to the UN Convention on Refugees and refuses to let them work or send their children to government schools, it is a precarious existence.

The chance of being resettled in a third country is remote—only between three and four per cent of the refugee population are likely to have that opportunity in any one year, according to experts.

Their only support comes from the United Nations High Commissioner for Refugees (UNHCR), which first opened an office in Malaysia to help the country cope with the 'boat people' who fled Vietnam in the 1970s, their own community groups and a small number of Malaysian civil society organisations. Together they operate mobile health clinics, run learning centres and help the refugees find ways to make a living.

The UNHCR compound is located in a colonial era bungalow that has long since disappeared behind a wall of portakabins and shipping containers where asylum seekers and refugees spend hours waiting (having spent months or even years awaiting an appointment) to relate their story to the harried officers who will decide whether they can be considered a refugee, and later on, whether they are a suitable candidate for resettlement.

It is an indication of how significant a place the UNHCR holds in their lives, that many arrive well before the gates open at 8am, and queue in the half-light for their chance to be heard.

While most asylum seekers have fled Myanmar, continuing conflict in the Middle East and South Asia has brought people from countries such as Yemen, Syria, Afghanistan and Pakistan; many of them thinking they will get a warm welcome in Malaysia because a majority of its population is Muslim. There are also a large number of Sri Lankan Tamils who fled the island during that country's long-running civil war.

There is hope that the new government will ratify the refugee convention and try to make the climate less hostile to those who have found sanctuary in Malaysia. Refugees with UNHCR cards can now access local healthcare services at a cheaper rate (although they sometimes run the risk of being referred to the immigration department for being 'illegal migrants'), but a pilot programme to provide work for Rohingya that was started under the previous administration has not proved successful. Few Rohingya wanted to work in the plantations industry, and many were afraid at the prospect of moving away from their own communities and established support networks.

MAIN HOLIDAYS

Thanks to Malaysia's diverse population, it can seem like every month has a celebration of one kind of another and there are numerous public holidays to ensure devotees can celebrate their most important festivals.

The main holidays are religious and celebrated across the country: Hari Raya Aidilfitri, (the Malay name for the Muslim festival of Eid), Chinese or Lunar New Year, Deepavali (the Hindu festival of lights) and Christmas. There is no holiday for Good Friday or Easter in Malaysia, and it is worth remembering that in the north-eastern states New Year's Day is a normal working day. Malaysia's diversity means it also has a wealth of smaller festivals that often aren't marked by public holidays but are worth your attention.

Hari Moyang

In a tent in clearing, the table is laden with freshly-steamed rice, curries, cakes and snacks, and bottles of sugary drinks to wash it all down. Outside, a man is

Mah Meri women at the annual Hari Moyang festival on Carey Island.

performing a tribal dance as women sing and musicians keep time with bamboo poles and drums. Their skirts, woven from palm leaves dried in the sun, rustle and swish as the women move.

Hari Moyang or Spirits' Day is one of the most important days in the year for the Mah Meri, the indigenous people who live on Carey Island, not far from Kuala Lumpur.

Despite rapid development and the spread of palm oil plantations across the landscape, they have held fast to their culture and traditions, honouring at least 700 gods and spirits that they believe inhabit the low-lying island.

Hari Moyang usually falls around February, but the actual date is only known when the village chiefs have made contact with the spirits. It's the Moyang themselves that decide when the festivities will be held.

Land and sea are both vital to the life of the Mah Meri who are thought to be the descendants of sea gypsies who once lived further south on the peninsula, and their rituals reflect the importance of nature to their lives. While the main event involves offerings, dancing and the village shaman dispensing blessings to a patient queue of Mah Meri and visitors, more intimate ceremonies take place along the shore and at sea.

GHOSTS AND SUPERSTITION

When I learned Malay, one of the teacher's favourite topics of discussion was ghosts. One of his most memorable stories involved the student hall of residence where he had been living during the holidays; dormitories are a popular location for Malay ghost stories.

The teacher was lying on his bed one evening and could hear the sound of a party taking place nearby. It was the end of term, so the teacher doubted there was anyone around to be having any kind of celebration, but he could definitely hear music, chatting and laughing. He thought he would go and join in. Following the music, and peals of laughter he made his way to the hall's common room. But when he opened the door, there was no one there. Nor was there any music.

The story did not end there. Our teacher told us he was a little unnerved by the occurrence. He was, after all, alone in the building. He went back to his room and tried to sleep. There was no more music, but there was a distinct chill and as he lay on the bed he could feel a great weight pressing down on his chest. It was getting hard for him to breathe, but no matter how he struggled he could not get away from whatever was holding him down. Increasingly desperate, and fearful, he turned to religion. Over and over he repeated verses from the Quran. First softly, then louder and louder. Finally, the pressure eased.

Ghosts, better known as hantu, are a big part of Malaysian life. Everyone, it seems, has a story to tell—relate your strange experience to a group of Malaysians and they will all—Malay, Chinese, Indian or 'lain-lain'—be clamouring to share the time they met a spirit or a ghost or experienced something strange.

Browse the shelves in any bookshop and they will be laden with ghost stories, tales of the supernatural and investigations into the mystical. Turn on the television or go to the movies and there will always be a spooky film to watch, many of them locally made.

The world may have sniggered (and some Malaysians too) when 'Raja Bomoh' turned up at the Kuala Lumpur International Airport in 2014 with a 'magic carpet', a few coconuts and a couple of bamboo cannons to help in the search for the missing MH370, but many take the work of traditional healers extremely seriously.

Indeed, Haron Din, who was the spiritual leader of Malaysia's Islamic party until his death in 2016, was a well-known bomoh (the Malay name for a shaman). The group he founded, known as Darussyifa, or House of Healing, is still run by his followers and is one of the most popular in the country.

The Malay fascination with the supernatural is deep-rooted and has been passed down through the generations, and it is shared by many other ethnicities in Malaysia.

Plenty will tell you that abandoned houses—their gardens overgrown—are occupied by ghosts who move in when living people do not (a ghost likes a nice house just as much as anyone else) or is haunted by the victims of those who were killed there. If it is an older building, then often you will learn that it was the site of executions by the Japanese during the occupation. Otherwise, the house was the scene of a suicide or a murder. Every neighbourhood seems to have at least one such house, the roof caved in, windows swinging open and the garden running to jungle.

For other people, it is numbers. Some are taboo, while others are lucky and the path to riches and success. In office buildings owned by a Chinese company or family you might find there are no floors 13 or 14 and that they are instead marked as 12A or 13A. For the Cantonese, the number four is ominous because it sounds the same as the word for death, while 14 sounds like 'must die' and 24 'easy to die'. The number 44 is also to be avoided; its connotations of death are doubled.

The luckiest number for all Chinese is eight because it sounds like 'wealth' and 'prosperity' and 88 is even better because it sounds like 'double happiness'. You will see these Chinese characters at every Chinese wedding complemented by decorations in red and gold (auspicious colours). On these occasions, money is given to the couple in red packets, known as 'ang pow', and the best guests will give crisp notes in denominations of eight.

On a quirkier note, do not be surprised to see cars slowing down so their occupants can note down the registration number of a vehicle that has been involved in a crash. Rather counterintuitively, the four digits are considered lucky for entering into the national lucky draw known as 4D.

Some Malaysian Chinese also believe in the idea of *feng shui*, the creation of spaces for the maximisation of *chi* (spirit) and good fortune, which can sometimes involve a complete architectural renovation (watch out for a front door at an angle), but can also be achieved through something as simple as a strategically placed coin or figurine.

Five of Malaysia's Most Well-Known Supernatural Creatures

A rather large number of Malaysian ghosts and monsters

appear to be women. Read into that what you will. Below are five that you might hear about while you are living in Malaysia:

Pontianak

The Pontianak (there's an Indonesian city named after the monster) is a fearsome female ghoul that is said to be the ghost of a woman who died while pregnant or giving birth. The creature takes on the appearance of a pale and beautiful maiden dressed in white, her long dark hair cascading around her shoulders, to lure unsuspecting men to their deaths; clawing at their bodies with her long nails and devouring their organs. Pontianak are said to live among banana trees, which is why some people do not plant them in their gardens, but the monster can become a real woman again if a nail is plunged into the back of its neck.

Orang Minyak

According to legend, the orang minyak—oily man—was a man who made a deal with the devil to give himself enormous power. But the agreement came at a heavy price; in order to develop extraordinary power he would have to rape 21 virgins within a week and promise to worship the devil. The creature, covered in black oil that makes him hard to catch, was made famous in a film by P. Ramlee back in 1959, but even today there are sporadic reports in the local media of 'orang minyak' appearing in local villages and terrorising young women.

Toyol

The toyol is a mischievous creature that is usually sent to do the bidding of a bomoh. Like many newborns (the toyol is said to be the reincarnation of a stillborn baby), toyol are small and hairless, but as spirits they have the ability to walk and, apparently, a penchant for sucking the blood from the toes of sleeping humans.

Penanggalan
One of the most fearsome of Malaysian spirits, the Penanggalan is said to have the head of a woman and the body of, well, entrails. Supposedly a normal human being during the day, as night falls the Penanggalan settles on the roof of a house ready to lap up the blood of the humans inside with its long tongue. Apparently, planting spiky plants around your home will keep the monster at bay.

Hantu Raya
Best described as a demon, the Hantu Raya is said to be the most dangerous of all Malaysia's supernatural creatures. Like the Toyol it does the bidding of a human master, but in exchange for wealth and success, the human must ensure the Hantu Raya's needs are met and promise to find another owner for the ghost before they die, which usually means the being is passed down from one generation to the next. People believe the ghost can possess its owner even if they are living.

Hungry Ghost Month
At the start of the seventh lunar month, the Gates of Hell are flung open and the dead walk among the living. For Chinese, whether Buddhist or Taoist, this is a month that is steeped in tradition; the time to prepare offerings of food and money (the special kind that can only be used in the underworld), and produce rollicking street performances to keep the ghosts happy and content during the few short weeks they are back on earth.

In cities like George Town or Melaka (or anywhere else that is home to large numbers of Malaysian Chinese) you will see small bonfires of paper offerings at the side of the road (sometimes in a red barrel, but often not), that are supposed to act as a guide for the homeless souls. This is hell money—yellow paper printed with red and gold lettering that is sold in large bags at the shops that line the streets close to many Chinese temples, folded and twisted ready for burning.

Chinese will also prepare food for the ghosts to place on an altar at home or at the temple, and light incense sticks. Particularly popular are cardboard effigies of the latest gadgets and fashion—iPhones, Prada bags, even ten-bedded mansions and Ferraris—so that the ghosts can live in style and keep up with the latest trends.

In many cities and towns, performers will also stage special shows for the spirits—traditional Chinese operas or more boisterous productions involving plenty of loud singing, stand-up comedy and dancing to keep the ghosts entertained while they are in the world of the living. It might seem that the front few rows are empty, but the best seats in the house are reserved the spirits.

There are a whole range of activities that are out of the question for the more traditional Chinese during the ghost month, although younger people tend to be a lot less concerned about the risks than the older generation. Hungry ghost month dos and don'ts include:

- Do not touch the offerings and try not to step on any that have been placed in the street.
- Try not to stay out late at night because that is when the ghosts are most powerful.
- Avoid moving into a new home or buying property during the month because of the risk of bad luck. It

is possible to view houses and apartments and even choose the one that you would most like to buy, but contracts should only be signed once hungry ghost month has finished.

- If you already have your own home, avoid doing any renovation.
- Business people should avoid doing deals.
- Avoid travelling, especially by plane or sea.
- Children should avoid swimming. Some Chinese believe that ghosts lurk under the water and will try to pull a child below the surface.
- Avoid opening an umbrella indoors.
- Do not kill any insects that you find in your home during the ghost month. For some Chinese, ants and other insects are reincarnated spirits and could be your deceased loved ones.
- Do not hang your clothes out on the line overnight because spirits will make a home in them.

MALAYSIAN POLITICS

For decades, Malaysia was ruled, in one form or another, by the same party—the United Malays National Organisation (UMNO), which was founded in the southern state of Johor in 1946 and played a crucial role in securing colonial Malaya's independence from Britain.

Established to fight for the rights of the ethnic Malays, the party created a grand coalition with other race-based parties, each representing the country's three main ethnic groups but together championing Malaysia's economic development.

As the years passed, UMNO became increasingly dominant in the Barisan National coalition, and corruption, often known by the euphemism of 'money politics' and enabled by an opaque system of government procurement, began eating away at the organisation.

At party convention after party convention, leaders would bemoan the prevalence of 'money politics'. Copious tears would shed. But even as Malaysians gossiped among themselves about the party leaders' dodgy dealings and flashy lifestyles, some of which were shared eagerly on social media platforms, nothing seemed to change.

Then, under the country's sixth prime minister, Najib Razak, public anger and corruption came to a head in the form of the misappropriation of billions of dollars from state investment fund 1MDB.

The wrongdoing was exposed in the London-based blog *Sarawak Report*, and *Wall Street Journal*, as well as braver local media like the financial newspaper *The Edge*. The scale of the alleged wrongdoing—the money funding, according to the Department of Justice in the US, a jet-set lifestyle of celebrity parties, luxury yachts, Manhattan penthouses, Hollywood movies and diamond jewellery—was mind-boggling to ordinary Malaysians.

Najib, who had come into office in 2009 as a reformer, responded not with transparency—although he did set up an investigation—but by battening down the hatches. He fired senior colleagues and the attorney general who had been about to lay charges against him, blocked Sarawak Report and other critical websites, and adopted ever more draconian measures to maintain his hold on power.

It was not enough. Malaysians were aching for change, tired of Barisan, UMNO, and, most of all Najib and his handbag-and-diamond-loving wife, Rosmah Mansor. In May 2018, after 61 years, the unthinkable happened. Despite numerous hurdles—from a compliant media to vastly unequal constituency sizes and financial resources that had many observers predicting yet another win for Barisan—Malaysians voted for change.

Ironically, the historic win for the opposition parties—challenging under the banner of Pakatan Harapan (Alliance of Hope) was led by a former UMNO leader—the country's fourth prime minister, nonagenarian Mahathir Mohamad who had returned to politics after 15 years in retirement, abandoning UMNO to establish his own party and then joining the opposition coalition.

In the process, he and Anwar Ibrahim, the former deputy he had sacked 20 years before and then jailed on charges of sodomy, made their peace. Such are the machinations and intrigues of politics in Malaysia.

The new government wasted no time in reviewing the policies and practices of its predecessor. Anwar was pardoned and released from jail where he was serving a second term for sodomy, a crime in Malaysia. And the investigation into 1MDB, which had continued in the US, Switzerland and a number of other countries around the world even as the domestic probe was closed down, resumed.

Both Najib and his wife were summoned to a reinvigorated anti-corruption commission where they were questioned for hours. Najib was charged with corruption and the first of a number of trials in relation to 1MDB started in Kuala Lumpur's High Court in April 2019. His wife and a number of former senior leaders are also facing trial. All deny wrongdoing.

In a sense, the election victory of 2018 was a return to the hope that existed in Malaysia's early years of independence.

Although UMNO's founding fathers were motivated by a concern that the Malays might be left behind in the shift towards independence if ethnic minorities, particularly the Chinese (already seen as more economically powerful), were given equal citizenship and status in the newly independent country, it was Tunku Abdul Rahman, the Kedahan prince who eventually became Malaysia's first Prime Minister, who deftly navigated the differences between the sides to secure the compromises necessary to build the nation.

The Malays got commitments on language, education and 'special rights' while the Indians, Chinese and others whose forefathers had come to Malaya during British rule secured the right to stay in the country on the basis of *jus soli*.

As the *New York Times* wrote on his death in December 1990: "He was able to walk the line between the two religions and win the trust of both. He became a success symbol for Chinese-Malay political cooperation and was known for his self-effacing wit and ability to move audiences with simply spoken common sense."

Tunku Abdul Rahman hoped the new country would be an example to the world. "I call upon you all to dedicate yourselves to the service of the new Malaysia: to work and strive with hand and brain to create a new nation, inspired by the ideals of justice and liberty—a beacon of light in a disturbed and distracted world," he told Malaysia's new citizens.

But in only a decade, and despite the Tunku's carefully devised compromises, deepening racial resentments put his vision at risk. The elections of 1969 were hard fought and when the opposition wrested control of four states, there were violent protests on the streets of Kuala Lumpur, an event still euphemistically known only by its date: May 1969.

Nearly 200 people, mostly Chinese, died in the violence as Malay mobs rampaged through parts of the capital. The unofficial death toll is thought to have been much higher, and the spectre of what happened that night—even with the relatively smooth handover of power when the opposition toppled BN in 2018—continues to haunt many older Malaysians.

The unrest enabled the UMNO-led government to quickly reassert control imposing a state of emergency and a raft of positive discrimination measures, known as the New Economic Policy or NEP, designed to rapidly improve the economic position of the Malays and reduce inequality between the races.

The NEP was supposed to have a finite existence, but the racial preferences it created, remain in force, albeit with some adjustments, even today.

Post-1969, Malaysia also became increasingly authoritarian. While it was never a country where people feared the knock of the door in the middle of the night, opposition politicians, activists and journalists were targets of periodic crackdowns under legislation, some of it dating from the colonial era, that criminalised dissent and allowed detention without trial for as long as two years.

The media was also hobbled by legislation requiring annual printing permits, and as newspapers and television news were gradually bought up by groups controlled by the ruling parties, the space for genuine debate on public policy diminished.

For most of the 1980s and 1990s, however, Malaysia's economy was growing fast; an 'Asian tiger' to rival Singapore, Taiwan and South Korea. With food on the table, rising incomes and even a new 'national' car, Malaysians felt they had much to be proud of and few were concerned about the political limitations under which they lived.

It took the Asian Financial Crisis and the sacking of Anwar Ibrahim in 1998 to shock Malaysians out of their wealth-induced stupor. Thousands flooded onto the streets in support of the former deputy prime minister, the demonstrations clashing awkwardly for the government with an official visit by Britain's Queen Elizabeth. Protesters shared developments with the wider public through photocopies and fax and as Malaysians began to sign up for the Internet, critical voices found a new platform; one where they could say what they wanted.

Anwar's supporters saw the downfall of Suharto in Indonesia and dreamed that Malaysia too could become a democracy. In the event, it took a further two decades.

THE MECHANICS OF PARLIAMENT

Malaysia is a parliamentary democracy with elections for the federal government taking place no more than five years apart at a date of the prime minister's choosing. Like its former colonial ruler, members of parliament are elected through the system of 'first past the post'—the winner is the person that gets the most votes, and the losing side gets no representation whether they get 0.9 per cent or 49.9 per cent of the votes. Some 222 seats are up for grabs at the federal level. The same system is used for the various state assemblies, which also sit for five-year terms.

Since independence, Malaysia's political parties have typically been race-based—UMNO representing the Malays, the Malaysian Chinese Association (MCA) for the Chinese and the Malaysian Indian Congress (MIC) for the Indians.

Pakatan Harapan's members include the race-based Parti Pribumi Bersatu Malaysia, which Mahathir founded after splitting from UMNO, as well as the more inclusive Parti

Keadilan Rakyat (Anwar's party) and the Democratic Action Party, which is often accused of being 'Chinese chauvinist' but whose membership is open to all. Amanah, meanwhile, is a progressive Islamic party whose members defected from the long-established, but increasingly conservative Parti Islam seMalaysia (PAS). PAS was once part of Pakatan, but moved closer to UMNO shortly before the 2018 election.

Sarawak and Sabah have a huge number of political parties that are indigenous to Borneo and UMNO is noticeably absent from Sarawakian politics. The upper house is known as the Senate and is an appointed body.

Until recently, Malaysian parliaments had seen little real debate over policy and it was rare, if ever, that a bill would go through committee stages or be returned for amendment. Indeed, under the Barisan Nasional government bills, particularly those likely to attract most controversy, were presented to lawmakers at the last minute with only a few hours for debate or discussion.

The Pakatan Harapan government came to power with a promise to strengthen parliament. An independent speaker has already been appointed, compared with the previous Barisan-supporting speaker who often refused motions to discuss issues sensitive to the government.

The now opposition Barisan Nasional has also appointed its members to a shadow cabinet to scrutinise key portfolios—a first for Malaysia—and a number of parliamentary committees have also been established, another first.

Staying Informed

The 2018 election gave new life to Malaysia's reticent media, which was facing the threat of additional restrictions under a broad and vaguely-worded 'Fake News Law'. The

BN's historic loss not only fuelled a surge of interest in news—boosting sales and audience—but also encouraged journalists to report more freely.

It is probably too early to say that the media landscape has irrevocably changed—many repressive laws remain on the books and the former ruling parties still control the major media companies—but the change in government provides an opportunity for the country's journalists to reconsider the purpose of their work and keep the government, business and politicians accountable.

Many Malaysians get their news through Facebook and WhatsApp, but *Malaysiakini* has developed into one of the most popular, and trusted online newspapers publishing in both English and Malay.

The biggest circulation English language daily is *The Star*, a tabloid whose biggest strength is R.AGE, a small team focussing on issues-based and investigative journalism.

On radio, BFM 89.9 has acquired quite a following in the Klang Valley. Its daily business coverage is supplemented with programmes on culture, the arts, music and even football in the evenings and at weekends.

The local Awani channel, part of Astro, has also become increasingly popular since the 2018 election and broadcasts some popular talk shows. BBC, CNN and Al Jazeera are all available on Malaysian fibre and satellite television, as well as a number of European and Asian news channels.

CHAPTER 4

FITTING IN

> ❝We put on new clothes to be ready to usher in a good new beginning.❞

— Datuk Jimmy Choo OBE

GREETINGS

Malaysians are generally a hospitable and friendly bunch of people, proud of their country and eager to make visitors and longer-term residents feel welcome. Greetings are warm, but public displays of affection are rare; indeed it is probably more true to say that they are frowned upon. A simple handshake will suffice, whether you are meeting a Malaysian of Malay, Chinese or Indian descent. Business cards remain important to many Malaysians so be sure to have a supply of cards with you at all times.

Ordinary Malaysians can be addressed as Encik/Makcik/Cik (Mr or Mrs/Ms). Children and young people will generally refer (politely) to older women as "aunty" and older men as "uncle". The Malay language reflects Malays' social structure providing different forms of address depending on who is speaking to whom, but forms of address are also complicated by differences between the written and spoken language, and the need to use different types of language to convey respect depending on who is involved in the conversation.

For instance, in written Malay the word for "you" is "anda" but in speech it is "awak" and "kamu" if a slightly older person is speaking to a younger one. The word for him or her is "dia" but becomes "beliau" when talking about someone who is respected such as a teacher, a doctor or a dignitary. For royalty, there is an even higher form of Malay.

TITLES

Malaysia has a labyrinthine system of honours, which can be awarded by the Agong, the Federal Territory, the royal houses of each state on the peninsula, and the governors of the four states without Sultans. The honours are supposed to recognise those who have contributed greatly to the country as a whole or the individual state, and while not hereditary, are highly sought after.

The most common titles are Dato' and Datuk ('datuk' is also the Malay word for 'grandfather'). Both sound the same in Malay. Anyone named a Dato' has been honoured by the state of Penang or one of the nine Sultans. Datuk comes from the Agong, the other three states headed by governors or the Federal Territory. In both cases, the wife of a man awarded the title is known as a Datin. Individual states have also created their own honours, such as Dato' Wira (Pahang) or Datin Paduka (Selangor).

Malaysia also has more exclusive titles. Tun existed for hundreds of years as a hereditary title given to noblemen, but is now conferred by the King on those deemed to have provided exceptional service to the nation. Only 35 people can hold the title at any one time and both men and women are eligible. With the exception of Najib Razak, all previous prime ministers of the country, including Najib's father, have been given the honour. The wife of a Tun is addressed as Toh Puan, but—just to confuse matters—a To' Puan is the wife of a Dato' from Terengganu.

> It is important to address a person who has a title with the honorific (unless they have told you otherwise) and to use the title in any formal speech or address.

The second most senior title in Malaysia is Tan Sri, which is made up of two separate rankings one of which is slightly higher than the other. There can only be 325 people with the title Tan Sri at any one time. Dato' Seri is the equivalent of Tan Sri at the state level—at least in the states that have Malay rulers. In the other states, the top title is Datuk Seri.

Honours are usually given out during the official celebration of the birthday of the King, the state rulers or Federal Territory Day (February 1). Foreigners are also eligible for the awards. People do not generally have their honours taken away if convicted of wrongdoing although there has been discussion on the issue.

Titled in Malaysia

Some of Malaysia's most well-known people, some of them globally renowned, have been awarded titles. Some examples: Tun Dr. Mahathir Mohamad, Prime Minister 1987–2003, 2018 to date; Tan Sri Michelle Yeoh, Actress; Tan Sri Dr. Jemilah Mahmood, founder of NGO Mercy Malaysia, Under Secretary General for Partnerships, International Federation of Red Cross and Red Crescent Societies; and Datuk Nicol David, World Squash Champion.

In the past, most members of the government, and the Cabinet in particular, tended to have titles. The government that took power had far fewer people with honorofics, but senior officials (the prime minister, deputy prime minister, menteri besar or chief minister, should be addressed as Yang Amat Berhormat (YAB), the right honourable.

Other members of the government or Members of Parliament are commonly known by the initials YB, which stands for Yang Berhormat (the honourable).

The complex system of monarchy that exists in Malaysia means there is an equally complex system of royal titles, that can seem overwhelming to anyone who is not themselves a royal. The King is officially known as the Yang di-Pertuan Agong, which translates as 'he who was made Lord' or 'King of Kings' and is elected by the other Sultans from the peninsula under a unique five-year system of rotation. The current King is the Sultan of Pahang and was installed in office in January 2019.

The King's official title is Kebawah Duli Yang Maha Mulia Seri Paduka Baginda Yang di-Pertuan Agong, and, should you ever find yourself invited to the palace, is addressed as Tuanku (Your majesty).

At the lower level there is Tengku and Tunku (prince or princess), with the difference in spelling reflecting the different states. Tengku applies to Pahang, Selangor, Kelantan and Terengganu while Tunku is used in Kedah, Johor and Negri Sembilan. To complicate matters further, Perlis calls its princes Syed, while Perak uses Raja.

DRESS

Malaysians are proud of their traditional dress and wear it frequently, particularly Malay women who wear the *baju kurung*, a loose outfit made up of a sarong skirt and top that comes almost to the knees, on an almost daily basis. Many like its forgiving shape, which also fits with the more conservative approach to fashion that has spread throughout West Malaysia in recent decades.

Many Malay women now also wear the headscarf, which is known as the '*tudung*' in Malay and is tied in a variety of styles and often fixed in place with gem-like clips or a strategically-placed brooch. The *tudung* business is huge with young women queuing to buy the latest scarves from the most fashionable brands. Only a tiny proportion of Malay women wear the *niqab* that covers their face, but it is also true that it is more common than it was 20 years ago, particularly among younger women.

The *baju kebaya* is a more figure-hugging outfit than the *baju kurung* and consists of a heavily-embroidered blouse that skims the hips, and a traditional *batik sarong* either cut to fit or tied in place. Malaysian women of all ethnicities, and even foreigners, like to wear the *kebaya*—younger women often wear the top with jeans—but it is most popular during special occasions like weddings, official dinners or the open houses that are held during Hari Raya and other major festivals.

The *kebaya* originated with Peranakan women, who fastened the top together with three delicate brooches in place of buttons and paired it with a sarong of hand-drawn *batik* and beaded shoes. Even today, the best *kebaya* are still to be found in Melaka and Penang. Men usually only wear traditional outfits for special occasions—at Hari Raya, weddings or other formal occasions.

Baju melayu is a long-sleeved top with a subtle mandarin collar that is worn with trousers and what is known as a *samping*, which is folded around the waist, a bit like a mini-skirt. While the shirt and trousers are usually made of a shiny fabric (polyester rather than silk these days), the *samping* is made of a traditional woven material known as *songket,* often in a colour that complements the *baju*. Malay men will often wear the outfit with a *songkok*—a black, velvet oval-shaped hat.

At other times Malaysian men of all ethnicities might wear *batik* shirts. The more stylish tend to opt for the restrained patterns and muted palette that define Indonesian *batik*, while others like the riotous explosion of colours and silkiest silk favoured by Malaysian designers. *Batik* shirts are

The colours on a *batik* cloth are traditionally painted rather than dyed.

also popular with non-Malaysians.

Other ethnic groups have their own traditional outfits, which have become part and parcel of Malaysia's tourist marketing campaigns, even though they might not be worn as regularly. For Chinese women, the *cheongsam* is a popular choice at Lunar New Year. Usually made from silk—stiffer silks skim the body to create a more flattering look—the dress has a high collar, cap sleeves and splits in the skirt; a floor-length *cheongsam* may be cut to the thigh, while the knee-length version has a more modest split. The dress is fastened at the shoulder with special fabric buttons. Designers have recently begun to give the dress a more contemporary look and shops like Nala Designs in Bangsar offer *cheongsam* in striking graphic prints.

Malaysian Indian woman, meanwhile, like to wear the *salwar kameez*—a long shirt over slim cut trousers—and, sometimes, a *sari*. More elaborate styles are reserved for weddings and other special occasions.

In the business world, aside from official functions, Malaysian dress codes are relatively relaxed and outside the world of banking and law, or the fancier office towers like KLCC, few men wear ties or jackets. For women in fields like accountancy and finance, shift dresses and skirt suits are common. In newer office buildings, shopping malls and cinemas, it is best to have a jacket or sweater on standby as the air-conditioning is usually extremely powerful.

On the whole, regardless of gender or religion Malaysians tend to dress more conservatively than their neighbours in Singapore or Thailand, even if they are not Muslim. Certainly, on returning to Malaysia after a business trip elsewhere, people—particularly women—seem very modestly dressed.

In recent years, there have been stories of women refused entry to government offices because their skirt was "too short" or their top "too skimpy", and men because they were wearing sandals (universally called "slippers" in Malaysia). It is usually best to err on the side of caution when visiting the immigration office or tax department, rather than run the risk of being told to leave and have to come back another day.

It is also worth noting that expectations of dress are considerably more conservative in the east coast states of the peninsula. In Kelantan and Terengganu where about 95 per cent of the population is Malay, it is not uncommon to see fully-robed women paddling in the sea and jumping over the waves. Perhaps unsurprisingly, away from resort areas, foreigners in bikinis and swimsuits tend to draw attention.

There are, of course, dress codes for visiting mosques, and larger ones will have a board outside showing the appropriate clothing for men and women. It is necessary to remove shoes before entering a Hindu temple, while Chinese (Taoist or Buddhist) temples are generally more relaxed.

In the evenings and weekends, Malaysians like nothing better than to hang around in an old T-shirt and shorts, although people tend to make more of an effort in the trendy cafés in more upmarket parts of Kuala Lumpur, aping the latest trends in London, New York and Tokyo.

And with a Louis Vuitton in virtually every city centre shopping mall, designer handbags are a crucial sign of status for wealthier women, and even the middle classes.

CHAPTER 5

PRACTICALITIES

Apa macam?

**— popular, casual greeting
and equivalent of "How's it going?"**

WHAT TO BRING

Malaysia is far from a hardship posting—housing is of a consistently high quality, it is easy to get around whether by road, rail or air, and foreigners have access to top-notch healthcare and highly-rated schools in languages from English to Japanese and French. It is no wonder that so many people move to Malaysia for a couple of years and end up staying for far longer.

What you bring will depend partly on whether you have already secured a job and have relocation benefits, or whether you are moving to the country in the hope of securing work. If it is the former, and you are moving an entire family rather than just yourself, then you may have an opportunity to fill a container with your favourite furniture and possessions from home. If it is the latter, then you will need to pack more astutely. Whichever you are, Malaysia is a hot and humid place, so summer clothing, swimwear and sandals are crucial (bear in mind it is not always easier to find women's shoes beyond a European size 39, and men's shoes also skew towards the smaller sizes). The dampness can also cause leather to go mouldy and elastic to lose its elasticity, which some people try to address by adding dehumidifiers to their wardrobes to soak up the moisture. However, if you store the items in an airy cupboard and use them regularly, there should not be any problems.

It is easy to buy furniture and electrical goods once you arrive in Malaysia. As well as Ikea, Malaysia has numerous furniture makers of its own and there are specialists in Western designer furniture as well as companies that restore antiques whether from Southeast Asia or further afield.

VISAS AND PERMITS

Malaysia's bureaucracy can seem overwhelming—numerous forms, requested one year in English and the next in Malay, demands for photos, marriage and educational certificates, letters of support and personal bonds—but the truth is that over the past few years the government has made a considerable effort to make the process easier, particularly for foreign professionals.

The eXpats Service Centre was established in 2007 and handles applications for employment passes issued to so-called foreign knowledge workers—generally highly-qualified people with expertise in multimedia or ICT, individuals with hard-to-find, but much sought-after skills, or people who work in the creative content industry—through an online application and tracking system. Passes are generally issued in about a month, but the process can sometimes take longer.

Every foreign knowledge worker needs an employment pass and, if they have a family, their spouse and children will need dependent passes. Common-law partners may also be able to apply for a social visit pass (long-term) as may parents, in-laws and children over the age of 18. Children attending school will need a 'permission to study' endorsement in their passport, in addition to the dependent pass. Spouses on dependent passes are not allowed to work. Same-sex marriages are not recognised in Malaysia.

One of the biggest challenges in Malaysia is not finding work, but finding a job that is well paid, particularly if you have come from a developed country where salaries tend to be higher. Malaysian pay, except at the very top, has changed little in the past two decades.

An employment pass requires a minimum salary of RM3,000 (US$715) a month, while the Residence Pass (Talent), an innovation that was introduced in 2011, demands at least five years working experience (three of them in Malaysia) and a minimum basic monthly salary of RM12,000 (US$2,900) a month. Anyone who secures the pass can live in the country and change jobs or even study, without having to get a new permit. Their spouse can also work. The RP-T is particularly targetted at those with expertise in key economic sectors like communications, education and business and financial services.

The RP-T lasts for a decade and, like employment passes that have been extended over ten years, it is not clear whether it can be renewed after that. Like many decisions in Malaysia, those made by immigration are shrouded in secrecy. Those who want to stay longer are advised to apply for permanent residence, but the requirements and process for securing PR have long been opaque. Getting approval can be a test of endurance and commitment spanning decades and is not even accorded to spouses of Malaysians, although they are apparently eligible to apply after a few years in the country. Applications for PR have to be made to the immigration office of the Malaysian state where you are living, rather than the head office in Putrajaya.

The Malaysia My Second Home (MM2H) programme is pitched at retirees looking to live out their golden years in the warmth of the tropics, and in 2018 was named by International Living as one of the best retirement programmes in the world. It offers a ten-year renewable residence pass for those with a monthly income of RM10,000 (US$2,400), but also requires a property investment of RM1 million (US$240,000) and that at least RM100,000 (US$240,00) is maintained in a fixed deposit throughout the decade of residence. MM2H holders over the age of 50 are allowed to take on a part-time job to a maximum of 20 hours a week.

ACCOMMODATION

Two decades ago, Mont Kiara was a development of a handful of high-rise apartment blocks with views of the Twin Towers, an international school and a modest plaza of shops and offices that quickly gave way to wooden village houses and thick jungle. Neighbouring Sri Hartamas was a small housing estate of tree-lined roads, overlooked by the forested hills of the Kiara Forest Park. Both had a somewhat sleepy feel; peaceful outposts at the end of a road that seemed to peter out into nothing.

But in the past 20 years, the two places have been transformed. First came the highway, as the road was widened and connected to other highways. Then, as the hangover from the Asian Financial Crisis lifted, developers came looking for cheap land and salivated at the thought of the profits to be made in an area that was just ten kilometres from the city centre. A construction boom began. New housing estates appeared in Sri Hartamas, climbing up the hills and encroaching into the jungle, followed by towering condominiums, a sprawling complex including a shopping centre, offices and serviced apartments, and a grandiose new palace—an entire forest uprooted for the purpose—for Malaysia's King. In Mont Kiara, new and ever more luxurious condominiums appeared, more shopping centres and gated communities. Dirt tracks became roads, forests disappeared, and hills were flattened to make way for all the construction.

Like many Asian cities, the pace of change in Kuala Lumpur, especially those used to the more sedate growth of Europe, can seem dizzying. But development, especially the construction of condominiums, means a wide choice of good quality accommodation, usually with swimming pools, gyms, and covered parking at attractive rents, especially in comparison with other major cities. There has also been an increase in the number of 'gated and guarded' communities in Kuala Lumpur, mostly on the outskirts of the city, while residents of some older housing estates club together to install boom gates and deploy guards along their streets (this can only be done with approval from the city authorities).

The capital has the greatest selection of housing for rent—from Mont Kiara's condominiums, to the leafy streets of semi-detached houses and bungalows in neighbouring Damansara Heights (one of KL's top addresses) to the buzzing enclave of Bangsar and the city centre itself where some of the country's most luxurious apartments designed by internationally-renowned architects have mushroomed around the Twin Towers, and in nearby Bukit Ceylon. Out in the city's east, at the foot of the mountains that border the city, the Ampang suburbs remain popular given the proximity of the International School of Kuala Lumpur (the junior and senior school campuses are both located in the area, but in different neighbourhoods).

Choosing where to live depends on a number of things— your commute to work and your appetite for traffic jams, schools (if you have children) and the suburb's proximity to public transport if you do not have a car. It can also come down to the very simple matter of whether you feel at home in the place; that gut feeling you get as soon as you first visit an area or walk into the house or apartment that you have come to view. Some people are willing to live an hour or so drive from Kuala Lumpur to enjoy the greenery and space of its outer fringes, while others like to be in the thick of the action, with the option to walk to and from work and from bar to bed.

While there has been an increase in the number of studio and one-bedroom apartments in KL, most of the stock is for two or three-bedroom flats. Older developments are unlikely to have such well-maintained facilities as their more modern counterparts, but on the other hand are likely to cost less and be more spacious.

If you are going to be living and working in Penang, your decision on a home is likely to depend not only on the location of your office, but also whether you want to have a sea view or live in a heritage building (with all the likely noise that entails).

Like KL, the pace of construction on the island has been rapid in recent years, with condominiums and villa developments appearing all along the seafront between the World Heritage site of George Town and Batu Ferringhi, the island's long-established beach resort, where vast land reclamation works have also caught the attention of concerned environmental groups. There is little in the way of public transport on Penang, beyond a few buses, so bear in mind that a car will be necessary and that congestion can be a problem at peak times, particularly along George Town's narrow streets, on the bridge that connects the island with the mainland and for the ferry to Butterworth. That said, there is an excellent free bus service that runs around the borders of the World Heritage district from the Ferry Terminal and Komtar—full name: Kompleks Tun Abdul Razak—the 65-storey skyscraper that was built in the 1970s, and still dominates the landscape.

In Johor, housing veers towards condos and gated communities with most construction focussed on the region known as Iskandar close to the second bridge to Singapore. Some of these projects are made up of hundreds of towering blocks of tightly-packed apartments more akin to a land-scarce city than a place like Johor, mostly designed to appeal to investors from mainland China. These have come in for particular criticism from the new government, which appears keen to interpret legislation relating to foreigners' buying property more strictly. There are also plenty of conventional housing estates, which have long been popular with Singaporean investors, but the pace of development has led to something of a glut, which means that market prices have declined and rents have become more competitive.

Whatever your preferences, a good property agent should be able to guide you in the right direction, and ensure you find the home that best suits your needs. There are also useful online sites where you can view properties for rent or sale (non-Malaysians can only buy properties worth more than RM1 million (US$240,000) and are not allowed to buy terraced homes), although the photos might not provide a reliable indication of what the property is actually like.

Once you have decided on a place, you will need to pay a deposit, which is made up of a booking fee (also known as an earnest deposit) to confirm your interest and ensure the landlord does not rent the property to another tenant), a refundable security deposit (usually equivalent to two months' rent) to cover damages or rent if the tenant absconds, and a deposit for utilities (about half a month's rent). The booking fee is normally paid to the property agent who hands it onto the landlord once the contract has been signed. Rentals lasting for three years or less require a tenancy agreement while longer arrangements are governed by a lease, and the security and utility deposits are payable once the contract is signed. All contracts are negotiable so be sure to read the agreement closely and make sure it includes provisions to cover the circumstances in which the landlord can raise rent and by how much, clearly defines the party responsible for repairs, and includes clauses that are important to you.

Most landlords will rent properties unfurnished or partially furnished although the kitchen will have cabinets and, possibly, appliances. Bear in mind that Malaysian homes often have "wet" kitchens for cooking—the hob will be installed in the backyard or on the kitchen/utility room balcony—and "dry" kitchens which are inside and have cupboards, worktops and other appliances. Ovens are more popular these days, particularly in newer buildings, but are far from ubiquitous in Malaysian kitchens.

Washing machines are generally top-loaders. If you want a front-loading machine you will probably have to buy it yourself. It pays to check your chosen property—and test any appliances—before you sign any rental agreement so that you can get the landlord to carry out any repairs, or get replacements, before you move in.

UTILITIES

Malaysia's utilities are considerably more reliable than they once were, and bills remain low compared with those in developed nations. Most water companies are owned by the individual states, while electricity is provided by the national power company, Tenaga Nasional, which is listed on the local stock exchange, but remains controlled by the government. Consumers are charged monthly in arrears with the unit cost of power rising according to how much each household uses (people who live in bigger houses, have their air-conditioning on all day or use a boiler rather than solar panels to heat water are likely to find themselves paying more).

Piped gas is rare although sometimes available in newer condominiums. Most Malaysians rely on bottled gas for cooking, and while that can sometimes mean running out halfway through cooking dinner, it is easy enough to call a provider and get a new bottle delivered (paying cash to the driver). Most people keep one bottle in reserve just in case.

Water from the taps is (officially) drinkable, although older pipes in less modern developments may mean it is cloudy or murky. Many Malaysians install filters and continue to boil their water before drinking it.

Power cuts and water shortages, although not completely unheard of, are far less frequent, but do not be surprised if, when there has been no rain for several weeks, water starts to be rationed or tankers appear on streets. Major disruption last hit KL in 2016, after weeks without rain boosted demand and put pressure on the surrounding reservoirs.

Residents are billed each month, according to their usage. If you do not pay, then the water company will disconnect the service (although this does not usually happen unless the bill has gone unpaid for six months or more). The same applies for electricity. Bills can be paid through online banking, and at the post office in cash. If you find you have been cut off, it is best to pay at the utility's office to be sure you will be reconnected as soon as possible.

KEEPING CONNECTED

There is growing competition when it comes to telecommunications, especially in mobile and the Internet, where there is a variety of providers and the government has promised to improve speeds to be more competitive with regional (and global) leaders in Singapore, South Korea and Japan.

For mobile, Malaysia has at least four major service providers offering prepaid and post-paid (pay upfront or pay monthly in arrears) voice and data plans promising fast and reliable coverage throughout the country. Of course, all claim their customers will be able to use their mobile from the streets of Kuala Lumpur to remote jungle villages, but it is worth checking such claims to make sure that you will be able to make calls and access data in the places you are most likely to go. This is particularly true if you will be based in Borneo or will be travelling there frequently because the coverage in East Malaysia has traditionally been less extensive.

Be aware that foreigners are charged a higher deposit than locals—usually at least RM1,000 (US$240)—even if you have a work permit or have been living in the country for a long time. You may also find that special offers on handsets and smartphone plans (say, the latest iPhone on installment) apply only to Malaysian customers even though most mobile providers lock their non-Malaysian postpaid subscribers into lengthy contracts (two years is the norm). These days, however, it is possible to switch providers and keep your existing number.

Another important factor is the amount of data offered. Most mobile phone companies provide a generous allowance for postpaid subscribers, which varies according to the monthly fee. Some may include all voice calls and supplementary lines, with data roaming offered at a flat daily rate. Work out your budget, check the small print and ask around to make sure you choose the service that best meets your needs.

DOMESTIC HELP

Not too long ago, I was chatting with a Cambodian salt miner in his bamboo shack on the country's southern coast. The work was difficult and, understandably, the man's children had decided not to follow their father into the salt trade. In fact, his daughter had gone to Malaysia to work, but he had not heard from her for a long time and was getting worried. She had signed up with an employment agency to become a domestic worker, lying about her date of birth so that she would meet the minimum age requirement. My colleagues and I promised to look for her when we returned to Kuala Lumpur.

Thousands of young women from around Southeast Asia head to Malaysia every year to work for Malaysian families— cleaning the house, cooking and looking after children and elderly parents. In 2017, there were estimated to be at least

250,000 domestic workers in the country, according to the Malaysian Maid Employers' Association, which uses the acronym MAMA.

Like the young Cambodian, they are mainly recruited through agencies in their homeland that charge a hefty fee to the family that is looking for help in exchange for providing training in domestic chores—from using an iron to cooking popular local dishes—to young women who may never previously have left their village, let alone their country. Some may have been brought up in places without running water or electricity.

The agencies send details about the young women they have trained to partners in Malaysia who create profiles for each, adding a photo of the young woman in uniform, for potential employers to browse. The charges involved are high—estimated at somewhere between RM12,000 (US$2,900) and RM18,000 (US$4,300)—some of which is paid by the employer and some by the woman herself through deductions from her monthly wages.

The government has been talking for some years about allowing families to hire women directly from selected countries around Southeast Asia. The most recent announcement was in the Budget for 2018, and applied only to Malaysians and permanent residents. It seems any foreigner looking for live-in help from overseas will still need to go through an agency, with all the ethical issues that raises.

In Malaysia, most homes (even small apartments and terraced houses) have a 'maid's room', which is usually next to the kitchen with a ceiling fan and space for a single bed. Those hired must be between 21 and 45 years old, and must also pass a medical at a government-approved clinic before they can start work.

But even when these women are treated well, their working conditions are often demanding. Government regulations stipulate that domestic workers should be allowed sufficient time to rest, but their working hours are often long, sometimes starting as early as 5am, days off are rare and the monthly pay low (the actual wage depends on the woman's nationality— those from the Philippines get the most thanks to determined government negotiators, while those from Cambodia and Myanmar tend to be paid the least).

Despite new regulations, the women often have their passports taken away. In the worst cases, they might face physical abuse or mental torture. About one in 20 of the women run away from their employers. In one of the most horrific cases, Adelina Lisao, a 21-year-old Indonesian woman was found lying outside the house next to the dog, covered with cuts and bruises, and emaciated. She died a day later in hospital and her employer was charged with murder.

Some of the abused find their way to Tenaganita, a local non-profit organisation that provides assistance to migrant workers, particularly women, in disputes over issues such as pay and working conditions. The name itself is a combination of the Malay words 'tenaga' (power) and 'wanita' (woman). The group operates a shelter and is often on the lookout for volunteers.

With the help of Tenaganita and the police, we tracked down the salt miner's daughter to a grand house in a small gated community in Ampang, a world away from the bamboo hut. It turned out the family did not like the then 18-year-old to call home because it 'upset' her and insisted that she had asked them to keep her wages back because she was worried her mother would gamble the money away. She was actually getting ready to fly home the next day and was thrilled to finally speak to her father over the phone, to tell him that she was coming home.

BANKING AND MONEY

When I first tried to open a bank account in Malaysia, the tellers were in the midst of a working dispute with their employer and queuing up in long lines to deposit bags of coins into accounts. It made the already difficult process even more stressful, but after an afternoon of waiting, a 'recommendation' from my employer, job contract and passport, I finally got myself a current account and an ATM card (for a fee).

Over the past few decades, Malaysia's banking system has weathered its fair share of financial storms—a Malaysian friend and former banker jokes, only partly in jest, that people should borrow from Malaysian banks and save with foreign ones—but after a series of forced mergers in the wake of the 1998 financial crisis, the system is in a much stronger financial position.

There are now eight Malaysian banks—the largest, Malayan Banking (better known as Maybank) reported a net profit of more than RM7.5 billion (US$1.78 billion) in 2018—and nearly 20 foreign banks, including HSBC and Standard Chartered. Every bank that operates in Malaysia, regardless of where it is now headquartered, is subject to regulation by the country's central bank, Bank Negara.

Malaysia also has a number of Islamic banks that offer Sharia-compliant products (interest is banned under Islamic law) and many non-Muslims choose to bank with them because the rates are competitive. Both conventional and Islamic banks offer a range of products including current and savings accounts, educational accounts for children expected to go on to college or university, car loans and mortgages. Bear in mind that Bank Negara sets an overall limit for the amount any foreigner can borrow from Malaysian sources. 'Non-resident' accounts (do not get confused with the fact that you will probably be resident for tax purposes) have special numbers that make them easily identifiable and incur stricter limits on the size of transfers and daily withdrawals.

The major local banks (Maybank, CIMB, Public Bank) operate branches in most cities, towns and suburbs, which are usually equipped with ATMs. Coverage in more rural areas is patchy so be sure to carry sufficient cash if you are visiting such places for any length of time.

The bigger institutions—local and foreign, conventional and Islamic—have formed a joint ATM network that ensures cash withdrawal costs remain low (RM1/US$0.24) even whenever any of their customers withdraws money from an ATM. It is also possible to use foreign cards with the Plus or UnionPay symbols at Malaysian bank machines. ATMs are generally housed in a room off the main banking hall so that they can be kept open after banking hours (branches generally operate from 9.30am–4pm) and where there are also cheque and cash deposit machines. Most have a security guard after working hours.

In recent years, there has been an attempt to get more people banking online by increasing charges for cheques and offering incentives for online cash transfers and bill payments. However, it is also true that cheques are still widely used between companies. They are not used in shops.

Credit cards (Visa and Mastercard) are widely accepted in Malaysia. Banks will generally offer platinum cards to their most well-heeled customers, but there are also gold cards and regular cards (the difference reflected in their annual fees and credit limits). All cards must be PIN-enabled although pay-wave is common for smaller transactions (generally to a maximum of around RM200/US$48).

With the multibillion dollar scandal surrounding state investment fund 1MDB, Malaysia's financial regulators have become increasingly strict about foreign exchange transactions. Be aware that if you receive money from overseas or want to send money internationally you are likely to get a call asking you to explain the origin of the money and its destination even for relatively small sums of a few hundred US dollars.

Ironically, given the concerns over money laundering, you will find money changers in nearly every shopping mall. These offer competitive foreign currency exchange—much better than the rates offered by the banks or at the airport. Do like Malaysians do and get your holiday money (or at least the first chunk of it) at the money changer before you leave. Ask local friends and colleagues for recommendations on the best places to change money.

SHOPPING

Along with eating, Malaysians love to shop, mostly in the air-conditioned shopping centres that can be found in every large town and provide much needed respite from the heat and humidity.

In big cities like KL, JB and Penang, malls generally open from 10am to 10pm and the centre management insists that all shops and kiosks abide by those hours. Shopping centres also house food courts, restaurant floors, clinics, cinemas and even theme parks and skating rinks. In Kuala Lumpur, you will find the now globally-ubiquitous designer shops, with branches of Prada, Louis Vuitton and Chanel in all the larger malls, alongside luxury Swiss watch manufacturers selling their products for often eye-watering sums.

At the cheaper end there is no shortage of H&Ms or Zaras, but Malaysia also has homegrown brands, including Seed and Padini, that sell reasonably-priced clothing that mimics global trends. These shops also sell lightweight clothing throughout the year, while the global brands follow the same spring/summer, autumn/winter collections in Europe and the US, which is useful if you are planning to spend any time in a colder climate. Of course, it is always possible to shop online, but bear in mind that any purchases from overseas—particularly those delivered by courier—will probably be taxed.

In recent years, as in many other big cities, there has been an increase in independent retailers, usually concentrated around older parts of the cities or in heritage buildings and focussing on reviving traditional, handcrafted goods with a more contemporary aesthetic. In KL, Nala, founded by a Dutch woman who was born in Singapore and has spent most of her life in Malaysia, has developed a reputation for creating Malaysian-inspired graphic prints that are silkscreened onto textiles and transformed into clothing, scarves, cushion covers and even wallpaper. Nala also has a popular café in the more upmarket suburb of Bangsar which holds regular food markets and celebratory events, as well as a design school for those keen to learn the techniques themselves.

A few doors from Nala, Kedai Bikin, is a great place to pick up good quality, one-of-a-kind Malaysian products, from handwoven baskets from Borneo to hand thrown ceramics (the tableware is popular with KL's most fashionable restaurants) and hand-drawn silk batik from the east coast. The brainchild of two enterprising Malaysian architects, the shop also sells its own line of contemporary furniture, some of it modelled on iconic designs of the 1950s.

In 2017, the 1950s Zhongshan Building in a largely forgotten part of the city was transformed from scruffy boarding house into a thriving creative hub boasting one of KL's best contemporary art galleries, an independent bookshop, vinyl stores, artist studios and a bakery clustered around a central courtyard.

SCHOOLS

Education is probably the single biggest concern for Malaysian parents who worry about the quality of teaching, standards of education generally and, above all, exam results (there are very few Malaysian middle-class children who escape the clutches of 'tuition').

Malaysian children start going to school in the year they turn seven at state-run schools, known as Sekolah Kebangsaan at the primary level and Sekolah Menengah at the secondary level, and all teaching takes place in Malay. At the primary level, Malaysians can also attend government-assisted schools where the teaching is in Chinese or Tamil. There are also numerous private schools offering the Malaysian curriculum or religious teaching (these are known as tahfiz schools and teach the Quran).

The academic year follows the calendar year with the main breaks at the end of May/beginning of June and from November until January. Most schools start early in the morning (at about 7am) and finish by lunchtime, although some may have a second, afternoon, session to enable them to teach more children.

Like parents the world over, Malaysian parents worry about standards and whether their children are learning the kind of knowledge and skills that will equip them for adult life. Despite an 'education blueprint' that was supposed to ensure students developed better critical thinking skills, Malaysian education remains quite traditional with a focus on rote learning, memorisation and frequent testing. In the last year of primary school, some schools spend the entire year preparing for the end of year exam that all Malaysian children are required to take, which is known as the UPSR (Ujian Pencapaian Sekolah Rendah). The obsession with exam results means Malaysian parents frequently send their children to tuition classes, both after school and at the weekend.

As in many countries, Malaysia also has 'elite' high schools, the most famous of which is Malay College Kuala Kangsar, a school that has educated many of the country's leading male (and Malay) figures in business and politics.

One of the most vociferous debates has been about language and the allegedly woeful standard of English teaching, and learning. Efforts to address the problem have focussed on teaching subjects such as Maths and Science in English in order to increase children's exposure to the language, but the government has flip-flopped on the policy a number of times in the face of criticism from Malay nationalists.

The long-running issues bedevilling Malaysia's education system have prompted many parents to look for alternatives. Some people choose to send their children to Malaysian curriculum private schools, others opt for home-schooling and a small, usually wealthy, minority to schools overseas, but many are now choosing international schools, particularly those offering the UK curriculum, in the belief that the teaching and the education that their children receive will be better.

A government decision to remove the limit on the number of Malaysian children allowed to attend international schools and to actively encourage their construction has also fuelled the sector's rapid growth. As a result, there are now a huge number of international schools in Malaysia (126 of them in 2017), mostly offering the UK curriculum, but also the Australian, US, Canadian, French, German, Japanese and even Indonesian syllabus.

School fees normally reflect the origin of the teachers. For a UK curriculum school, those with teachers hired from the UK will tend to be the most expensive, while the cheaper schools will have teachers from countries such as India and Pakistan. It is also worth noting that some of the schools that charge higher fees include the costs of after-school activities like sports.

Another factor is location, particularly in Kuala Lumpur. While a few schools are in more central parts of the city, the trend has been to move to the farther suburbs where it is possible to build large campuses surrounded by greenery and with plenty of space for sports fields—the Australian school is in the far south, as is the secondary campus for the Alice

Smith School, one of the leading UK curriculum schools. The International School of Kuala Lumpur, which offers US schooling, is in the eastern suburbs.

Most schools offer teaching from primary through to secondary and sixth form—although the primary school may often be in a different location to the senior school (the Alice Smith Primary School, for example, is on a hill near the former royal palace close to the city centre). Given the rapid expansion of international schools, it is advisable to focus on those that have accreditation such as FOBISIA or CoIS (these schools will often hold sports competitions together or with other schools in the region), and to visit the campus for yourself. Schools usually organise annual open days for new parents and offer guided tours by appointment. Some require children to sit entry or placement tests.

In recent years, Malaysian campuses of some British independent schools have also opened, including Epsom College (the alma mater of AirAsia boss Tony Fernandes who was instrumental in getting the school to open in Malaysia) and Marlborough College. Such schools are mostly in the EduCity area of Johor and also offer boarding.

There is also St. Joseph's Institution, a campus of the highly regarded school of the same name that was founded by the La Salle Brothers in Singapore. Some of the schools offer scholarships.

Most private and international schools hold regular parent-teacher meetings and teachers are often keen to share exam results because they know that Malaysian parents expect high grades. At one primary school parent-teacher conference when my daughter was about eight, I was surprised when one teacher opened our conversation by apologising for the fact that my daughter had 'only' got 85 percent in their particular subject. When I told her it didn't matter, the teacher looked astonished.

DRIVING

Nearly every Malaysian has a car, or at least a motorcycle, and at peak times it can seem like every single one of them is on the road. Only recently has Malaysia begun to develop its public transport system—mainly in KL and Penang—and having a car will make your everyday life considerably easier, especially if you have children. It will also give you the freedom to enjoy all the country has to offer, whether that is a nearby theme park, a jungle retreat or the cultural and culinary delights of Melaka and Penang.

All drivers and their cars need to be licensed. An International Driving Licence allows foreign nationals to drive on Malaysian roads for three months, but anyone staying longer is advised to get a Malaysian one.

The Malaysian government has bilateral agreements with some countries, including Australia, Japan, Iran, Iraq and a number of European nations, to recognise their nationals' driving licences (bear in mind that if it is in a language other than English it will first have to be translated).

On paper the procedure for getting the Malaysian licence might seem quite onerous, but it is actually quite straightforward and simple enough to handle on your own. You will need to have your photo taken at the Road Transport Department in your state in order to get the licence, and the cost depends on the length of the licence (maximum of five years each time). It can be renewed every five years (just remember to bring enough cash), but as of writing foreigners will need to return to the Road Transport Department to do this, while Malaysians can do their renewal at the Post Office.

If you have not passed your test at home, it is possible to take driving lessons and take a test in Malaysia. Candidates are only allowed to take the practical part of the test, which takes place on a special course rather than a public road, if they complete a classroom course and pass an exam on the Highway Code. Successful candidates are issued with a preliminary licence requiring them to display a red 'P' on their vehicle's front and rear windscreens for the first two years after passing their test.

Cars in Malaysia are expensive, thanks to high import taxes and excise duties designed to protect the local carmakers— Proton (bought by China's Geely in 2018 but still positioning itself as a 'Malaysian' car) and Perodua. Taxes have been declining over recent years and are lower for vehicles assembled in the Association of Southeast Asian Nations (Asean), but buying a car still demands a considerable financial outlay.

Perodua is the biggest selling brand in Malaysia and its Myvi is ubiquitous, but Japanese and Korean manufacturers are hugely popular with Malaysians, selling vehicles that are considered to be good value for money and safe (attractive, extended warranties also help). European cars, including Mercedes, BMW, Volkswagen and Renault, are widely seen as 'luxury' vehicles and priced accordingly. Given the economics of the car business in Malaysia, manufacturers tend to bring only the most popular brands and models so there is not the breadth of choice found in more developed countries.

Two terms you should aim to understand when buying an imported vehicle are CBU (Completely Built-Up) which means the car was manufactured outside Malaysia in its entirety, and CKD (Completely Knocked-Down), which means the vehicle's components and panels were made overseas, but it was put together in Malaysia. CKDs may also use locally-made tyres, windows and headlights. The tax on a CKD car is considerably less than it is for a fully-imported vehicle.

Some Mercedes, BMWs and VWs are assembled in Malaysia to keep the prices more competitive, while some Malaysian car companies have been licensed to build certain brands, such as Peugeot and Renault. The designs of many of these vehicles, particularly the interior, are often tweaked for Malaysian tastes. Note too that Malaysians' preference is for automatic transmission rather than manual, and for saloon cars, SUVs and MPVs rather than hatchbacks.

Buying a new car is usually quite straightforward. As elsewhere in the world, manufacturers have brochures and price lists on their websites (bear in mind the prices in East Malaysia are higher) and offer test drives.

The manufacturer may also offer financing (balloon payments have become popular recently) but will certainly be able to assist with bank loans—designated as 'hire purchase' in Malaysia and available for as long as nine years—as well as insurance. While Malaysians can generally borrow as much as 85 per cent, it is much more difficult for foreigners to get such a margin of financing, and they may be asked to provide a local guarantor.

You can bid for a special number if you want (a strangely popular pastime for Malaysians) or take whatever is given to you (each state's plate starts with a different letter). All number plates should be black with standard white lettering or there is the risk of a fine.

Buying secondhand often means a better deal since wealthier Malaysians like to change their cars quite frequently. Given that there is no requirement for roadworthiness, you should be aware of the risks and either know cars yourself or take along someone who does. It is also possible to buy 'pre-owned' cars direct from the manufacturers which sometimes come with a limited warranty.

Malaysian roads themselves can be feral places. Although road laws are being better enforced, it is not uncommon to see drivers speeding down the emergency lane to avoid traffic jams, weaving in and out of traffic or even driving with a child sitting in their lap (there is no rule requiring children to be strapped into a special seat and many allow their children to sit unrestrained and even stand between the two front seats). The speed limit for the highway is usually 110km/hour, national roads 90km/h and state roads 80 km/h. Most highways have tolls and cash payments are being phased out. It is best to buy a Touch n Go card, which can be topped up at supermarkets, convenience stores and petrol stations or at the highway toll booth (expect a long queue) or a Smart Tag, which allows you to drive through the designated lane without having to stop.

Malaysians' general deference means that anyone who is in an expensive car or has the special plates given to MPs, lawyers and those with titles need only flash their lights for the cars in front to pull to over, regardless of whether it is actually safe to do so. The King often travels in a motorcade of blue flashing lights with police motorcycle outriders.

The Malaysian tapir frequently wanders onto roads, where it risks being run over by vehicles. Road signs warn drivers to watch out for them.

Road signs are mostly similar to those in use internationally although the text may be in Malay. In more rural parts do keep alert for wildlife particularly at night—road accidents are one of the most common causes of death for the endangered tapir, whose black and white markings make it hard to spot in the dark. Elephants and tigers sometimes stray onto highways too although the Wildlife Department has recently built viaducts in known crossing areas to keep animals—and people—safe. Other potential hazards are cows, dogs and slow-moving lorries, particularly on inclines.

While the number of road accidents in Malaysia, has declined in recent years, there is no getting away from the fact that Malaysian roads can be dangerous

The highways have regular rest-stops offering fuel, toilets, local delicacies and usually a fast-food joint or two. They get extremely busy during the major public holidays.

places. Some 6,740 people lost their lives on the country's roads in 2017, which works out at roughly 18 people every day. Partly this is down to poor driving—many Malaysians drive as if theirs is the only vehicle in road and motorcyclists weave in and out of traffic with sometimes scant regard for the rules of the road—but the country also does not require cars to meet a certain standard of roadworthiness, which means that older vehicles are sometimes not properly maintained.

Another factor is the weather. During heavy downpours when the amount of water hitting the windscreen obscures the drivers' vision and huge puddles—even lakes—form on poorly graded roads and near blocked drains, the number of accidents increases markedly. Many Malaysians also dislike driving during the heat of the day and prefer to get behind the wheel when it is cooler—in the early morning or in the evening and into the night—another time when accidents tend to occur.

If you are unfortunate enough to be involved in an accident, do not panic. If it is a minor incident (say, a misjudged manoeuvre in a car park) you might be able to reach some kind of agreement with the other driver(s). Although insurance is compulsory it may not be financially savvy to claim for a small amount if the excess on a policy is nearly as much.

For larger accidents where there are no injuries the drivers should exchange details (for themselves and the vehicle) and insurance information (without admitting any blame) and lodge a report with the traffic police (bear in mind, this can be done only at certain police stations). You should take photos of the damage in case there are any disagreements later. The police attend only the most serious of accidents, generally where there has been loss of life. The officer at the station will guide you through the process of making your statement and you will then have to wait to see a more senior officer who will apportion blame and fine the offending party (RM300/ US$72 at time of writing). You can use the police report to file your insurance claim. For major accidents—ones that cause serious damage or harm to life—the police will attend the scene and the vehicles involved should not be moved.

If your car breaks down on the highway, pull over onto the emergency lane and use the nearest emergency phone to call for help. The highway operator will dispatch one of their roadside assistance teams.

It is also sensible to be a member of the Automobile Association of Malaysia, which provides a roadside assistance service. They will sometimes dispatch a mechanic by motorbike if they think the problem can be rectified easily, but they can also tow your car back home or to an approved garage, if necessary. If you buy a new car, you may also be offered an emergency assistance package with the manufacturer or your insurer. These are generally more useful in cities than in rural areas.

Be aware that during an accident or a breakdown, tow trucks often appear (as if by magic). Be very careful before you think about using one of these, no matter how persistent they are. They are likely to charge you an inflated amount for moving your vehicle and may not be entirely trustworthy. They could also turn out to be entirely the opposite. It is a decision you will need to make at the time.

As ever, the best advice is to ensure your car is serviced regularly and make sure it is roadworthy before setting off on any longer journey, especially if you will be travelling to more remote parts of the country where settlements are few and far between, and help might be some distance away.

Malay on the Roads	
ikut kiri	keep left
terus	straight on
kanan	right
awas	caution
dilarang masuk	no entry
kenderaan berat	heavy vehicle (lorry)
kenderaan ringan	private vehicle (car)
had laju	speed limit
kurangkan laju	reduce speed
peringatan	reminder
persimpangan	junction
selekoh	bend
jalan	road
lebuhraya	highway
lorong	lane
zon tunda	towing zone (usually accompanied by image of a car being towed away)

Uniquely Malaysian Road Manners

When you are driving around Malaysia, you may see a vehicle—usually a van or a lorry—at the side of the road or even on the carriageway with a leafy green branch sticking out at the back. This is the old-school Malaysian equivalent of a red emergency triangle and means the vehicle has broken down. Note that emergency triangles are now becoming more common.

When it rains, it is normal to turn on the headlights, but some Malaysians still persist with the old habit of turning on their hazard lights. Thanks to regular public service radio announcements it is not as common a practice as it used to be, but be aware that this might happen.

Motorcyclists are notorious for their daredevil approach to the roads, jumping red lights, weaving in and out of traffic and using city streets as race tracks after dark. Worse, many fail to maintain their bikes properly and ride without a properly functioning headlight or rear-light and rarely bother with their indicators. If you are in heavy city traffic, always think of motorcyclists and do not ever expect them to give way even if you are indicating your intention to move.

Parking

Given the number of cars on Malaysian roads, it is perhaps no surprise that parking, particularly in the big cities, can be a real test of endurance.

Many shop-house developments make little provision for parking so finding a space is difficult (unless you arrive early) and double, and even triple, parking is common. The convention is to leave your mobile number on a piece of paper on the windscreen so the other drivers can find you if they return to their vehicles before you return to yours, but on many occasions the culprit is impossible to find, and the hapless boxed-in driver is forced to use their horn until the double-parker appears.

Traffic wardens often make the rounds of such areas, leaving pink tickets in the windscreens of those parked on yellow lines, corners or double-parked. Some officers will drive around in their van first blaring a siren to warn errant parkers of their arrival.

Some areas are designated towing zones—you will see the yellow road sign with a car being towed and the words '*zon tunda'*—and, occasionally, a truck will appear to transport the offending vehicles to the pound. The challenge for the driver is then to find out what has happened to their vehicle (it pays to have someone with you who can speak Malay). Some councils and car park operators threaten clamping to those who park illegally, but this is rarely enforced.

Most shopping centres have extensive car parks, but on busy days even those might not be able to cope with the demand and drivers are left circling the lot waiting for others to return and free up a space. Most offer valet parking for a fee, which is popular with the kind of people who tend to drive expensive cars.

In most offices, spaces are paid for on a monthly or quarterly basis. Some offer 'reserved' spaces to those who are prepared to pay a premium or are in senior corporate roles. Abandoned lots and building sites are also turned into open-air car parks until construction starts, offering cheaper rates.

HEALTH

Do not let the fantastical names of tropical diseases put you off, Malaysia is generally a safe place in which to live. Your chances of contracting a nasty illness, getting bitten by a snake or attacked by a wild animal are quite small and healthcare is both reliable and affordable (and probably covered in your health insurance policy anyway). It is even possible to drink the tap water, although in older developments the age of the pipes means the water sometimes comes emerges brown so many Malaysians install filters, boil the water or buy bottled.

Of course, the heat and humidity make any tropical climate the ideal environment for viruses, bacteria and fungi to thrive so it is sensible to be aware of the most common illnesses.

Chikungunya

Chikungunya is a virus carried by mosquitoes, which causes fever and often severe joint pains and headaches. There is no vaccine and treatment focusses on the symptoms—getting plenty of rest and drinking lots of fluids. Most people get better within a week, but the joint pain can persist for months. The best way to protect yourself against it is to avoid being bitten.

Dengue

Dengue is a virus carried by the female Aedes mosquito (Aedes aegypti) and is probably the biggest disease risk you will face while living in Malaysia, particularly as it is largely an illness of urban areas. Dengue is generally more debilitative than dangerous (the symptoms are similar to Chikungunya), but it is exhausting. Most people require a few days or even weeks off work before they recover their full strength.

Doctors will check for dengue using a simple blood test as soon as you detail your symptoms—headaches, joint pain, fever and sometimes a rash. If it is found to be positive you can expect to spend a few days in hospital on a drip. Your doctor is required to notify the Ministry of Health if the diagnosis is confirmed and inspectors will be sent to your office or home (wherever you may have contracted the disease) to inspect the area. Outbreaks are mapped and 'hotspots' identified. Anyone found to have areas where mosquitoes can breed (they can reproduce in water the size of a 20-cent coin) will be fined.

A vaccine developed by the French pharmaceutical giant Sanofi-Pasteur was thought to be a breakthrough, but it has not proved as effective as expected. The best way to protect against dengue is to avoid being bitten. Make sure there are no places for the Aedes mosquito to breed by cleaning away any standing or stagnant water around your home (in potted plants or buckets, for example), and use repellents (Mosiguard is effective). City authorities fog residential areas regularly and especially after a case of dengue has been reported.

Hand, Foot and Mouth Disease (HFMD)

Another common disease in Malaysia (and Singapore), HFMD usually affects babies and young children under the age of five. However, it is possible for adults to contract the disease and the effect can be quite severe.

The symptoms include a fever, sore throat and tiredness. The distinctive blisters and ulcers usually develop in the mouth and on hands and feet a few days after the child is infected. Since the disease is spread through coughs, sneezes and the fluid from the blisters, HFMD can be transmitted quickly within childcare centres or at indoor gymnasiums. If an outbreak is reported, centres will often close.

Heat

Never underestimate the strength of the sun. Kuala Lumpur is only three degrees north of the equator and the heat can be intense, especially in the hours around midday. If you're outside use sun screens with a high protection factor (35 or more), wear sunglasses and a hat, and drink plenty of water. Too much exposure can cause prickly heat, painful sunburn and increase the risk of skin cancer. It is not for nothing that the Asian people who work outside will generally wear long-sleeved shirts, trousers and a wide-brimmed hat.

The high humidity also increases the chance of dehydration—locals swear by electrolyte drinks like 100 Plus

to combat the effects. Worst of all is heat stroke, symptoms include a high temperature, flushed skin and a racing pulse, which could land you in hospital.

Malaria

Malaria is rare in Malaysia these days, and I have not heard of anyone taking anti-malarial tablets, but the decision is yours. If travelling to a more remote part of the country, say in Borneo, you may want to take precautions. Again, the best advice is to avoid getting bitten so cover up, use repellent, sleep under a mosquito net or use a mosquito coil (a more common approach in Malaysia).

Rabies

Rabies is a viral disease of the nervous system, most commonly associated with dogs, which is fatal if those bitten do not start a vaccination programme within a day or two of being attacked. Although the disease is endemic to Malaysia, outbreaks are exceedingly rare especially on the peninsula where stray dogs are not as common as they are in Borneo. An outbreak of rabies was declared in Sarawak in July 2017 leading to the enforcement of a quarantine and a vaccination drive for pets and strays.

Stomach Upsets

The food is one of Malaysia's great wonders, and in recent years local authorities have made great efforts to improve standards of hygiene at street stalls and local restaurants. A popular banana leaf place in Bangsar was shut down after a video showing the staff washing the plates in a dirty roadside drain went viral. One of Penang's most famous *char kuey teow* joints was also forced to close for two weeks to clean up sufficiently to satisfy the health inspectors.

Nevertheless, stomach upsets are always a risk. Mostly they are quite minor and resolve themselves after a day or two. The best way to stay healthy is to eat at popular places (where food turnover is high), choose freshly cooked dishes rather than anything that has been sitting around for a while and follow basic hygiene standards (wash your hands before eating).

Toxic Stuff

Anyone coming from genteel northern climates may find the list of Malaysia's venomous snakes rather alarming. King Cobras, Spitting Cobras, Banded Kraits and numerous kinds of Pit Vipers can all be found in Malaysia, including the cities, but chances are you will never see one. In 20 years of living in Malaysia, the only snake I have seen was a luminous green whip snake (its bite is painful but the venom not dangerous to life) that had managed to slither its way into a first-floor apartment via a palm frond and was being wrangled into a gunny sack by ten firefighters.

Mostly snakes are rather timid creatures that prefer to keep away from people, but if you live in a house with a

> Snakes can and do find their way into homes, as a friend discovered when she walked downstairs one evening to be confronted by a cobra making itself at home in her living room. As it slithered away, she rushed off to the housing estate's security guards to get them to remove it from the house. When they got back the guards spotted the snake stretched out against the skirting board and grabbed it. The good news: My friend has lived in Malaysia for 25 years, always leaves her patio doors open and has had only one snake encounter in the entire time.

garden, particularly if your home is in a more secluded or forested neighbourhood (or near empty plots of land) then the chances of seeing a snake are higher. It is sensible to do what you can to make sure snakes will not find your garden an attractive place to stay. Cut any grass or lawns regularly and avoid keeping piles of wood and debris—these are the kind of places snakes love to hide.

The fire service (Bomba) and Civil Defence Force are trained to capture any snakes you find in your home or garden. If you are bitten by a venomous snake it is better to head to the Emergency ward of a government hospital because they have a store of anti-venom, and are part of a rapid response network.

As well as snakes, Malaysia also has insects that can give a nasty bite. If you leave a pair of closed toe shoes outside your door, always shake them out and check what is inside before you put them on.

CLINICS AND HOSPITALS

There are numerous doctors' surgeries and clinics in residential estates around the country and they often open from early in the morning until late in the evening. Ask friends or work colleagues for recommendations. Standards of care are generally quite good—many doctors train overseas in the US, Australia and the UK—and a consultation is not expensive, although most seem quite keen to prescribe medication even for a common cold. Many doctors also hold surgeries in private hospitals, although these will be more expensive.

Pharmacies are generally well-stocked and open late. Some treatments and preparations (such as cortisol) are on the controlled-list and require the assistance of the pharmacist. You will need to sign a special book if you buy any of these.

In the past, many people chose to go to Singapore for specialist treatment. Some still do today, but as part of its attempt to develop a 'medical tourism' industry, Malaysia now offers quality care at an affordable price. The best private hospitals are generally in KL and Penang, and some government hospitals also operate private wings.

Maternity care is good and most Malaysian women will see the specialist each month during their pregnancy before having their baby in hospital (government or private). Many foreigners also choose to give birth in Malaysia, although it is worth checking the citizenship requirements of your home country beforehand. For example, the UK requires a female citizen born overseas to give birth in Britain if they want their own child to have their citizenship, while Malaysian mothers who give birth overseas cannot pass on their Malaysian citizenship to their child, and children born in Malaysia do not get an automatic right to citizenship.

Once your child is born, you will need to register the birth both in Malaysia and at your respective embassy. The hospital will usually provide you with the forms that allow you to register the birth and get the Birth Certificate. They will also do early tests to make sure the baby is healthy and assign you a paediatrician who will ensure your newborn gets all the appropriate vaccinations according to the Malaysian schedule. Most women are out of hospital in a couple of days, and although midwives are not so common in Malaysia, there are some who will visit the new mother and baby at home to make sure both are well.

Be aware that Malaysians love babies and children, especially if they are blonde-haired and blue-eyed. Do not be alarmed if people want to coo over your infant or pinch your toddler's cheek, but do let them know (politely) if you would rather they did not.

GETTING MARRIED

For those who dream of getting married on a tropical beach next to azure seas, Malaysia offers the ideal opportunity to make that dream a reality. Many of the luxury hotels in island resorts such as Langkawi offer wedding packages that include a ceremony on the beach and a celebration, but it is also possible to find a venue and make all the arrangements yourself.

The paperwork will be different depending on whether the two people getting married are a Malaysian and a foreigner or two foreigners, but your embassy or high commission should be able to advise. If you decide you want to marry a Malaysian Muslim you will need to convert to Islam (and attend pre-wedding classes at the mosque) before the ceremony can go ahead. Many people in this situation also choose to adopt a Muslim name at the time of their marriage. Any children must also be brought up as Muslims.

DEATHS

A Malaysian friend was called out to the morgue in the middle of the night after an uncle—a Singaporean—died suddenly while on an evening stroll with his wife during a weekend getaway in Genting Highlands. While the police were on the scene relatively quickly, his wife was left with the awful task of bringing his body back to KL—and onward to Singapore—while struggling to cope with her own grief. My friend helped her deal with the Malaysian authorities—morgue, hospital, police and undertakers—while she awaited consular assistance.

In the event, the undertaker about whom she had initially felt quite sceptical proved the hero of the hour—dealing with the legalities, finding a coffin of their choosing and arranging a van to bring the uncle's body back to Singapore.

It is also possible to be buried or cremated in Malaysia. There are burial grounds and gardens of remembrance catering to all the main religions, and undertakers who can arrange services, wakes and burial or cremation. The largest is probably Nirvana, which is listed on the Kuala Lumpur Stock Exchange and operates a large centre in Kuala Lumpur. While the building is in a strange position squeezed between highways and flyovers, the staff are unfailingly reassuring and respectful to those mourning their loss.

Transporting a body back to a home country can be difficult, but it is not impossible providing the paperwork is completed. It is usually easier to have the body cremated first.

THE 'HAZE'

Southeast Asia is supposed to have two seasons, wet (the monsoon) and dry, but 20 years after forest fires first blanketed the region in a choking smog the joke is now that there is a third—the haze season.

The fires began as plantation owners in Indonesia and parts of Malaysia sought to clear forested land quickly and cheaply to expand their businesses. Soon, local communities were shrouded in thick smoke, which gradually spread across borders to envelop Singapore and parts of Malaysia. The sky turned a sickening yellow and buildings disappeared behind a haze of microscopic smoke particles that grounded planes and forced schools to close. Worse, the smell of burning hung in the air, making throats sore and eyes sting. The longer-term health consequences remain unknown but people in the worst-affected areas reported respiratory problems and asthma.

Indonesia's government has long promised to tackle the problem, and Singapore has tried to develop a cross-border response, but fears the smoke will return continue.

Peak haze 'season' usually occurs sometime between July and October, and can be made worse by natural climatic events, say, for example, an El Nino that reduces rainfall over the parts of Indonesia—Sumatra and Kalimantan (Borneo)—where forest clearance is the biggest problem. The smoke created by the fires includes a range of noxious gases and particulate matter including sulphur dioxide, nitrogen dioxide and carbon monoxide, which can irritate the eyes, nose and throat of even a healthy person and cause respiratory problems. The risks are higher for children, the elderly and those who already have chronic diseases like asthma or chronic obstructive pulmonary disease.

Most people use the Air Pollutant Index (API), which measures pollution in major towns and cities during the haze season, to decide how best to cope with the situation. The API divides air quality into five ranges: good (0–50), moderate (51–100), unhealthy (101–200), very unhealthy (201–300) and hazardous (300+).

As the air quality gets worse, you will often see Malaysians wearing face masks (the kind usually worn by construction workers to protect them from dust), and most people reduce the amount of outdoor exercise that they do and try to stay inside. Once the reading gets to the 'very unhealthy' range the government may instruct schools to close (bear in mind that while most international and private schools are air-conditioned, most government ones are not). In 2015, some 7,000 schools were closed because of the haze.

CHAPTER 6

SEDAP!

❝To understand Malaysian food is to understand history. Food travels and evolves, so we can never 100 per cent claim that 'Malaysian food' belongs to us. We're just lucky to have it all.❞

— Chef Wan, celebrity chef

Malaysians love eating, and it shows in the country's language and culture, where migration and inter-marriage have created a fusion of flavours, and entirely new culinary styles. To eat Malaysian is to know Malaysia. Food helps bring people together and is at the centre of nearly every national celebration. The Malay words for tasty and delicious—'*sedap*' and '*lazat*'—are popular with all kinds of Malaysians, and when arriving at someone's home the standard greeting is not hello, but the question, have you eaten: "Sudah makan?" Malaysians eat out regularly—sometimes it can be cheaper than cooking at home—hanging out at makeshift stalls set up by the side of the road or beneath the trees, neighbourhood restaurants (known as *koptiam* or *mamak*, some of which are open around the clock), and indulging in the lavish buffets that are common in four and five-star hotels. Foodies can also visit the growing number of fine dining restaurants, while those in search of a quick bite are devotees of KFC, McDonalds and the other fast-food outlets that have appeared in towns and cities throughout the country.

At a business meeting, particularly in government departments or more traditional offices, visitors are routinely offered tea and coffee (beware of the sugar), and a selection of local snacks, while in towns throughout Malaysia, people gather at the local *kopitiam* to drink tea (or a beer if they're not Muslim) at all hours of the day snacking on a plate of fried noodles or rice, and catching up on the latest gossip.

Impassioned debates over which town or city has the best food—Penang usually wins out with Melaka a close second—are surprisingly common, and Malaysians think nothing of organising a holiday road-trip around their favourite eating spots. On special occasions, each community is eager to share the numerous specialities that are the focus of their festive tables, and families will often hold what are known as 'open houses' to celebrate with family and friends. Even the government holds its own 'open house' during major public holidays. In theory, the 'open house' means anyone can join in, but these days most are by invitation. While many dishes are still thought of as particular to each ethnic group, there are others that have become so popular they have become truly Malaysian dishes.

TRULY MALAYSIA
Nasi Lemak
Nasi lemak (or fatty rice) in its most basic form, wrapped in a banana leaf, is one of the country's most popular breakfast dishes. The rice is cooked in coconut milk giving it a creamy taste and is served with a spicy chilli paste known as *sambal*, half an egg, peanuts, deep-fried anchovies (*ikan bilis*) and a few slices of cucumber. Fancier versions might include fried chicken, squid cooked in a spicy sauce or a meat curry.

Roti Canai
Another breakfast staple is an Indian flat bread about the size of a small dinner plate known as *roti canai*. The preparation is as theatrical as the bread is delicious to eat. The cook slaps

the dough repeatedly on the worktop, spreading it out until wafer thin, folding it over and then repeating the exercise before throwing the roti on the hot plate to cook. It is ready in a couple of minutes and after a final flourish—pressing the sides together with the inside of their palms—the cook sends it off; a light, fluffy bread that is at its most delicious and moreish when hot and fresh. *Roti canai* is usually served with curry sauce and *dhal*, but these days there are numerous options from sugar to sardines, and the *rotis* (*roti* means bread in Malay) themselves can also come in a smaller, thicker version known as *roti bom*.

Char Kuey Teow

Char kuey teow is a fried flat rice noodle (the *char* comes from the Hokkien word for fried while *kuey teow* is the type of noodle) with egg, fishcake, chives, juicy prawns and cockles that can be found everywhere from hawker stalls to posh hotels throughout Malaysia. The cook breaks the egg into a smoking hot wok and quickly adds the other ingredients along with light and dark soy sauces and a dollop of chilli; scraping and scooping the noodles in and out of the fierce heat with a metal spatula. Some ingredients might be removed to cater to Muslims—traditionally Malaysian Chinese use pork lard for the dish—but others have also been added as chefs and hawkers seek to stamp their mark on one of the nation's most-loved dishes.

Laksa

There are numerous types of *laksa*—a spicy noodle soup, which takes its name from the laksa leaf—in Malaysia, and nearly every state seems to have its own version. The most famous is probably what is known as *Nyonya laksa*, an unctuous mix of coconut curry soup laden with puffs of tofu, prawns, fish balls and topped with half a boiled egg and a spoonful of sambal chilli. Other popular *laksas* include *Sarawak laksa*, which is said to have originated from the wok of an entrepreneurial ethnic Chinese hawker in 1945. The paste that gives the soup its distinctive flavour is a closely guarded secret, but the soup is served with ribbons of omelette, prawns and chicken slices, a garnish of coriander leaves, sambal and lime. *Johor laksa*, meanwhile, is distinct for its use of spaghetti rather than Asian-style noodles and its fishy soup is like a thick gravy topped with cucumber, green beans and local herbs. *Assam laksa*, is said to be one of the healthier laksas. The soup is made with mackerel and has a distinctive sour flavour from the tamarind. For many Malaysians, it is a must-have dish on any trip to Penang.

Satay

The morsels of chicken, beef, and even pork, cooked over a charcoal grill and served with a spicy sweet peanut sauce are ubiquitous across Malaysia. Indeed, *satay* is the signature dish on the national airline. The best *satay* is said to come from the town of Kajang, just south of Kuala Lumpur but slowly being absorbed into the city's suburbs. Conveniently, it is now the last stop on the MRT, which triggered huge queues at the *satay* stalls when the line first opened.

Satay is usually served as a snack alongside a Malay-style dumpling of rice wrapped in woven coconut leaves, known as *ketupat*, chopped cucumber and onion. The *ketupat's* distinctive diamond shape is a popular decoration during Hari Raya Aidilfitri and other festive occasions, when *ketupat*-inspired lights are hung along the roadside and outside people's homes.

Chicken Rice

Chicken rice is one of Malaysia's most delicious meals and hugely popular with children. The combination of juicy, poached chicken and tasty rice (it gets its flavour from being cooked in the chicken juices) with just the right amount of soy sauce and sesame oil to liven the dish is sublime, especially when accompanied with chili and ginger. Chicken rice came to Malaysia with migrants from Hainan in southern China in the early 19th century, and the recipe has changed little. There are some variations—in Melaka, the rice is usually shaped into balls, while the Malays seem to prefer roasted over steamed chicken—but the dish is so delicious there is little need for innovation. Chicken rice stalls can be found throughout Malaysia, distinguished by the whole chickens (white for steamed, brown for roasted) hanging at the counter at the entrance. Be sure to ask for breast meat, if you do not want any bones.

Banana Leaf Rice

Eating banana leaf rice is an integral part of Malaysian life. A clean banana leaf is placed in front of each diner and a generous serving of steamed white rice placed on top. The waiter (they are always male) will then bring over a choice of curries and vegetables—what you get depends on what is been cooked that day—while another vat of sauces— usually a couple of curry gravies and a *dhal* are left on the table for diners to add as they go along. You can also order fried chicken, fish or other meats. The whole dish is usually scooped up with your fingers (right hand only, please) which requires quite a bit of practice. Most restaurants will provide cutlery for those who are squeamish about eating with their hands or simply not skilled enough to do so. When you have finished your meal, fold the banana leaf towards you (covering any leftovers) to show you have enjoyed your meal. Do not fold it away from you—a practice generally reserved for funerals and other solemn occasions. The waiter will tot up what you have eaten and you pay at the cashier in the front of the shop when it is time to leave.

Rendang

When the judges of the British TV cooking competition, *Masterchef*, suggested *rendang* should be crispy, the whole of Malaysia exploded in outrage. *Rendang,* the country's 30 million people agreed, should never be crispy. A traditional Malay dish, *rendang* gets its intense flavour from being cooked for hours over a low heat. Usually made from beef, chicken is also a popular choice for the dry curry, which is a must-have at any special occasion from weddings to Hari Raya Aidilfitri. *Rendang* is traditionally served with steamed, white rice.

DESSERT, SNACKS AND CAKE

It is often claimed that Southeast Asian cooking does not have dessert or cake, which, like most sweeping generalisations, is not really true. It is simply that people in the region have a different approach to sweet things. In a hot, sweaty climate people want snacks and desserts that cool, refresh and replace salts lost in the heat, so Malaysians have developed a taste for what may seem to outsiders like an eclectic range of snacks and desserts, generally involving palm sugar, coconut, rice flour, and local spices, which provide both flavour and colour.

Confusingly, the word '*kuih*', which is the Malay word usually used for the sweet snacks offered with tea and coffee, as well as during festive occasions, also refers to savoury snacks—in essence, anything that is not eaten as part of a main meal, often cloyingly sweet and sometimes not sweet at all. Certainly, unless you are coming from elsewhere in Asia, desserts in Malaysia will be unlike anything you have ever tasted before.

Malaysia has a host of moreish snacks to offer from fried banana (*pisang goreng*)—best served hot from the wok when the inside is gooey and sweet and the batter crisp—to ice-based desserts such as *cendol* and *ais kacang*, which is sometimes known as ABC. While *cendol* is a refreshing mix of coconut milk with strings of pandan jelly, sweetened red beans and palm sugar (the best *cendol* has *gula melaka*) on a bed of shaved rice, *ais kacang* (iced beans) is a cone of shaved ice drenched in colourful syrups, topped with red beans, nuts, jelly, fruit and even corn. It is a riot of colour, and hugely effective against the heat.

The combination of shaved ice, pandan jelly strands, red bean and fresh coconut milk that make up a cendol is the perfect cool-me-down on a hot day.

During festival times, Malaysians stock up on jars of local cookies including love letters (thin wafers folded into fan shapes), *kueh bangkit* (a light coconut cream biscuit) and, the most popular of all, pineapple tarts. The best of these luscious little morsels have a soft, buttery base topped with a dollop of pineapple jam caramelised to a golden brown.

Mango pudding, a kind of mango-flavoured jelly, is popular at Chinese restaurants as are small steamed buns filled with lotus paste or red bean. Other desserts tend towards a combination of salty and sweet, or an earthy flavour, and often take the form of a soup containing glutinous rice balls, fruit and even vegetables. Mooncakes, brought out only during the Autumn Festival, traditionally contain lotus bean paste and an egg yolk (to symbolise the moon), but in recent years chefs have experimented with new flavours and combinations, and it is now possible to buy mooncakes made of ice cream or even chocolate. The fantastically-named *bubur cha cha* is

Freshly baked mooncakes cooling on a rack.

> Just before Christmas we decided to get all our friends together for a festive tea. The table was filled with delicious foods – from chocolate chip cookies to Malaysian curry puffs and pasta salads – and, in the centre, a magnificent Yule Log that a friend had bought at a local bakery. As I was making another pot of tea in the kitchen, the children decided they couldn't wait any longer for the cake, but when they tried to cut it discovered that it wasn't the chocolate sponge we were all expecting, but a beautifully decorated piece of polystyrene. We are still trying to work out how and why the shop assistants sold it to our friend, and how none of them, and none of us noticed.

not a dance, but a sweet soup filled with yam, taro, sweet potato and bananas that has its roots in Nyonya culture.

Indians too have a taste for a sweet treat, like the deep-fried syrup and cardamom-soaked balls of *gulab jamun*, but Malaysians generally are more keen on the savoury snacks, particularly the spirals of crunchy fried *muruku*. The lightly-spiced snack originated in southern India but is now a must have for all Malaysians.

There are so many different foods in Malaysia it is impossible to get bored. Try the divine lacy-pancake that is *roti jala* topped with chicken curry, the sublime coconut sauce atop the grilled chicken of *ayam percik*, myriad fresh salads, and oodles of noodles. For many foreigners in Malaysia, the food is what they miss most when they return home.

COFFEE AND TEA

Long before Malaysians adopted the globalised coffee culture of espressos, lattes and flat whites, they would while away the hours drinking *teh tarik* (which translates into pulled tea)—sweet, milky tea thrown to a froth by its flamboyant maker, or myriad other variations on one of the world's most popular drinks (from the plain to the sweet and the milky). These classic *kopitiams* continue to serve the older generation, but

Café culture has taken off in Malaysia and there are plenty of places to enjoy espresso or Japanese-style drip coffee.

also younger Malaysians looking for a quick, cheap drink alongside a traditional breakfast.

But the coffee culture that has swept much of the rest of the world, has breathed new life into Malaysia's heritage buildings and industrial districts from Sandakan on Sabah's eastern shore to KK and Kuching, JB, KL and George Town as cafés have mushroomed across Malaysia. Of course, not all the coffee is good, but word-of-mouth and trial of error will help you find a favourite.

While most cafés specialise in Italian-style espresso drinks using beans roasted either locally or in Italy or Australia, aficionados have also developed a taste for Japan's intense and aromatic drip and cold-brew coffees. In these cafés you will find glass towers lined up along the counter (although they might also have an espresso machine to cater to more mainstream tastes) through which the coffee is slowly dripped. They usually import their beans from Japan.

Still, even with the growth of a coffee scene, there are

times when a traditional brew is what hits the spot—perhaps with that great slab of *kaya* toast or a fresh-off-the-stove *roti canai*—and Malaysia's more traditional approach to coffee and tea is still easily found at *kopitiams* and *mamak shops* across the country.

LOCAL TEA AND COFFEE

Be aware that if you order straight tea (*teh*), you will get a large glass of tea and condensed milk. For black tea, you need to ask for '*Teh-O-Kosong*'. If you do not want tooth-tingling sweet tea order '*kurang manis*' (less sweet) or '*kosong*' (no sugar, literally 'nothing'). Indeed, it is best to remember that in Malaysia, all drinks come sweetened with sugar or syrup by default, so it is best to let the waiter know straightaway if you do not want sugar. More terms to know:

- **Teh**: Tea with condensed milk (and probably an awful lot of sugar too)
- **Teh O**: Tea with sugar
- **Teh O-Kosong**: Tea with no milk or sugar
- **Teh C**: Tea with evaporated milk and sugar
- **Teh C-Kosong**: Tea with evaporated milk, but no sugar
- **Teh Tarik**: Pulled tea, made with condensed milk
- **Teh Halia**: Ginger tea
- **Kopi**: Coffee with condensed milk
- **Kopi O**: Sweetened black coffee (more like an Americano than an Espresso)
- **Kopi C**: Coffee with evaporated milk and sugar
- **Kopi C-Kosong**: Coffee with evaporated milk, no sugar
- **Kopi C Ais**: Iced coffee with evaporated milk and sugar

THE COLONIAL 'CLASSICS'

A chop is supposed to be a thick slice of meat, usually pork or lamb, that is cut along the ribs. So what to make of the Malaysian 'chicken chop' that can be found on menus from five-star hotels to neighbourhood coffee shops, and even in the chilled chicken section of the 21st century supermarket?

The chicken chop has its origins in Malaysia's colonial past when locally-hired cooks, generally from Hainan in southern China, improvised 'English' dishes for their homesick colonial bosses. The food they came up with was a unique hybrid that combined local ingredients with British culinary traditions in what can be seen as one of the first examples of fusion cooking, according to academic Cecilia Leong-Salobir, a researcher in colonial food culture in Malaysia, Singapore and India.

Poultry, rather than cows and pigs—which in any case are forbidden to Muslims—were plentiful in colonial times and chicken became a substitute for many of the meats the colonial rulers enjoyed back home but struggled to find in the tropics.

The chicken chop—a thigh or leg with the bone removed—was fried and slathered in a sweet tomatoey-sauce including (from the British side) ketchup and Worcester sauce, and (from Asia) oyster and soy sauces with garlic and, sometimes ginger, heated in a pan with slices of onion and fresh tomato until thick and unctuous. In the past, it would be served not only at home, but also in the clubs frequented by the British, as well as the hill station, and the rest-houses where they liked to break their journey on long trips between the major towns and cities.

These days the dish remains a mainstay of traditional coffee shops—notably the Coliseum and Yut Kee in Kuala Lumpur—and is probably the best-known culinary legacy from colonial times. But ingenious chefs also cooked up plenty of other fusion dishes from curry puffs, an Anglicised version of the traditional Indian *samosa*, to *kedgeree*, a rice-based dish with curry spices, eggs and fish.

Not too long ago, KL retained a number of old-fashioned restaurants which traded on nostalgia and curiosity about the past. Colonial classics featured heavily on the menus, the serving staff seemed to have been there since before independence, and it was possible to drink gin and tonic on the veranda in wicker chairs. Hefty land prices, developers greedy for profits and changing tastes—younger Malaysians have less appetite for the culinary oddities of the past—have prompted many to close but the Coliseum soldiers on, a throwback to another age.

DURIANS

With a spiky casing the colour of sage, buttery yellow flesh and a pungent odour that some compare to the stench of rotting flesh, the durian is a fruit unlike any other. The distinctive smell means countries across Southeast Asia have banned the durian in confined spaces—you will often see warnings in hotels and on public transport (a black outline of the fruit with a red line through it) indicating durian is off-limits.

But the fruit inspires intense devotion—its creamy, custardy flesh is considered an aphrodisiac—and once the fruiting season rolls around, Malaysians cannot get enough durian, queuing up at roadside stalls to gorge on their favourite variety or taking to the road to sample the produce of some of the country's best durian orchards.

The durian is known as the 'King of Fruits' in Southeast Asia and grows across the region, with peak season (depending on the monsoons) usually falling around the middle of the year. *Durio zibethenus*, to give the durian its formal name, grows as high as 45 metres and takes between three and four months to ripen, dropping to the ground (some can be as large as a football) when it is ready. The trees are grown on plantations (it takes at least four years for the tree to reach maturity), but also in the wild where the stinky fruit is particularly sought after by orang utans who break open the shell, feast on the fruit inside and spit out the seeds, playing a major role in the species' dispersal.

Malaysian durians can be found across the country and are exported to neighbouring Singapore as well as to China. There are numerous different varieties and tasting notes can read almost like those of a wine connoisseur. Singapore's *The Straits Times* describes the Black Pearl, which is grown in Johor as, 'slightly bitter, smooth and creamy' while another durian known as XO and grown in Johor and the highlands has, 'bitter and extremely soft, fleshy meat with an almost alcoholic taste'. Not all foreigners are able to get past the durian's pungent smell to taste the fruit, but Malaysians can point you to the best stalls and ensure you try the best examples of this most Asian of food experiences.

Cempedak is as stinky as durian, as I discovered one day when we bought one of the green spiky fruits from a roadside stall, put it in the car boot and forgot about it. The next day, we opened the car door to an overpowering stench of ripe cempedak that hours of open windows could barely budge. Luckily (for us) it was a rental car.

EATING AT HOME
Markets

In the not too distant past, Malaysia's supermarkets were rather tatty affairs with a limited selection of goods and—aside from a few family-owned grocers—little in the way of international food products. But thanks to a new breed of food and retail entrepreneurs, and a curiosity for new tastes among Malaysia's ever-richer middle class, supermarkets in the capital and elsewhere, including Penang, now offer customers a vast range of products. Alongside Malaysian basics—noodles, sauces, rice and the chocolatey malt drink called Milo—there is food not only from Australia, Europe and the US, but also from Japan and South Korea. Some shops have their own food courts, in-house bakeries, hipster coffee bars, and sushi counters while others offer groceries from European grocery brands like Waitrose and Casino.

Supermarkets are most often found in the basement of shopping centres including BIG (Ben's Independent Grocer), Village Grocer, Jaya Grocer, Isetan and AEON (both Japanese brands). Unsurprisingly, Japanese supermarkets generally offer high quality sushi and fish. Hypermarkets such as Tesco, from the UK, and Giant, a Hong Kong-based retailer, have vast warehouse-style outlets in the suburbs. They generally cater to a more local crowd, but also offer competitive prices on everything from food to clothing, outdoor furniture and electrical items. Most offer online shopping and will deliver non-perishable goods to your door, but it is also possible to get others to do your shopping for you through apps like HappyFresh and SmartShopper.

One thing to bear in mind when it comes to cooking at home in Malaysia, is that it is often cheaper to eat out than it is to prepare a meal at home.

If you like pork, you will find that it is kept in a separate non-*halal* section of the supermarket. If you buy bacon, sausages or any other product with pork in it (or even artificial pork flavour) you will also need to pay for it at the non-*halal* cashier, rather than with everything else at the main check-out. The same goes for wine and alcohol (although not always beer and cider), which means that you can end up paying at three separate areas within one supermarket.

While wines used to come predominantly from Australia, New Zealand and the US, Malaysian specialist wine retailers now bring vintages from across the world and prices are increasingly competitive. Select food halls of Marks and Spencer, the UK food chain, offer a decent selection of wines from France, Spain, Italy and other countries at attractive prices. Bear in mind that alcohol is only sold until 9pm and cannot be bought by Muslims or anyone below the age of 21.

Many Malaysians still prefer to visit the fresh food markets, which usually take place in the early morning or in the evening when it is cooler. 'Wet' markets, where meat and fish are sold, are not for the faint-hearted; the sight of freshly chopped meat, piles of fish, and live chickens confined in often filthy crates before they are sold and slaughtered, is a visceral and pungent introduction to food culture in Southeast Asia. Few stalls have refrigeration and rely on insulated ice-boxes to keep their produce fresh. As the ice melts, the water seeps onto the uneven floors making closed-toe shoes with a good grip vital (unless you want to slip over in the murky water or cover your toes with it).

The most famous morning markets in KL (they usually close by lunchtime) are probably in Pudu and Chow Kit in the city centre, and Taman Tun Dr Ismail, a more upmarket (and clean) offering in the western suburbs. In Penang, the

Campbell Street Market is a delightful old colonial structure in the heart of George Town, which was built in 1900, although the stalls now spill onto the streets outside. Even though markets can be hot, smelly and crowded many Malaysians still prefer them because they think the food is fresher and the pricing more competitive. Indeed, when Malaysians go food shopping they usually say they are going 'marketing', which perhaps gives some indication of how much they value the traditional markets.

As in markets the world over, shoppers stroll among the stalls and are faced with a bewildering (at least to outsiders) array of fruit, vegetables and spices. Sometimes, the stallholder will put the produce into small plastic baskets, say, five apples or five oranges in each, but it's just as likely the fruit and vegetables will be piled on the table, with an old-fashioned standalone weighing scale next to a thick wad of pink plastic bags (it is worth noting that there is a growing movement towards reusable plastics and bags in the major cities and plastic carriers are charged) so many shoppers now bring their own. The best local fruit appears according to season while fruit like apples and oranges are imported from Australia, China and further afield and available year round.

Most markets also have cooked food sections—a magnet to many food cognoscenti—offering an array of local dishes from bowls of steaming hot soup, noodles straight from the wok, freshly-cooked *roti canai*, local coffee (*kopi*) and *kuih*. The stallholders set up tables in the shade, sometimes beneath colourful umbrellas or a large tree, but takeaway is also common. Just ask to *tapau* (pronounced 'tar-pow' and meaning 'pack' in Hokkien) or *bungkus* (pronounced 'boongkoos' and meaning 'wrap' in Malay). Hot food will be deftly wrapped in waxed paper and drinks poured into clear plastic bags and spun around to seal the top to make it easier to carry.

During festivals, night markets might offer seasonal specialities. During Ramadan, food stalls are set up in the afternoon so Malay Muslims can buy food to break the fast, but since many of the dishes can be found only during the fasting month, other Malaysians also visit the markets to enjoy the food. At Hari Raya, for instance, stalls pop up to sell *lemang*, a sticky rice cooked in coconut milk, wrapped in banana leaf and steamed over coals inside a hollowed-out bamboo pole. The rice is served with *serunding*—dry and spicy strands of meat or chicken.

The Night Market—A Malaysian Tradition

Every Sunday afternoon, drivers stop their beaten-up vans and cars along the kerb in the fashionable Kuala Lumpur suburb of Bangsar to set up their stalls for the weekly night market. They quickly set about constructing roadside grills for satay or chicken wings, and lay out pots of homemade curries and *laksas* ready for the crowds. Beneath blue canopies provided by the city council, other stallholders prepare trays of *kuih* or pile their tables with vegetables and a mind-boggling variety of tropical fruit. Depending on the season, there could be anything from mangosteens to mangoes, durians and rambutans.

Night markets continue to thrive even in an era of digital distraction, providing a fascinating insight into Malaysian life and traditions. They are of varying quality—I once went to one in Terengganu that seemed to offer little but cheap China-made clothes and a frightening array of rather large knives—but in the northeastern state of Kelantan, the market in the state capital of Kota Bharu offers delicious food—the *ayam percik* (a barbecued chicken in a secret sauce) is a must-try—and an array of medicinal treatments for men looking to boost their libido. It also closes for an hour or so during evening prayers and anyone eating at that time is politely asked to pack up their food and eat it elsewhere (somewhere inside). In Sabah and Sarawak, the markets are known as 'tamu' and are often held in the morning. Particularly in smaller towns and villages, night markets are a way to catch up with the community and relax a little in the cool of the evening, and they're also an opportunity to sample some of the best of Malaysian food.

EATING OUT

In most Western cultures, families visit a restaurant as part of a celebration. They do that in Malaysia too—witness the trend among Chinese to have their reunion dinner at a fancy restaurant or the groups of young Malaysians celebrating a friend's birthday at a café—but Malaysians also eat out as a matter of course, because the coffee shop is where people of all kinds (from the titled to the pensioner) can hang out with their friends, chat, gossip and eat tasty and reasonably priced food.

The cheapest place to eat out is on the street, and Malaysia—notably Penang and Melaka—is renowned for the quality of its food stalls. Where once the stallholder would carry their mobile kitchen through the streets on a yoke around their neck, these days they are more likely to be using a stainless-steel cart on wheels that can be pushed or attached to a motorbike. Some stalls are permanent and simply packed away and kept by the side of the road or down an alleyway outside opening hours. In Penang, around Lebuh Chulia, cooks start setting up chairs and tables along the street as evening approaches and are quickly doing a roaring trade in noodle soups, *satay* and *laksa*. In KL, stalls normally appear near large office towers at breakfast and lunch (these tend to be less formal affairs and probably unlicensed—where food is cooked at the seller's home and laid out in large plastic boxes on a table). Others appear at the roadside, in shady spots (I recall once reading a newspaper guide to the best of KL hawker food which showed the stall's address as 'beneath the large tree' in one of the suburbs) as well as around the night markets that take place regularly around the city.

A step up from the street stalls, at least in terms of

A cook at work at her street stall.

hygiene, most shopping centres now operate food courts or hawker centres which are popular with the lunch crowd (air-conditioning helps). Some of these, notably in KLCC, only offer *halal* food so if you are craving pork then you will need to go elsewhere. The food court in the basement of Lot 10 along KL's Bukit Bintang strip was devised as a showcase of Malaysia's best Chinese hawkers, at least according to its owners, and serves good hokkien noodles and *bak kut teh*—a herby pork stew that is popular for breakfast. The food court that opened in 2018 in the basement of the tower that houses the Four Seasons Hotel, right next door to KLCC, also serves pork dishes. It was packed from the first day.

HALAL PRODUCTS

The *halal* industry is a multibillion dollar business and covers not only food, but a huge variety of products and services from cosmetics to medicines and holidays. As Malaysia's government-backed Halal Industry Development

Corporation, which was set up a decade ago, puts it, "Halal is not merely a way of life—it is a global industry."

For many years, *halal* mostly applied to food, denoting products that were suitable for observant Muslims to eat (*halal* means 'permissible'). Most people know that Muslims do not eat pork, which is considered *haram* (forbidden), but for any meat to be *halal* it must be slaughtered a certain way.

In Malaysia, food products (all beef and lamb sold in Malaysian supermarkets is *halal*) and restaurants serving such foods are checked by the religious authorities and given a stamp of approval—a distinctive *halal* logo that is usually displayed in the window or stamped on a product's packaging.

But with around 1.8 billion Muslims around the world, the *halal* brand has expanded and at the end of 2017, the value of Malaysia's *halal* exports topped 43 billion ringgit, making the country the centre of the global *halal* industry.

EATING AT RESTAURANTS

In the 1980s, Malaysia's dining scene revolved around the five-star hotels and beach resorts that were beginning to open as the country's economy expanded. Independent restaurants were few and far between.

Fast forward thirty years, and it is no longer necessary to step into the lobby of a hotel to find a decent dining experience and while Malaysia may not (yet) have any Michelin-starred restaurants, Kuala Lumpur has a thriving dining scene, fed by local chefs trained in some of the world's best kitchens and a growing number of wealthy Malaysians eager to spend money on enjoying themselves.

In KL, Changkat Bukit Bintang has a clutch of boisterous bars and restaurants that are popular with the after-work crowd. In the area's quieter streets, in shophouses and bungalows dating from the early 20th century, there is a hugely popular Malay fine-dining restaurant (Bijan), places catering to Korean and Western tastes as well as the capital's pre-eminent jazz club No Black Tie.

Another popular place—on the 23rd floor of the Norman Foster-designed Troika Residences, and a significant number of steps up in sophistication—is Troika Sky Dining. The brainchild of self-taught chef Chris Bauer and Ipoh-born Eddy Chew, the restaurants boast stupendous views of the Twin Towers with menus specialising in South American-inspired grills (Fuego) and Italian trattoria-style food (Strato). Bauer himself heads the kitchen at their flagship venue, Cantaloupe, which builds on the success of Frangipani, their original foray into KL's dining scene, which was at the centre of Changkat's early popularity.

The upper levels of the city's ever-growing number of skyscrapers, particularly in and around the Twin Towers, are popular locations for restaurants whether it is the Malaysian outpost of Japanese-Peruvian restaurant Nobu, the swish offerings at the Four Seasons and the Grand Hyatt, all of which boast breathtaking views of the KLCC Park and in the case of the two hotels, the Towers themselves. There is no restaurant at the top of the Twin Towers—the space is instead occupied by a penthouse that was once an office for Mahathir Mohamad when he was an adviser to the national oil company.

Malaysia also boasts an impressive number of high-quality Japanese restaurants, the consequence of a Mahathir-led drive to lure Japanese investment in the 1980s known as the 'Look East' policy. The Lot 10 Shopping Centre has two floors devoted to Japanese dining—on one floor a spacious food court for Japanese specialities, like curry *udon*, some of them brought into Malaysia for the first time, and a clutch of more expensive restaurants, the ceiling draped with orangey-red cloths. Many restaurants are helmed by Japanese chefs, particularly around suburbs such as Mont Kiara that are popular with Japanese. In recent years, Korean restaurants have also begun to open, capitalising on young Malaysians passion for K-Pop and all things Korean.

The Japanese-Korean wave has also hit Penang, but the island's thriving food culture, and the relatively smaller number of expat residents means fewer fancy restaurants. Steak Frites is a pleasant place in an old shophouse in the World Heritage area that serves one dish only—steak frites. Around the corner the Nyonya restaurant in the luxurious Seven Terraces Hotel is buzzing every night, and a hugely popular place for a celebration. The dishes are inspired by recipes from the owner's grandmother. There is also a fine Italian restaurant—the owner is Venetian—that is beneath the charming Campbell House boutique hotel.

CHAPTER 7

ENJOYING MALAYSIA

❝Now that we are rich, we do not talk about the past; to study history is backward-looking and we are only concerned with the future.❞

— **Tash Aw,** *The Face: Strangers on a Pier*

GETTING OUT AND ABOUT

One of the joys of living in Malaysia is the chance to travel; an opportunity to experience first-hand the country's enormous geographical and cultural diversity.

The forests of the main range offer ancient jungles where elephant, tiger, tapir and other rare fauna still roam, and while the peninsula's east coast might be more conservative in its culture than the west it offers seemingly endless, almost deserted, sandy beaches and laid-back island resorts. There is history too in the form of the old cities of Melaka, George Town (Penang) and Ipoh, which also come with a well-deserved reputation for serving up some of the country's most delicious dishes.

A mural of oversized takeaway drinks in bags, on a wall in Ipoh.

And then there is Malaysian Borneo. In some ways the states of Sarawak and Sabah seem like another country, a feeling that is underlined by the fact they have their own immigration rules—there must be few places where in the world where a second stamp of arrival is necessary when travelling in different parts of the same country.

People from Sabah and Sarawak also pride themselves on having a more relaxed approach to ethnicity and religion than people on the peninsula and have a strong sense of pride in their own history and culture.

Borneo's indigenous people tend to live along the major rivers in longhouse homes—rather like a row of terraced houses—which are elevated on stilts and share a common veranda. While the days of headhunting are long gone, and many of Sarawak's indigenous people—have become Christians, others still practise their traditional beliefs, and some do both—giving their Christianity a local flavour.

Some of the Penan, arguably Sarawak's most marginalised people, continue to live a semi-nomadic existence, even as palm oil estates gobble up vast tracts of the forest that once provided them with all they needed to survive. Despite that, Borneo still offers a once-in-a-lifetime chance to get close to some of the world's most iconic species and explore (with experienced guides) jungle that seems to have been barely touched by humans, including the Danum Valley, and the World Heritage sites of Mulu and Mount Kinabalu.

A night in a longhouse

The sun had disappeared suddenly behind the forest, leaving the longhouse in darkness and the trees ghostly shadows against the sky. Suddenly, a diesel generator shuddered into life and fluorescent lights flickered on around the settlement. We could hear the sound of cooking—metal spatulas scraping against woks—and women laughing with their children as they prepared for bed, followed by dogs barking and yelping as they fought over some scraps. A rat scurried across the rafters.

The longhouse was about a 10-hour drive along a back-breaking logging track from the coastal town of Miri and the villagers, from the Kenyah tribe, had kindly agreed to put us up for the night.

As there was no piped water, we changed into our sarongs, slipped on our flip flops and headed down to the river that ran behind the building. Sliding down the banks, the water soothed our shaken bones and came as welcome relief after a long day in the heat, humidity and dust. We floated on our backs in the shallow waters, picking out the star formations, the stretch of river our private bath in the wilderness.

While we were bathing, our hosts had been cooking dinner on the gas stove at the back of their section of the longhouse. Lunch at the Penan village further up the track had been wild boar—its coarse hair still attached to each chewy chunk of meat. It looked like dinner would be the tins of corned beef our guide had asked us to bring, with some ginger, garlic and chilli to give the dish a bit of a kick.

No one stayed up late—generators are expensive to run so most communities use them for only a few hours of the day—so we rolled out our sleeping bags on the floor and tried to sleep.

The longhouse walls were thin and ended well before they got to the roof. Men snored. Dogs barked and rats scratched and scurried across the rafters. There was the occasional sound of a baby crying and couples getting amorous. Then, finally, the silence fell.

PLANE TRAVEL

The rapid growth of low-cost aviation over the past 15 years has made it cheaper and easier to travel not only in and around Malaysia, but to the rest of Asia and beyond. There are 21 airports (five offering international connections) across Malaysia, as well as 18 landing strips in more remote areas.

In Kuala Lumpur, budget carriers (AirAsia, JetStar Asia, Malindo) operate out of the cavernous klia2, a terminal that opened in 2014 and is touted as the world's only airport terminal designed to cater specifically to low-cost carriers. Its size means distances between gates are significant—it was only after the terminal opened that anyone thought travellators might be useful—but electric buggies are provided for the less mobile. The terminal itself is part of a large shopping centre, which is convenient for an arriving passenger who needs to stock up on food or essentials before heading home, but something of a nuisance for departing passengers trying to manoeuvre their baggage through the mall and the crowds.

The main airport, Kuala Lumpur International Airport, is next door and opened to much fanfare in June 1998 just as the Asian Financial Crisis plunged the region's economies into recession. Designed by the Japanese architect, Kisho Kurokawa, it was carved out of a palm oil plantation (and is surrounded by rows of oil palms), some 50 kilometres south of the city.

The terminal building has the glass, steel and soaring roof of the typical modern airport, but a distinctively Malaysian look—there is even a mini-rainforest (open to transit passengers) in the middle of the satellite terminal.

KLIA is the base for the national carrier, Malaysia Airlines, and offers flights to 120 destinations around the world. It is particularly well connected to cities across Southeast Asia and the Asia-Pacific and is part of the One World Alliance that also includes carriers like British Airways and Japan Airlines.

When KLIA opened, the original airport at Subang (now surrounded by the city suburbs), was expected to close, but the terminal has been renovated and remains in operation for local and regional flights on smaller, turboprop planes. The airport also caters to private jets and helicopters.

KLIA and klia2 are connected to the city by train—the KLIA Ekspres and a cheaper stopping service—and passengers can take city cabs as well as the so-called KLIA Limo to their final destination as well. The train journey takes about half an hour. There is a five-star hotel next to the terminal that is useful if you have an early departure, and do not want to get up too early.

In Borneo, the larger cities have regular connections to the peninsula with direct flights available from Kota Kinabalu, Sandakan, Kuching, Miri and Bintulu. Onward connections are usually by turboprop, while remote towns depend on Twin Otters—19-seater propeller planes that have strict weight rules and do not fly when the weather is bad. Every passenger and their luggage is weighed before boarding, and it is entirely possible you will be travelling with crates of chickens as well as other basic supplies for outlying settlements. The fleet is based in Miri and provides an essential lifeline for communities without links by road.

ROAD TRAVEL

Even though cars are an expensive proposition, in housing estates throughout the land, there are probably as many of them as there are people. In swankier districts, there may be five or six vehicles in the front yard, parked behind electric gates, the point of which becomes abundantly clear as soon as it rains.

For years, Malaysians drove Japanese vehicles—they were reliable and not too expensive. But in the 1980s, then prime minister Mahathir Mohamad had an idea. He would create a national car company to produce a Malaysian car, and he would get the Japanese to help.

The first Proton Saga rolled off the production line in 1985, a localised version of a Mitsubishi and with none of the import duties and taxes associated with vehicles brought in from overseas. The economy was doing well, and more Malaysians were tempted to buy themselves a car with their newfound wealth. They turned to Proton.

By the 1990s, seven of every ten cars on Malaysian roads was made by Proton, and a second 'national' carmaker had also started manufacturing vehicles too. The first of Perodua's small, nippy cars rolled off the production line in 1993, based on models made by Japan's Daihatsu and designed to appeal to younger buyers. Few of the cars made by either of the national producers had much in the way of safety features, and the electric windows were notorious for breaking, but buyers did not seem to mind. Protons and Peroduas got them to where they needed to go cheaply and efficiently.

Mahathir also moved to improve the road network, creating the first highway—to link the country's south (and Singapore) to the north nearly 750 kilometres away. These days most people the take North South Highway for granted, but when it first opened in 1994, it would not be overstating its impact to say it changed the peninsula, connecting towns along the west coast and—for good or bad—fuelling economic development. No longer did drivers have to dawdle behind slow-moving trucks on the single carriageway of the old federal route one, they could speed at 110 kilometres an hour along the three-lane tolled highway and take a break at the purpose-built rest areas along the way.

Express bus services upgraded their services too, offering passengers fast connections between Malaysia's major cities and towns. Some, particularly between KL and Singapore, began to differentiate themselves with the kind of generously padded seats more usually found in airlines' business class cabins with food served by uniformed attendants. Whatever the type of bus, most Malaysians seem content to pull the curtains and sleep away the journey, however long it may be.

These days the highway is not always as free-flowing as it used to be. Traffic accidents are all too common, quickly causing tailbacks, and at holiday times, it is best not to travel by car or bus at all. During my first Hari Raya in Malaysia, I drove up to Penang to celebrate with friends. On the way back to Kuala Lumpur, the traffic jam started at the junction for Cameron Highlands, 125 kilometres north of the capital. Drivers whizzed down the emergency lane, while others tried to wait out the jam in the nearest rest stop. Most just sat in their vehicles edging slowly towards KL.

Away from holidays, the highways (there is a second one goes across the main range from Kuala Lumpur to Kuantan to link the relatively poorer states of the east with the more prosperous west, and another further north called the Gerik highway that achieves a similar feat), provide an easy way to get around. Before the east coast highway opened, a car journey to the country's northeastern states was long and tedious and involved traversing hectare after hectare of regimented plantations. For people heading to Kelantan it involved the rather more fascinating road through the jungle that still occupies much of the heart of the Malaysian peninsula.

Even with the highways, West Malaysia maintains a fairly extensive network of federal roads in various states of repair. Trucks laden with timber or palm oil are a common sight on these roads and accidents are not uncommon. Indeed, considering its size and wealth, Malaysia has a high level of road fatalities—on average about 300 people are killed on the roads every day, many of them motorcyclists.

It is vital to stay alert when driving in Malaysia, not only for other drivers, some of whom have a rather relaxed relationship with the rules of the road, but also for animals. (In 2017, I was astonished to see a herd of cattle wandering around the northbound carriageway of the North South Highway and hundreds of cars at a standstill waiting for them to move). Sadly, some of Malaysia's most iconic wildlife including tapir, tiger and elephants sometimes stray onto roads (including the highways). Signs usually warn drivers of the risk while wildlife viaducts have also been built at known crossing points so animals can walk safely below.

The road system in Sabah and Sarawak is less developed beyond the major cities, and air and boat remain the only way that some communities are able to keep in touch with the outside world. Some make use of the network of rough, unsealed roads that have developed to meet the needs of the logging and plantation industries. Most of the logging tracks are hugely rutted and passable only in a 4WD (or the huge trucks for which they were built), but they are also vital links for remote communities.

In recent years, Malaysia has been working to improve its rail network to relieve some of the pressure on the peninsula's roads. The main railway line, running from Singapore to the border with Thailand, was built by the British and has changed little since. The train between Singapore and Kuala Lumpur trundles along at 40 kilometres an hour and takes a leisurely eight hours to complete the journey. Plans to build a high-speed line on the route were shelved in 2018, after the new government took power, but improvements to the existing track are continuing which should speed up the journey. The section from Kuala Lumpur to Butterworth (Penang) has already been upgraded. All trains are air-conditioned with reserved seating, making the train a viable alternative to cars and buses for visiting cities such as Ipoh (two hours) and Penang (four hours plus the ferry).

Boat services are also available to connect coastal ports with outlying islands on the east coast. Mersing is the gateway to many of the resort islands in the southern part of the South China Sea with regular services to Tioman, while Kuala Besut is the jumping off point for the Perhentian Islands in the northeast. At most ports along the coast it is also possible to arrange private speedboat transfers. On the west coast, there are ferries to Sumatra from Melaka, while boats run from Penang to Langkawi as well as Sumatra and Phuket.

THE ARTS

Malaysian contemporary art has long tended to float beneath the radar of many international collectors, but the country boasts a small, thriving art scene centred around a handful of art schools and galleries that stage regular, high-quality shows. Many young artists also take residencies overseas as a way of developing their practice.

Ilham is arguably Kuala Lumpur's best gallery. The brainchild of renowned Sabah-born regional art curator Valentine Willie, it opened in a Norman Foster-designed building close to the Twin Towers in 2015. The gallery, which operates as a public rather than a commercial operation, stages between three and four exhibitions a year, complemented by a series of talks, panel discussions and workshops from local and visiting experts.

Its opening show was a survey on the work of one of the country's most renowned portraitists Hossein Enas, while in 2018 it staged a show by Latiff Mohidin, a modernist master who made his name with the highly sought-after *Pago Pago* series in the 1960s.

Other notable galleries include Taksu, Richard Koh and Wei Ling Gallery.

Taksu is housed in an old bungalow in the Keramat area of Kuala Lumpur and is one of the stalwarts of the art scene, having been in operation for more than 20 years. It shows the work of contemporary artists from Malaysia and Southeast Asia and has a sister gallery in Singapore.

Ilham is probably Malaysia's leading non-commercial art gallery. It is situated in a Norman Foster-designed building in Kuala Lumpur and offers regular talks and workshops.

Richard Koh operates from a terraced house with a distinctive white façade in the Kuala Lumpur suburb of Bangsar. One of the city's newer galleries, Richard Koh hangs regular shows by both up-and-coming and established artists from around Southeast Asia.

The eponymous Wei Ling Gallery and Wei Ling Contemporary are owned by Lim Wei Ling, the daughter of Jimmy Lim, one of Malaysia's foremost architects. The main gallery is housed in a stunning shophouse conversion on the edge of Brickfields that was once her father's office while the contemporary gallery is on the roof of The Gardens Mall. Wei Ling specialises in contemporary art from Malaysia and the region.

In a class of its own is Rimbun Dahan, the country estate of the architect Hijjas Kasturi and his wife Angela. A 40 minute drive northwest of Kuala Lumpur, depending on the traffic, Rimbun Dahan is set in a lush, natural garden dotted with contemporary sculptures collected by the Kasturis. It offers residencies to artists and performers from around the region who are invited to live and work on the estate for anything from a month to a year. Its annual residency show is hugely popular and there are also studio visits, dance performances and guided tours of the garden, which is planted with native species. The Kasturis also operate a small, luxury resort—The Kasturi—on the beach near Cherating where they run a turtle sanctuary. Artist residencies are also planned.

In Penang, the declaration of George Town as a World Heritage site prompted renewed interest in the state's heritage as well as the adaptive reuse of old buildings for creative people and businesses.

Hin Bus Depot is a gallery and arts centre that offers a roster of often avant garde shows, as well as studio space, craft workshops, a regular market and café. There is also the

The annual George Town Festival uses the city as its canvas.

George Town Festival each July—turning the city into a canvas for performance and art (the murals that adorn the walls of many buildings in the historic zone were commissioned as part of the festival)—as well as the Literary Festival in November.

Kuala Lumpur has had less success with its festivals, but it does boast a world-class classical concert hall in the Dewan Filharmonic Petronas beneath the Twin Towers, which is the home of the

The art deco-style former bus garage, Hin Bus Depot in George Town, Penang, is now a thriving community arts space.

Malaysian Philharmonic Orchestra. Many of the musicians are from eastern Europe, but a growing number of Asians have joined the orchestra and its family shows on Sunday are enormously popular.

Internationally renowned performers including Kiri Te Kanawa and Vladimir Ashkenazy have performed at the hall and tickets for the shows by guest performers are quickly sold out. Each year's season begins around the end of September and runs until July and MPO friends get early access to the box office. Bear in mind, that the concert hall operates a dress code and men are supposed to wear batik shirts or jackets. The latter are available to borrow.

The capital also has a small, but dedicated performing arts scene centred around KLPac, a theatre and performance space built out of the old railway sheds in Sentul, as well as DPac out in the new suburb of Damansara Perdana which stage mostly local productions, and the occasional international touring event.

KLPac also offers affordable courses in the performing arts—from dramatic speaking to hip hop and gamelan—which are open to children and adults in the evenings or at the weekend. There is a centre in Penang too—PenangPac.

Ramli Ibrahim, who turned 65 in 2018, is one of the world's foremost exponents of Odissi, an Indian dance that was close to dying out in the 1950s, and established the Sutra Dance Theatre in 1983. Frequently described as a legend, Ramli was awarded India's Padma Shri Award for his contributions to Indian dance. Sutra organises regular performances of Odissi, other forms of classical Indian dance and Malaysian contemporary dance. It also runs classes for children.

Dama ('big horse' in Mandarin) started off as a Chinese

orchestra in 1994 and quickly won critical acclaim for its performances. The company has now forged a reputation for its musical theatre and stage productions and has toured internationally.

Of course, censorship is an ever-present concern. In recent years, a portrait of a transgender woman and a gay activist were removed from an exhibition in Penang after Muslim conservatives complained that looking at the pictures would unduly 'influence' young people, while paintings have been taken down and books of cartoons seized—the artist detained for sedition—for being too political or criticising the government.

In 2019, a play that was supposed to be staged at Penang Pac was cancelled at the last minute after conservatives objected. The playwright had earlier changed the name of the play to remove the word 'sex' from the title, but it was not enough to assuage the critics.

CINEMA

There is no shortage of Hollywood blockbusters, Bollywood spectaculars, Korean love stories or Hong Kong dramas on Malaysian cinema screens. There is even a small domestic industry, which veers between edgy independent-style films to cop flicks and lavishly produced drama usually in Malay, but sometimes in Chinese or Tamil.

The big-ticket shows will generally get a Malaysian release ahead of the US or Europe, but arthouse films or even thoughtful dramas rarely get screen time unless as part of an embassy-organised film festival.

Cinemas themselves are dominated by two main operators—TGV (Tanjong Golden Village) and GSC (Golden Screen Cinemas) and are not only extremely comfortable (the air-conditioning is strong so do not forget to bring a sweater to keep warm) but also affordably priced. There are no arthouse-type cinemas.

Fancier, reclining seats are available at a higher price at cinemas offering Gold Class halls. The usual popcorn and junk food are sold near the ticketing booths (most people buy their tickets online or through an app) and Malaysians enjoy munching their way through the movies.

Once the lights go down (assuming you are not in parts of the northeast where lights can remain on to prevent any canoodling), be prepared to sit through reams of commercials and previews before the main event. Be prepared too for censorship. Far from an exact science, all kinds of violence appear to be allowed but the slightest kiss is swiftly cut. Malaysia does have a limited classification system, but that does not seem to have any bearing on what is or is not cut.

Malaysia Film Classification

Film classification was first introduced in what was then Malaya in 1953 with films assessed as suitable either for 'Public Viewing' or 'Adults Only'. The system was refined in 1996 when the classifications were renamed U and 18, and the latter divided into four categories. In 2010, 'parental guidance' was introduced as a classification creating a middle ground for films that did not really fit into either of the two existing categories. The last revision took place in 2012 when PG13 was renamed P13.

U: Universal. For all ages. The film 'portrays good values, decency and positive lessons, as well as entertaining [sic],' according to the Ministry of Home Affairs which has ultimate responsibility for censorship.

P13: Viewers under 13 years of age require the supervision of parents or guardians while viewing. Scenes in the film might contain elements of horror or be scary and also include, in the words of the Ministry, 'negative acts, suspense and frantic elements (but not excessive) and elements that can disturb a child's emotion.'

18: Films for people of 18 and above. Such movies contain elements of horror, gore, and violence, but not too much, 'adult scenes' that are not too excessive, and social, sensitive political or religious elements that require a high-level understanding.

Censorship means some films never make it to Malaysia at all, including the *The Wolf of Wall Street* starring Leonardo DiCaprio, somewhat of an irony given that the tale of financial debauchery was allegedly financed by money stolen from the state fund 1MDB. In 1995, *Babe*, the gentle story of a little pig with big ambitions, was banned for fear it would offend Muslims (it was eventually released on video). Many Steven Spielberg films, including the Oscar-winning *Schindler's List*, have also failed to make it to the big screen in Malaysia, while more recently it was the Disney live action remake of *Beauty and the Beast* that caught the censors attention.

Even films that make it to the screen might be heavily edited in order to meet the requirements of the censorship board (some directors and producers refuse to comply with the cuts, withdrawing their film from exhibition instead). Note that censors do not normally worry if their cuts make the story impossible to follow.

Fans of arthouse films and documentaries should look out for Malaysia's film festivals. The first European Union Film Festival took place in 2000 and is now one of the year's cultural highlights. The 2018 edition took place in cinemas in KL, Penang, JB, Kuching and Kota Kinabalu between October and December, offering film fans the chance to watch 21 award-winning movies from 17 countries, with some of the shows screened for free. There is also a Japanese Film Festival organised by the embassy and two locally-organised independent showcases of film—the Freedom Film Fest and Eco Film Fest—that take place over a week showcasing short and feature-length documentaries as well as talks and workshops focussing on democracy and the environment.

NIGHTLIFE

Despite a rather staid international image and the regular risk of police raids, KL has long been something of a party hub with bars and clubs open, and the drink flowing freely until the early hours; the sticky-carpeted rooms, throbbing music, alcohol and drugs of the city's late 1990s clubbing scene are recalled with vivid intensity in Bernice Chauly's 2017 novel, *Once We Were There*.

One of the most enduringly popular clubs in a notoriously fickle scene remains Zouk, the Malaysian outpost of the original Singapore club. Housed for ten years in a purpose-built marshmallow-like building on Jalan Ampang (now occupied by a branch of the nasi kandar joint, Pelita), Zouk was packing in the punters at TREC (Taste, Relish, Experience, Celebrate) off Jalan Tun Razak at the time of writing. Often described as a superclub, Zouk is famous for its variety of dance spaces, and internationally-renowned DJs. It also has two restaurants and a VIP lounge, known as Imperial, that is designed to cater to KL's super rich. A password-activated lift ensures only those in the know gain access to this exclusive playground.

Elsewhere in the city, the discreet and cosy has become

increasingly popular with piano bars, jazz clubs and cocktail bars hidden away in unlikely suburban settings. The pioneer of the genre, No Black Tie, first opened its doors on Jalan Mesui in the city centre in 1998 and hosts regular shows not only by some of Malaysia's best singers and musicians, but also performers from around the region and beyond.

SPORT, CLUBS AND GYMS

Malaysia's searing heat and often stifling climate means most people head out for a run, walk or cycle when it is cooler—either in the early morning or late afternoon. At these times, it is usual to see Malaysians out and about—eager runners with their dogs at their side, lycra-clad men and women on the latest racing bikes, dog walkers and elderly couples taking a gentle stroll around the neighbourhood.

The country's most popular sport is badminton. It is the one sport that gets everyone in front of the television to watch the national team even though Malaysian competitors seem to be forever the runners-up rather than the champions. Squash is popular too, with young people inspired to take up the sport by the incredible success of nine-time women's world champion Nicol David.

Malaysia hosts a regular roster of competitive events from more relaxed fun runs and walks to marathons, triathlons and Iron Man, most of which will be timed to start early in the morning to avoid the worst of the heat. The most popular races are the Standard Chartered Marathon which starts and ends in Dataran Merdeka each September and OCBC Cycle in November. There are also regular biathlons and triathlons, which include shorter races for children. The Port Dickson Triathlon each April is one of the most popular events.

For the less serious athlete, Hari Sukan Malaysia (National

Sports Day) takes place every October and is an opportunity to try out a range of different sports with events taking place across the country—from the National Stadium in Bukit Jalil to neighbourhood sports centres.

THE GREAT OUTDOORS

Rounding a bend in the river, as the sun begins to drop, our guide catches sight of a grey shape barely distinguishable from the bushes along the banks of the river. He slows the engine and turns to us—a finger to his lips. We drift silently in the boat, scanning the undergrowth for wildlife, as a group of elephants emerge from the trees, plunge into the river and begin to drink and bathe, sucking the water into their trunks and splashing it over their backs.

The Asian elephant (including the pygmy elephant that lives in Sabah) is only one of the iconic animals. There is also the critically-endangered Malayan tiger, orang utan, and the unique monochromatic Malayan tapir, as well as Borneo's distinctive helmeted hornbill, rare orchids and the world's biggest flowering plants, which Sir Stamford Raffles discovered in 1818 and named after himself. "It is perhaps the largest and most magnificent flower in the world," Raffles observed. It also, by all accounts, stinks.

Some of the most popular places to see wildlife are in Taman Negara in the peninsula, and along the Kinabatangan River in Sabah, but lesser known parks also offer those with time, patience and a high tolerance for leeches the chance to see animals in a rainforest environment millennia-old.

The government says at least 50 per cent of Malaysia will be maintained as 'forest' but logging and plantations remain existential threats to the rainforest and the flora, fauna and people that depend on the forest for their survival.

The Malayan Tapir is a distinctive black and white creature with a stubby trunk. It lives only in Peninsular Malaysia.

Environmental activists have become increasingly vocal in recent years, forcing the end of illegal bauxite mining in Pahang that had left roads red with sediment, and campaigning against an Australian-run rare earths plant nearby. In the forest itself, researchers and non-governmental organisations and civil society are on-the-ground helping mitigate conflicts between animals and people—mainly elephants—tackling poachers and enlisting the orang asli (the people who know the forest better than anyone) in national efforts to save the tiger.

VOLUNTEERING

From schools for refugee children to wildlife surveys and helping out at soup kitchens, there are many opportunities to get

Malaysia is one of the most bio-diverse nations in the world with 152,000 species of animal life and 15,000 plants, hanging on amid the monoculture of palm oil and durian plantations.

involved in helping others whether in KL or further afield. Most organisations publicise their needs through expatriate associations (a work permit is not necessary for voluntary work) or on local radio, while others rely on word-of-mouth.

Teaching is a popular activity for spouses of foreigners working in Malaysia, and refugee schools are always on the lookout for effective teachers, especially those who can teach the core subjects like Maths and English.

Bear in mind, that most of the schools operate from community halls or shophouses, relying on donations for books and other resources, and may not follow any kind of curriculum. Some are chaotic—I once walked in on a group of Chin children from Myanmar running riot around the elderly foreign woman who was trying to get them to sit down and do some drawing. Others run like well-oiled machines—when I visited a school for Sri Lankan refugee children they all stood up at their desks and greeted me by name before returning diligently to their work.

Volunteers need to decide on their strengths and work out how they might be able to help the school while recognising that the need may be for fundraising or administration rather than teaching.

Voluntary work in the environmental sector has also expanded in recent years. One of the most popular opportunities is to join a MyCat trek organised by the WWF to join the rangers to map tigers and assess risks to the animal and its forest habitat. Most of the jungle walks last for three days (they are not too physically arduous) and can be booked online through the MyCat website. Longer treks are available for the more adventurous.

MUST-SEES

Batu Caves

Watched over by a statue of Lord Murugan, a Hindu deity, the limestone caves on the outskirts of Kuala Lumpur are home to numerous shrines and temples. Worshippers and tourists must climb 272 steps and brave the monkeys to reach the top. The temple is at its most vibrant during the Thaipusam festival.

Cameron Highlands

Malaysia's biggest hill station. Discovered in 1885 by William Cameron, a surveyor with the British colonial government, it was developed into a hill resort in 1925. The area, some 1,800 metres above sea level, is famous for its tea plantations and cooler weather. Development of agriculture and housing has been rapid in recent years, however.

Taman Negara

Peninsular Malaysia's first and largest national park spans 4,343 square kilometres in the centre of the country and is a sanctuary for the country's most iconic and elusive animals—tigers, tapir, leopards and elephants. Most people access the park by the Jerantut River, but you will (probably) have to get well off the beaten path to spot any of the more elusive animals.

Kinabalu National Park and Mount Kinabalu

The highest point in Malaysia and the first place in Malaysia to be listed as a UNESCO World Heritage site, the mountain is clearly visible from Sabah's capital Kota Kinabalu although the granite-spired summit is often hidden in cloud. Most people aim to reach the summit at dawn then return down the mountain. Porters run up and down with practised ease.

The Kinabatangan River

At 550 kilometres, the chocolatey-brown river is the longest in Sabah and the second-longest in Malaysia. Much of the forest along the river's banks has been designated a wildlife sanctuary and a stay at one of the lodges provides ample opportunity to see proboscis monkeys, elephants, crocodiles and even orang utans.

Gunung Mulu National Park

The World Heritage-listed Gunung Mulu National Park is home to some of the world's most spectacular caves, pristine tropical rainforest and unique rock formations. The Deer Cave is more than 2 kilometres long and 174 metres high, making it the largest cave in the world that is open to the public. At least two million bats live in the cave.

Langkawi

The Langkawi archipelago in Malaysia's northwest is made up of 99 islands. The northern beaches of the main island overlooking the Andaman Sea are home to some of the world's most sublime resorts promising turquoise waters, stunning architecture and ancient, almost untouched rainforest. UNESCO awarded Langkawi Geopark status in 2007 in recognition of its mangrove-fringed limestone karsts, ancient forests and unusual freshwater lakes.

The Kilim Geoforest Park is a unique estuarine network of mangroves and limestone karst formations.

A boat ride through the Kilim Geoforest Park is a popular activity for people visiting Langkawi.

Petronas Twin Towers

The world's tallest buildings when they were finished in 1998, the Cesar Pelli-designed towers have become an icon of Kuala Lumpur and Malaysia. Each tower has 88 storeys (one was built by Korean contractors and the other by the Japanese), and visitors are taken to the connecting bridge on the 41st floor. The Philharmonic Hall on the ground floor hosts orchestras, jazz and hugely popular family shows.

George Town and Melaka World Heritage Sites

The joint UNESCO-listed cities of George Town (Penang) and Melaka provide a fascinating insight into Malaysia's past and the lives of the so-called Straits Chinese or Peranakans. It is easy to stroll the old streets (especially during the week when it is less busy) soaking up the atmosphere and enjoying some of the best food Asia has to offer.

Sepilok Orang Utan Rehabilitation Centre

The Sepilok centre was founded in 1964 and is one of only four in the world. It extends over 4,000 hectares close to Sandakan in Sabah and is supposed to provide a space for once captive and injured orang utans to recover so they can eventually return to the wild.

We had spent about half an hour at the salt lick—a clearing in the jungle—where complex minerals lure wildlife including elephants and tapir out of the forest to feed. Nature being what nature is, the only signs of wildlife we saw were football-sized dollops of elephant dung and giant footprints, but when we got back on our boat we became all too aware that other less easy to spot animals had been there too. Leeches. Scores of them, searching, sniffing, hungry for blood and racing up our trouser legs. I managed to flick some off the fabric and into the water. Another walker did the same—little brown lines, probably no more than 1cm long—spinning through the air and into the milky brown river. We weren't entirely successful. There were simply too many. Some stuck around on the edge of the boat, sensing their next meal, and a few found their way through. I didn't know that at the time. Only later, when I discovered the tell-tale patches of blood on my socks.

Leeches are harmless, of course, and there are plenty of ways to deal with them if they make you squeamish. You can opt for leech socks, long trousers, long socks and lashings of Mosiguard, or you can follow the locals' lead and ignore them altogether.

CHAPTER 8

THE LANGUAGE(S)

‘Makan already?’

— common greeting

Malaysians, particularly in the main cities, speak good English and it is easy to live in Kuala Lumpur and never feel the need to learn Malay or any of the other languages spoken across the country. That would be a shame.

The Dewan Bahasa dan Pustaka, much like the Académie Française in France, was established to act as an official authority on Malay and produce textbooks for the new country's schools. Within five years the agency had managed to publish a total of 14.5 million books under 381 different titles from nursery rhymes to philosophy and science.

A decade after independence, then Prime Minister Tunku Abdul Rahman told parliament that "the national language was the one and only means of binding together the peoples of various origins in the country and achieving the goal of loyalty, thus providing a guarantee of peace and harmony."

Nowadays, Malay is the language of government, official announcements and events, and countless newspapers, magazines and television dramas. It is also the language of instruction in state schools.

Malay (known officially as Bahasa Malaysia or Bahasa Melayu—'bahasa' means language) was proclaimed the country's national language shortly after Malaya got its independence.

An Austronesian language, Malay is a window into the country's history and culture, evolving alongside the waves of trade and migration that shaped modern Malaysia. The language has different forms depending on the context, and a host of words borrowed from a variety of other sources including Arabic, Sanskrit, Portuguese, Dutch and even some Chinese dialects. The earliest written records of the language are Sumatran inscriptions written in an alphabet from southern India and dating from the late 7th century.

Even away from the royal courts, Malay retains a certain formality and politeness and most Malay speakers will do their best to avoid using words such as 'you' (*anda/awak*), 'he' or 'she' (*dia*) or, even 'I' (*saya*). Instead, they will refer to an individual by name, title or position, and may even do this when referring to themselves—a mother talking to her child, for example, might call herself '*mak*' rather than '*saya*'.

If you are speaking to an older man you might address him as '*encik*', while an older woman might be called '*puan*' (in more relaxed settings such as market you could also use '*makcik*'—auntie). It's also acceptable to use a person's job as a form of address—'*cikgu*' for teacher, for example—or a title (Tan Sri, Datuk etc) if the person has one. This politeness also explains some expressions in Malaysian English where older women might be addressed as 'auntie' or 'madam'.

It is often said that Malay is an 'easy' language, which is true in the sense that there appear to be no tenses, and plurals can be made simply by repeating a word, but like most things that appear easy on the surface, it is actually a lot more complicated.

The type of language that is used depends on the context so the kind of Malay that is spoken in a royal household or in the presence of royalty is markedly different to the language of everyday conversation or so-called '*pasar* Malay' (literally market Malay).

On top of that, many words are shortened or even changed in everyday speech (which can come as something of a surprise if you have been schooled in a more formal, written Malay), and there are also seven different dialects in regular use around the country. The language spoken in Kelantan can seem utterly unintelligible even to a Malay speaker from Kuala Lumpur.

MALAY PRONUNCIATION

Pronunciation is relatively straightforward, and most Malay words are spoken as they are written. For the vowels:

- The letter 'a' is usually a short, hard 'ah'
- The letter 'e' is pronounced in the same way as the English 'pet'
- The letter 'i' like 'pit'
- The letter 'o' like 'pot'
- And the letter 'u' like 'put'

There are, of course, some exceptions:

- *Meja* (table) is pronounced 'may-ja'
- The sound 'sh' is written as 'sy' as in *Syariah* law or *syarikat* (a company)
- The sound 'ch' is written as a 'c' as in *cucu* (grandchild) or *cahaya* (light)

It is polite to address someone by their name or title. The latter can come in quite handy if you have forgotten someone's name.

USEFUL MALAY WORDS AND PHRASES

Rosak. You will see this everywhere—on doors, escalators, parking machines… It means 'broken'.

tandas	toilet
tandas awam	public toilet
awas	caution
dilarang	prohibited
boleh	can/possible
ya	yes
tidak (or tak)	no
tarik	pull
tolak	push
mana	where
berapa?	how much?
harga	price
mahal	expensive
murah	cheap
selamat pagi	good morning
selamat tengah hari	good afternoon (early afternoon around lunchtime)
selamat malam	good evening/good night
apa khabar?	how are you?
khabar baik	I'm well, thank you. (this is the only acceptable reply)
selamat tinggal	goodbye
jumpa lagi	see you soon

maaf	sorry/excuse me
terima kasih	thank you
siapa	who
nama saya...	my name is...

The Dewan Pustaka frequently reviews the language as the ultimate arbiter of acceptable usage. It publishes the Kamus Dewan—the Malay dictionary of record—with recent additions including *swafoto* (selfie) and *sohor kini* (trending).

MANGLISH

While English is widely spoken among Malaysians, it has some local idiosyncrasies—usually the result of a direct translation or trying to use English in the same way as Malay, Mandarin or a Chinese dialect. To increase the confusion, at least to the uninitiated, Malaysians often add words from their native languages to English.

In business situations, particularly in emails, Malaysians will tend to say that they will 'revert' to you when they mean they will reply to you.

'Where do you stay?' rather than 'Where do you live?'

'Send' means to give someone a lift or take them somewhere as in: 'I'll send you home.' 'Fetch' is used when a Malaysian is going to collect someone. 'I'll fetch you from school.'

There is some confusion too over the use of the word 'borrow'. Malaysians will often say 'borrow' when they mean 'lend'. As in: 'Can you borrow me your book?'

'Open/close the light' rather than turn on or turn off the light.

The word 'friend' can be used as a verb as in: 'Can I friend you?'

'Take' is often used as a substitute for eat or like when talking about food. A Malaysian might ask you whether you 'take' spicy food when they are curious about whether you are able to tolerate spicy food.

'Boss' is commonly used when talking to a waiter, especially in a local *mamak* shop.

Malaysians love the word 'boleh' and use it liberally in English, too. If you ask whether a person can do something they're likely to reply 'boleh' or 'can'.

For some Malaysians (and Singaporeans) 'doing the marketing' means doing their weekly shop in the market or supermarket.

Then there are the colonial holdovers including 'outstation', which remains quite common. The term means a person is away from home—visiting another city, another state or another country.

All Kinds of Can

Malaysians love the word 'can'. But while a simple response of 'can' might mean a Malaysian is willing to do something, there are many nuances in the way the word is used, so it is worth paying attention to the speaker's expression and their tone of voice.

'Can lah' is a gentle way of signalling agreement.

'Can ah' carries a range of possible meanings from a question enquiring whether that individual is allowed to do something to whether an action is itself allowed.

On the negative side, 'cannot' clearly means 'no'. But so does the question, 'How can?'

On the other hand, 'also can' generally indicates the

speaker has some reservations about the suggestion. 'See first lah' is another way of suggesting some concern about what is being proposed.

JAWI

It was not until the mid-20th century, as the British deepened their control over their colonies in what is now Malaysia, that the Romanised alphabet for Malay achieved widespread popularity. For hundreds of years before that the language was written in an Arabic script known as Jawi, which was expanded to accommodate Malay sounds and vowels.

Legends and folk tales that had been passed down through the generations were written down in Jawi as poetry (*pantun* and *syair*), stories (*hikayat*) and couplets (*gurindram*), and some of the language's great literary works, including the story of Hang Tuah and the parable of Sang Kancil, the mouse deer, were first written down in Jawi.

The script was widely used not only in the royal courts, but also among ordinary people and even senior British civil servants who were posted to the territory in the late 19th century.

Until the 1980s, the script was taught in Malaysian schools and there were Jawi newspapers too—with the Malay language Utusan Melayu publishing a Jawi edition until 2006. These days, however, while it is common to find older Malaysians of all ethnicities able to understand Jawi, the script has been largely replaced by Romanised Malay and many younger Malaysians struggle to understand it. Street names may still appear in Jawi with the Romanised Malay beneath in many states of the peninsular, but there is growing concern that the script may die out as younger generations focus on English, Chinese, Japanese and even Korean.

OTHER LANGUAGES

As a multicultural nation, Malaysians speak a wealth of languages. It is not uncommon, especially among the ethnic minorities. to find people who can speak four or five languages (although they may not be able to read or write all of them) including Malay and English.

Mandarin and Chinese Dialects

The country's ethnic Chinese came predominantly from southern China and brought their local languages with them. The most common of the so-called dialects is Hokkien, but you will also hear Cantonese (especially in KL) and Hakka. Other less common dialects include Teochew, Foochow, and Hainanese. After decades and even centuries in Malaysia, Malay words have also crept into the vocabulary of many Chinese dialects too.

Alongside the rise of mainland China and the global push for a 'standardised' Chinese, Mandarin has become increasingly common as a form of communication.

Malaysia has a vibrant Mandarin language press, regular news bulletins in Mandarin, a thriving Mando-pop scene and plenty of dramas and soap operas to cater to the Chinese-speaking community, or anyone else who is interested. Mandarin is also the language of instruction in the country's government-aided Chinese schools, while those at mainstream government schools may find they have the option to learn Mandarin.

Mastering Mandarin starts young and children are required to memorise individual characters and practise writing them out over and over again. They must also remember the four different tones of the language. Although Malaysia uses simplified characters, it is a tough language to learn and many adult Malaysian Chinese, particularly those who attended mainstream government schools, are unable to read or write the language. For people who have grown up with the Roman alphabet, Mandarin is even tougher.

Indian Languages

Tamil is the most common of the Indian languages spoken in Malaysia, and a number of Tamil schools are supported by the government. There are also Tamil language newspapers, regular news broadcasts in the language and dedicated Tamil television. Other languages include Hindi, Malayalam, Punjabi and Telugu.

Indigenous Languages

The peoples of Borneo speak a variety of native languages, usually in addition to Malay, including Iban, Kadazan and Bidayuh, which are also Austronesian languages. English is also common.

Peranakan or Baba Malay

Peranakan, or Baba Malay, is a mix of Hokkien and Malay that developed as a result of inter-marriage between local Malay women and ethnic Chinese men, predominantly in Penang, Melaka and Singapore. It is mostly spoken by the older generation, but you may recognise some of the words when you wander around these historic cities. For example, '*bibik*' is a form of address for an elderly woman while '*bikin*' means make.

Bahasa Rojak

Given their language abilities, it is not uncommon to find a Malaysian who starts talking in one language and switches to another and even throw in words and expressions from a third. Like the spicy mixed salad, it is a melange of different languages that together make sense.

'You *memang gila betul lah*' is a mix of English, Malay and Manglish that translates as: 'You are really crazy.'

LEARNING MALAY

The government often talks about trying to make Malay more popular, but the reality is that it is often easier to find a teacher of French, Japanese, Mandarin or Korean in Malaysia than it is to find someone who teaches Malay.

The National University of Malaysia (UKM) used to offer an intensive class over a three-month period which was a great way to get started with the language (even if the Malay that was taught was rather formal), but the class no longer seems to be available.

There are private language schools that offer classes and some teachers may come to your office for an agreed fee. There are also a number of books that are designed to help you teach yourself Malay. Since the language is constantly evolving, and new words are added regularly, an up-to-date edition is crucial.

Although many Malaysians like to speak English, it is also worth making the effort to converse with your colleagues in Malay to practise and learn new words. Other tactics that can speed the acquisition of the language include writing emails in Malay, watching TV with the subtitles (English/Malay or Malay/English) and setting a daily target of words to learn. Listening to Malay radio channels (the presenters tend to speak extremely quickly) and reading Malay media are also helpful.

CHAPTER 9

WORKING IN MALAYSIA

'Malaysia Boleh!'

— popular saying

In a country where English is widely spoken (sometimes to a higher standard than countries where English is the first and only language of communication) and people dress mostly in Western-style clothes, it would be easy to assume that Malaysia's working culture is similarly globalised.

In some senses it is. If you are working with a multinational, it is unlikely you will see much immediate difference in the working environment, but beneath the surface it is clear that Malaysians have a quite different approach to work; a reflection of the country's diversity and its geographic location in Asia.

Skyscrapers have sprouted across Kuala Lumpur in recent years, providing state-of-the-art offices to multinationals, large local companies and tech firms. These are 'Class A' buildings providing internet and phone connectivity, fast lifts, efficient air-conditioning systems and clean toilets. Not all buildings are like this though. In smaller towns, offices and government departments can be decidedly creaky.

MALAYSIAN RUBBER TIME

Malaysians have a somewhat elastic relationship with time, summed up in the joke that the country operates on 'Malaysia Rubber Time'. Malaysians are routinely late, whether for an in-house meeting or one outside. For meetings in the office, some consultants say Malaysians need to be 'corralled' into attending. Outside the office and despite the proliferation of apps to help those with poor time-keeping, the latecomer will probably blame the traffic, heavy rain, or both. Beware the person who tells you they are 'on their way' or 'five minutes away'. They rarely are. It is probably best to accept that Malaysians will always be late and plan accordingly.

MEETING AND GREETING

Like other Asian countries, Malaysians have a tendency to defer to those who are more senior to them, whether in age or position. Although there are increasing mutterings about their value, titles are all important. If someone has been given such an honour then you should address them with that title unless they have told you otherwise. And always use royal titles.

For the ethnic Chinese it is important to show respect to the older generation and younger Malaysians will address those older than them as 'auntie' or 'uncle'. Such terms of address might sound odd to a Westerner, but it is a term of respect. Married women will often be addressed as 'Madam', which can be a little disconcerting.

In a business setting, Malaysians will usually shake hands when greeting each other. For Malay men this does not always mean a firm grip. For some (prime minister Mahathir Mohamad, for instance) it is more like a pass across the palms.

There are some business consultants who say Malay men and women do not shake hands for religious reasons— instead placing their hands on their hearts. In more than 20 years in Malaysia, dealing with people of all backgrounds, I have never found this to be the case. The only place I have seen such a greeting used is in hotels. The hand-on-the-heart gesture seems to be more a marketing tool of the tourism promotion board than a longstanding, traditional welcome.

However, if you are male and meeting a Malay woman who has chosen to wear the headscarf, you should wait for her to extend her hand before you do. Most will be willing to shake hands, but a polite nod and a smile will do if she prefers not to.

Malaysians also like to exchange business cards when they first meet. As an indication of the business card's importance, most companies will ensure their new recruits have a box of cards waiting for them on their first day of work. When someone offers you their card, it is polite to study the card for a little bit and even to make a comment on the design before putting it away in your wallet.

While some people, particularly below senior level or in 'creative' industries may make do with a missed call to a phone to share their contact details, cards remain useful reminders of people and meetings, and provide a useful opportunity for small talk.

Government Name Tags
Malaysian officials—from the prime minister downwards—wear name tags on their left lapel whether they are elected politicians or civil servants. Mahathir introduced the policy, along with a requirement for all staff to clock-in and clock-out, back in the 1980s as a way to improve transparency and accountability, but after he retired in 2003 it was less rigidly enforced. Now that Mahathir is back, so are the tags. On the plus side, it means that it is easy to identify the official you are dealing with, whatever the government department.

In the office, Malaysians traditional deference means younger workers are unlikely to question what a boss is doing (even if they worry it is wrong) or leave the office before the most senior employee has done so. As a result, it is common for Malaysians to spend long hours at work, not because they necessarily have work to do, but because they do not want to be the first to leave.

DOING BUSINESS

Relationships are the key to successful business dealings. In practice, this means that anyone who is working or doing business in the country does an awful of tea drinking and pleasant chit-chat with every person they meet. It is best to keep any conversation away from the sensitive issues (ethnicity and religion) and keep to generalities like the traffic and the weather. A few words of Malay can help smooth new encounters, even something as anodyne as '*selamat pagi*' (good morning) or '*selamat petang*' (good afternoon). Malaysians love it when foreigners try to speak their language and do not seem to care too much about anyone's pronunciation. It is the fact that someone tried that matters more.

Some business people like to do their deals on the golf course. Some test their partners out at karaoke. Whatever their preference, Malaysian business people are unlikely to jump quickly into a deal and will take their time to reach a decision.

Generally, they are reluctant to give an outright no to a request even when they know there is no chance that they will agree to it. Instead, they will find a million and one excuses not to say yes, and constantly delay and defer until the other party gives up. Likewise, they are unlikely to say yes immediately even if they are absolutely thrilled at the deal's prospects. Patience and understanding are crucial assets when it comes to working and doing business in Malaysia.

Malaysians are not as superstitious as some of their regional neighbours, at least when it comes to business, but do not be surprised if they opt for a date that is considered to be particularly auspicious to sign a document. For the Chinese, this may be chosen at a temple. A Malay might consult the *bomoh* and not only over the best date to sign an agreement. A company planning a large outdoor event may also consult the traditional healer to ensure that it does not rain.

Malaysians of all types enjoy an official event with speeches, ribbon-cutting and a VIP (usually a local politician or minister). Whether in a luxury hotel or outside at a ground-breaking ceremony, chairs are generally arranged with plush sofas at the front (for the VIP) and chairs of declining order of comfort for everyone else, reflecting everyone's relative stature. The more important the VIP guest, the fancier the event, but there will nearly always be food. Unless it is Ramadan (the fasting month), in which case an event may be scheduled for the late afternoon or early evening so everyone can break fast together.

SENSITIVITIES

Malaysia has long portrayed itself as a moderate Muslim country, but it is also true that many of the country's Muslims are considerably more conservative in their interpretation of their religion than they were in the past.

Muslims are supposed to pray five times a day, but Friday prayers are sacrosanct, and while most Malay women (and Malaysia's non-Muslims) will take the opportunity to head to the mall or enjoy a longer lunch, Malay men are expected to go to the mosque (there is talk in some states of prosecuting those who do not go to prayers). Most men will disappear around 12.30pm, carrying a prayer mat and wearing flip-flops so they are better prepared for their ablutions (the washing of feet prior to prayers). Most will not return until around 3pm.

Given Muslim prayer requirements, larger offices and public

spaces often have a small *surau* or prayer room. In smaller offices, Muslim staff may simply find a quiet space for their prayers, which could be a meeting room or an empty office. Be respectful of anyone you see carrying out their prayers.

Most company canteens, especially in government-linked businesses or major blue-chip firms, are *halal*. Smaller businesses with pantries may simply choose not to serve pork or advise staff who bring their own food not to eat any pork dishes while at the office.

Barefoot in the office

At some companies, particularly those run by Malays, it may be necessary to leave your shoes at the door. I remember arriving at Neelofa, a trendy hijab manufacturer founded by one of the country's most well-known actresses and models, to discover a pile of shoes outside. Inside, scores of women—barefoot or in socks—were browsing the rails for the latest headscarves.

GOVERNMENT OFFICES

Government offices are staffed overwhelmingly by Malaysia's ethnic Malays so it helps to be able to understand a few words of Malay (if only to find the right floor or to understand your queue number).

In reality, most foreigners will only need to go to government offices for business purposes (for meetings with senior civil servants or government ministers and deputy ministers) because Malaysians mostly navigate the nitty-gritty of forms and approvals that cover all manner of issues from immigration to tax. For higher-level meetings expect to be greeted with tooth-tinglingly sweet tea (even if you ask for no sugar, be prepared for the fact that it is likely still to have a teaspoon or two) and a selection of local Malay *kueh* or snacks like curry puffs. You may be offered coffee, but whatever the drink you should take a sip to be polite. Likewise with food, even if it is just a nibble.

Usually an agency or company will insist on giving you a memento of your visit; a plaque, a notebook, or something small, and they will probably all want a photo to commemorate the event and share on social media.

Anti-corruption policies are being tightened, especially under the new government, and it is common to see banners in government offices and government-linked companies explaining that gifts and hampers (popular gifts during the festive seasons) will not be accepted.

WORKING DAYS AND HOLIDAYS

Thanks to a federal political system and its multicultural population, Malaysia has a lot of public holidays. The major ones are Chinese New Year, Hari Raya Aidilfitri (Eid), Deepavali and Christmas, and a host of smaller festivals including Thaipusam (a festival unique to Tamils—Malaysia's population is one of the biggest in the world) and Nuzul al-Quran (the day marking the revelation of the Quran), are recognised throughout the country.

Each state also has its own holidays, mostly for its respective Sultan's birthday. In Borneo, the biggest festival is probably Hari Gawai (the harvest festival celebrated by the indigenous people). It is worth noting that some states (Kelantan, Kedah and Terengganu) do not recognise January 1 as a holiday, and in these states, as well as Johor, the working week runs from Sunday to Thursday.

The central bank maintains a list of all the holidays, and while employers are not required to recognise *all* the holidays, they must honour 11 of the national-level holidays, five of which are non-negotiable (depending on the state).

It is also not necessary for companies to honour the state holidays except for royal birthdays. In practice most companies seem to close their offices for most of them.

TAXATION

Only about 2.27 million Malaysians pay income tax. Most pay nothing because they simply do not earn enough to reach the threshold, which is RM3,100 (US$740) a month.

Malaysia operates a progressive taxation system and most people who are employed (the vast majority of expatriates) have their tax deducted monthly at source. The top rate (at time of writing) was 28 per cent (annual income of RM1 million/US$240,000) with a personal allowance for all individual taxpayers of RM9,000 (US$2,146).

Compared with many developed countries Malaysia offers little in the way of tax relief, but contributions to pensions and life insurance policies are deductible. There are also allowances for non-working spouses, children, those who care for elderly parents or disabled family members and a variety of 'lifestyle' reliefs covering reading and sport.

Be aware that the number of days that you are in the country will affect your tax status. If you are only in Malaysia for between 60 and 182 days then you are not considered a resident for tax purposes and will have to pay a flat rate tax of 28 per cent on all your earnings (non-residents do not receive allowances or relief). You can use the arrival and departure stamps in your passport to keep a tally on the number of days if you are a frequent traveller.

Malaysia's tax year follows the calendar year and every employee is required to file a tax return (known as the BE form, which is usually completed and calculated online) by the end of April the following year. Your employer will usually give you what is known as an EA form a couple of months beforehand, which details your income, and how much tax you have paid. Be aware that if you have 'home' flights these are taxable, and you will probably have to make an additional payment because employers do not include such benefits in the calculation of the monthly tax deduction. There are also sections to declare income from dividends and property rental in Malaysia. If you have an income from a business in Malaysia then you will need to complete what is known as a B form (also online), but you have until the end of June to do so. You are also expected to pay any tax owing by the submission date.

When you resign from a job (and you are on an employment pass that is tied to that job) you will need to clear your tax before you leave. Employers generally handle this. Any outstanding tax will need to be settled although any overpayment will be refunded.

Be aware that Malaysia's tax department has the power to carry out audits of individual tax payers for as many as seven years after a return has been filed and paid. It can also prevent those who fail to pay tax from leaving the country. Generally, officials only take this step once all other avenues have been exhausted.

> Malaysia has strict labour laws that are designed to protect workers and employees. This is a good thing, but it also means that if you are a manager or employer you must first make a serious attempt to help an employee improve before you can be justified in letting them go. At one place I was working, we had a team member who was not doing his job as it needed to be done. With the help of HR, we worked out an improvement plan, and then kept a detailed record of every meeting and conversation that took place about his performance. Each time, he insisted he wanted to improve, but the next day would carry on as before. It was only after two years, and a file full of evidence, that we were able to let him go.

CHAPTER 10

MALAYSIA IN BRIEF

*Genggamlah ia yang terdaya
sebelum ia hilang selama-lamanya.*

(Hold on to what you have,
before it's gone forever.)

— **Latiff Mohidin,** *Catatan Dua Baris*

Official Name
Malaysia

Capital
Kuala Lumpur

Administrative Centre
Putrajaya

Timezone
GMT +8

Telephone Country Code
+60

Flag
Made up of 14 equal-sized horizontal stripes in alternate red and white with a golden crescent and 14-pointed star on a dark blue rectangle in the top left-hand corner. It is often called the Jalur Gemilang (Stripes of Glory).

National Anthem
Negaraku (My Country)

Climate

Tropical. The southwest monsoon is between May and October, while the northeast monsoon is from October to February.

Land

Malaysia is made up of two distinct areas. West Malaysia or Peninsular Malaysia (divided into 11 states south of Thailand) and, across the South China Sea in Borneo, East Malaysia (Sabah and Sarawak).

Geographical coordinates

2 30 N, 112 30 E

Area

Total 329,847 square kilometres (Land: 328,657 square kilometres; Sea: 1,190 square kilometres)

Highest point

Mount Kinabalu (Sabah) at 4,095 metres

Natural resources

Natural gas, oil, palm oil, timber, bauxite, copper, iron, tin and rubber

Population

31.4 million (2017 estimate), with 80 per cent living in peninsular Malaysia.

Ethnic groups

Malays and indigenous people (known as *bumiputras*) 62 per cent, Chinese 21 per cent, Indian six per cent and others one per cent. About 10 per cent are non-citizens.

Languages and dialects
Bahasa Malaysia (the official language), English, Chinese languages (Mandarin, Cantonese, Hokkien, Hakka, Foochow, Hainanese), Tamil, Telugu, Malayalam and Punjabi. In Borneo there are numerous indigenous languages, including Iban and Kadazan.

Religion
Islam, Buddhism, Christianity, Hindu, Taoism, Sikh, Animism

Political system
Federal system with a constitutional monarchy. Parliament is based in Kuala Lumpur and made up of a 222-seat elected lower house (Dewan Rakyat) and an unelected 70-seat upper house (Dewan Negara). Every state has its own hereditary ruler except for Penang, Melaka, Sabah and Sarawak, which all have governors who are appointed by the federal government.

Main political parties
Democratic Action Party (DAP), People's Justice Party (Keadilan), Malaysian United Indigenous Party (PPBM) and National Trust Party (Amanah), United Malays National Organisation (UMNO), Malaysian Islamic Party (PAS), Malaysian Chinese Association (MCA), Malaysian Indian Congress (MIC)

Administrative divisions
Johor, Kedah, Kelantan, Melaka, Negri Sembilan, Pahang, Perak, Perlis, Pulau Pinang, Selangor, Terengganu (in the

Peninsular) and Sabah, and Sarawak (in Borneo). There are also three Federal Territories—Kuala Lumpur, Putrajaya and Labuan.

Legal system

English common law and Islamic law (with jurisdiction over Muslims in civil cases). The country's highest court is the Federal Court.

Industries

Peninsular Malaysia: palm oil and rubber processing, petroleum and natural gas, electronics and semiconductors, pharmaceuticals and medical technology, timber, tourism; Sabah: petroleum and natural gas, logging, tourism; Sarawak: petroleum and natural gas, logging

Exports

palm oil, timber, electronics and electronic equipment, oil and liquefied natural gas, solar panels, rubber and textiles

Imports

electronics, chemicals, iron and steel, vehicles

Major sea ports

Port Klang, Penang, Tanjung Pelepas, Bintulu. Large China-funded facilities under construction in Kuantan and Melaka.

Airports

The major gateway is the Kuala Lumpur International Airport. Malaysia Airports runs the country's major airports, with the exception of Johor Bahru, which is privately-operated.

Major airlines
AirAsia, Malaysia Airlines, Malindo Air

FAMOUS MALAYSIANS
Jemilah Mahmood
Dr Jemilah Mahmood was a doctor in Kuala Lumpur's eastern suburb of Ampang when she founded humanitarian relief organisation MERCY Malaysia in 2009. Over the next decade she deployed MERCY's corps of volunteer doctors and health workers into disaster zones across Asia and the Middle East. Her work attracted the attention of the UN where she was appointed an adviser to then Secretary-General Ban Ki-moon's Central Emergency Response Fund before heading the secretariat of the World Humanitarian Summit. In 2016, she joined the International Federation of the Red Cross.

Jimmy Choo
A shoemaker extraordinaire, Choo was born in Penang in 1961, and launched his own shoe label after moving to London. He opened his first shop in the city in 1986 and, having caught the attention of the fashion set and Princess Diana, co-founded his own brand—Jimmy Choo Ltd—with *Vogue* stylist Tamara Mellon a decade later. Choo has sold his stake in that business, but he continues to make handcrafted shoes as Jimmy Choo Couture.

Lat
Born Mohamad Nor Khalid in a village near Ipoh, Lat published his first cartoon as a teenager. Renowned for his distinctive drawing style, his cartoons with their subtle humour appeal across religion, race and culture. He is most

famous for the semi-autobiographical book, *Kampung Boy*, about a mischievous young boy with a mop of unruly dark hair (like Lat himself) who is constantly getting into trouble with his elders. Lat's reputation is such that he has long been allowed to poke fun at the country's sometimes ridiculous politics in a way that few others are able to.

Latiff Mohidin
Latiff Mohidin is arguably Malaysia's leading artist. Born in Penang in 1941, he is most famous for his series of sketches and paintings called *Pago Pago*, the product of a journey around Southeast Asia he made in the mid-1960s after returning from Berlin where he was a student. In 2018, Latiff was honoured with a show at the Pompidou Centre in Paris, organised in conjunction with the National Art Gallery in Singapore.

Lee Chong Wei
Lee Chong Wei started playing badminton at the age of 11, joined the national squad at 17 and has dominated the game in Malaysia for the past decade. A three-time Olympic silver medallist, Lee was ranked number one in the world over 199 consecutive weeks from August 2008 until June 2012.

Michelle Yeoh
Ipoh-born Michelle Yeoh won the Miss Malaysia title in 1983 when she was 20 years old before being spotted by a Hong Kong production firm and establishing herself as a star of Asian martial arts and action movies, with a reputation for doing her own stunts. Yeoh rose to international prominence starring alongside Pierce Brosnan in the 1997 James Bond

film, *Tomorrow Never Dies* and went on to appear in such critically-acclaimed movies as *Crouching Tiger*, *Hidden Dragon*. She plays Federation Captain Philippa Georgiou in *Star Trek: Discovery* franchise and most recently appeared as the icy matriarch Eleanor Young in *Crazy Rich Asians*.

Nicol David

Penang-born and Amsterdam-based Nicol David is one of the world's greatest-ever squash players. From August 2006, David was ranked the world's top squash player for 108 months in a row—an incredible nine years. She has also won the World Open title a record-breaking eight times. Her success in squash is a world away from her childhood ambition of following in her father's footsteps and becoming an engineer. David retired from the competitive game in 2019.

P. Ramlee and Saloma

A legendary Malaysian who worked as an actor, director, composer and songwriter. P. Ramlee was born Teuku Zakaria in Penang in 1929 when it was still part of the Straits Settlements and got the name Ramlee at school. By the time he died in 1973, at the age of just 44, he had acted in 66 movies and directed 25, and was famous not only in Malaysia, but also Singapore and Indonesia. His films are classics of Malay cinema and a window into a Malaysia and a way of life that has largely disappeared. His third wife, Singapore-born singer Saloma, was the epitome of 1960s Malaysian chic in her traditional kebaya, cat's eye make-up and coiffed hair. Together they were, as a local newspaper wrote in 2014, Malaysia's first (and perhaps only) celebrity power couple.

Ridzuan Puzi

Diagnosed with cerebral palsy when he was just a year old, Ridzuan won a gold medal and a place in Malaysian hearts in the Rio Games of 2016. Ridzuan's gold in the 100 metres T36 event was the first Malaysia had ever won at a Paralympics. The Perlis-born athlete followed up on his Paralympic success by breaking the world record with a time of 11.87 seconds at the Asian Games in Jakarta in 2018.

Tash Aw

Born in Taiwan to Malaysian parents and now living in London, Tash Aw spent his childhood in Malaysia. The author of the novels *The Harmony Silk Factory*, *Map of the Invisible World* and *Five Star Billionaire* has twice been longlisted for the Man Booker Prize. His only work of non-fiction, *The Face: Strangers on a Pier*, is a moving exploration of the migrant experience and an insight into life in Malaysia.

Tony Fernandes

The ebullient founder of AirAsia was an executive in the music industry before finding his niche in aviation after he convinced Mahathir, then nearing the end of his first stint as prime minister, to sell him the country's debt-ridden second airline for just one ringgit in 2001. Fernandes transformed the airline into one of the world's leading low-cost carriers offering flights across the Asia-Pacific. Fernandes was born in Malaysia but went to boarding school in the UK and graduated from the London School of Economics. He also owns the London-based football club Queens Park Rangers and has dabbled in Formula One.

Yuna

Born Yunalis Mat Zara'ai in the northern state of Kedah in 1986, Yuna is a self-taught Malaysian singer-songwriter who was discovered on MySpace. Now based in Los Angeles, she is most well-known for her duet with Usher on the single, *Crush*, which got to number three on the Billboard R&B chart and *Shine Your Way* (with Owl City) the theme song for the animated movie, *The Croods*.

Zeti Akhtar Aziz

Johor-born Zeti Akhtar Aziz was the first woman to head Malaysia's central bank, winning Mahathir's trust as acting governor when the country pegged the ringgit and introduced capital controls in the wake of the Asian Financial Crisis. Zeti was formally made governor in 2000 and held the position until 2016. She was appointed to the Council of Elders, the advisory body of eminent economists and financial experts for Malaysia's new government, in 2018.

CULTURE QUIZ

SITUATION 1

You're driving along the street in Kuala Lumpur and make a left turn at a red light in the mistaken belief it is allowed. Shortly after you turn the corner, you notice that a police patrol car is signalling you to pull over. You stop by the kerb and wind down your window as the officer walks towards the car. What do you do next?

A Hand over your driving licence and wait for the officer to explain the offence and write out a ticket.

B Hand over your driving licence, apologise and hope the officer will be charmed into letting you go without a fine.

C Give the officer a sly look and ask: "How can we settle this?"

Comments

A The action of a law-abiding resident.

B Always worth a try.

C 'How can we settle this?' is the Malaysian invitation to bribery and the subject of many an amusing dinner party tale. But while Malaysians will often laugh about traffic offences (and wait months until there is a discount before paying their fines), there is a genuine effort in the police force to stamp out corruption and it seems to be making headway. Do not contribute to a culture of corruption. You would not offer to bribe an officer at home so do not do it in Malaysia.

SITUATION 2

You have arranged an office meeting for 9.30am. At 9.15am one of your staff calls to let you know that they are running a 'bit late' probably 'because of the rain' but are on their way. What do you do?

Ⓐ Get angry and shout at them about their tardiness.

Ⓑ Listen to their story and explain, politely, that you value punctuality and expect your staff to be on time.

Comments

Ⓐ Screaming and shouting never achieves much, and even less in Malaysia. Don't let your frustration bubble over.

Ⓑ Malaysians are notorious for being poor timekeepers—hence the phrase 'Malaysian Rubber Time'. A Malaysian who tells you they are 'on their way' is probably just reversing their car out of their driveway. Explain the importance of punctuality, and tell them they should join the meeting as soon as they arrive at the office.

SITUATION 3

You need to go to the immigration office (or any other government department) and have taken a day off to do so. What should you wear?

Ⓐ A suit.

Ⓑ Shorts, T-Shirt and sandals.

Ⓒ Casual, but smart clothes.

Comments

Ⓐ Probably a bit much. And hot.

Ⓑ Too casual. Think about the kind of dress you would adopt visiting a government department at home. It is highly unlikely you would dress as if you were heading to the beach or hanging out with friends at home.

Ⓒ The best bet. Women should make sure any skirt is at the knee or below (trousers are an easier option) and their shoulders are covered. Some government offices and law courts have signs outside explaining the dress code.

SITUATION 4

You are invited to a Chinese wedding banquet. The invitation says the event is taking place in the ballroom of one Kuala Lumpur's fanciest hotels and starts at 7.30pm. There is no mention of a wedding list or gifts. What do you do?

Ⓐ Arrive at 7.30pm dressed in the most glamorous outfit you can find with a beautifully-wrapped toaster as a gift for the happy couple.

Ⓑ Arrive at 7.30pm, smartly dressed with an *angpow* filled with crisp new notes (in RM50s or RM100s) that roughly match the likely cost per head of the banquet.

Ⓒ Arrive at 8.00pm, dressed smartly and clutching an *angpow* filled with crisp new notes.

Comments

Ⓐ If you get to the banquet at 7.30pm you will probably find you are one of the earliest to arrive. You might, however, find it a good opportunity to mingle and chat with the other early birds or improve your karaoke skills. If you wear your most-glamorous outfit you might feel a little over-dressed but you can always check with the family ahead of time. Generally, the posher the venue the more glamorous the clothes. You might not want to bring a toaster though.

Ⓑ Cash is king when it comes to Chinese weddings so bring the *angpow* and, clinical as it may sound, many guests really do work out how much to put inside the envelope on the basis of the swankiness of the venue.

Ⓒ Arriving at 8.00pm means most people will have arrived and you will not have to wait too long for the start of the banquet proper.

SITUATION 5

You are invited to a house-warming at the house of your Muslim neighbour who you are just getting to know. They are perhaps more than an acquaintance, but not quite a good friend. You have heard that they enjoy a good Bordeaux and are thinking about bringing a bottle. A few other people are going too, but you are not sure who. What do you do?

Ⓐ Take along the bottle of Bordeaux and offer it to your host.

Ⓑ Err on the side of caution and take along some chocolates or something else sweet.

Ⓒ Show up empty-handed.

Comments

Ⓐ Not a good idea. Some Muslims do drink, but it is not something they tend to publicise.

Ⓑ A much better approach. Malaysians are generally appreciative of chocolates, cookies and cakes. If it is a speciality from your home country so much the better. Make sure it's pork-free.

Ⓒ Not advisable. You would not arrive at a party in your home country without a gift for the host. It is the same in Malaysia.

DOS AND DON'TS

DOS

- Learn a bit of Malay. Malaysians are always thrilled when a foreigner starts off a presentation with '*selamat datang*' no matter how badly they might say it. Malaysians love to talk politics, and the state of the nation, so do try to join in, but try not to tell them how they should do things.
- Use your right hand when paying for goods, eating or shaking hands. The left hand is seen as unclean.
- Be careful about numbers. Malaysians are quite superstitious and the Chinese in particular are fascinated by lucky and unlucky numbers. One number you definitely want to avoid is the number four (which sounds like the word for death in Chinese).
- Make sure you are appropriately dressed when visiting a government office. It is not necessary to wear a formal outfit or suit, but dress respectfully. The same goes for temples and mosques. Some may even post a dress code on a signboard outside. Anyone who is incorrectly dressed risks being sent away.
- Turn your mobile phone off in the cinema or during events. There will be regular reminders, but there is always someone who forgets. Do not be that person.
- Be aware that sodomy remains a criminal offence in Malaysia and that gay people are often the targets of attack by religious officials and politicians. While acceptance and understanding is growing among younger Malaysians, the level of vitriol directed at this minority group is often alarming.

- Be aware that a white person may well be called *mat salleh* or *ang moh* although not always to their face. These terms are not meant to be rude, although it can seem that way.
- Be aware that Malaysia has no legislation on race relations or equal opportunities.
- Try any food or drink that is offered—even just a tiny bite is enough.
- Try to use the LRT and MRT to get around if you live close to one of the stations. The trains are clean and generally reliable.
- Be careful when flagging down taxis. Drivers frequently refuse to turn on the meter, claiming rain or traffic or any other excuse they can come up with. Do not be taken for a ride. You can book taxis through Grab or get the number of a driver who impressed you and make them your regular.
- Keep to the speed limit. Fines are issued direct to your home address and you will not be able to renew your car tax if they are not paid.
- Get a Touch N Go card. Most tolled roads no longer accept cash. You can buy the card wherever you see the Touch N Go logo and add cash at petrol stations, newsagents and even on the road itself (look for the lane marked '*Tambah Nilai*') although there is usually a long queue.

DON'TS

- Wear your shoes inside someone's home. Slip them off before you enter. The same applies to Hindu temples and mosques.

- Point with you index finger, which is considered rude. Use your thumb instead.

- Kiss in public. Locals never do, regardless of ethnicity or religion. Physical displays of affection are even more frowned upon in the conservative states of the east coast.

- Forget the word '*makan*'. It is possibly the most important one in Malaysia and means 'eat'.

- Malaysians sometimes like to eat more traditional foods (banana leaf rice, for instance) with their hands, but they will only ever use their right hand. Do not use your left hand to eat, pass, touch or handle any food.

- Use your mobile phone when driving. It is an offence (even if you see lots of Malaysians doing the same).

RESOURCE GUIDE

COMMUNICATIONS

Phone area codes for fixed lines:

* **Kuala Lumpur**   03
* **Kedah/Perlis/Penang**   04
* **Perak**   05
* **Melaka/Negri Sembilan**   06
* **Johor**   07
* **Kelantan/Terengganu/Pahang**   09
* **Sarawak**   082–086
* **Sabah**   087–089

The main mobile operators are Celcom (part of Telekom Malaysia), Maxis and Digi. Mobile numbers start with 010/0 11/012/013/014/016/017/018/019 depending on whether they are pre-paid or post-paid numbers and are followed by seven digits. Mobile phone numbers are linked to individuals rather than the operators. Companies have branches in all the main shopping centres.

Internet services are provided by Telekom (Unifi), Maxis, Time, Yes and other smaller operators. You can sign up at their outlets in the shopping malls or online. It will usually take a few days before the service is operational.

Websites for the major mobile and internet providers (they are also active on social media):

https://www.maxis.com.my/en/personal/support.html
https://unifi.com.my/personal
https://www.time.com.my
https://www.yes.my

Astro is the only satellite pay-TV company. It offers a variety of international and domestic channels. You will need to get an approved technician to install the dish and connect the service. The different packages are explained on the website: www.astro.com.my. Netflix, iFlix and other online streaming apps are also available.

Post offices (Pejabat Pos) operate in most towns in Malaysia. They offer a range of services including car tax renewal, tax and bill payment.

TRAVEL

Airlines

Malaysia has three main airlines, which offer frequent fare deals. Most people book online, although it is still possible to go through a travel agent or to book direct with the airline.

www.malaysiaairlines.com

www.fireflyz.com.my (part of Malaysia Airlines. Flies from the old airport at Subang)

www.airasia.com

www.malindoair.com

Airports

Arrivals and departures for the main Kuala Lumpur International Airport are available online at www.klia.com.my. The website also has information on the facilities available at each of the two terminals—the main terminal for full-service carriers and klia2 for low-cost carriers like AirAsia.

An express train runs from KL Sentral to KLIA every 15 mins from 0500 to 0040 (last departure). The journey takes 26 minutes with a stop at the main terminal (directly beneath arrivals) followed by the klia2 terminal. There is also a cheaper commuter train, which takes longer. Tickers are usually

cheaper bought online in advance. www.kliaekspres.com.
There are also bus services to the airport. Taxis and airport
limousines—despite the name no fancier than an average
car—are available, but many people now use Grab to book
either a taxi or a private car.

Railway
Malaysia's railway company is Keretapi Tanah Melayu Berhad
(KTMB). You can buy tickets at railway stations including KL
Sentral or online at www.ktmb.com.my for most destinations.
Demand is usually high over the festive seasons so it is wise
to book ahead if you want to travel at those times.

EMERGENCIES
Be aware that the person who answers the phone may not
speak English, especially outside the major towns.
- **Emergency (Police, Fire (Bomba), Ambulance)**
  999 or 112
- **Telekom Malaysia**
  100
- **Tenaga Nasional (electricity, street lights)**
  15454
- **Syabas (water)**
  1800 88 5252 www.syabas.com.my
- **Alam Flora (rubbish, neighbourhood cleanliness)**
  1800 88 7472
- **Department of Environment (to report open burning)**
  1800 88 2727
- **Dewan Bandaraya Kuala Lumpur (KL City Hall)**
  www.dbkl.gov.my
  24-hour hotline (for all complaints)   1800 88 3255
  Enforcement emergency (24 hours)   03 4024 4424

Snakes/bee hives (24 hours)   03 9284 3434

HOSPITALS
Kuala Lumpur and Selangor
- **Kuala Lumpur General Hospital (government)**
  03 2165 5555
- **University of Malaya Medical Centre**
  03 7949 4422 (general), 03 7949 2500 (ambulance)
- **Pantai Hospital Kuala Lumpur**
  03 2296 0888 (general), 03 2296 0999
  (emergency/ambulance)
- **Gleneagles Hospital**
  03 4141 3000 (general). Appointments can also be
  made via WhatsApp on 016 339 3000 during office
  hours. 03 4141 3131 (ambulance)
- **KPJ Ampang Puteri Hospital**
  03 4289 5000 (general)
- **Prince Court Medical Centre**
  03 2160 0000 (24 hours). Appointments can also
  be made via WhatsApp on 012 999 7262 during
  office hours. 03 2160 0999 (emergency).
- **Subang Jaya Medical Centre / ParkCity Medical
  Centre / Ara Damansara Medical Centre**
  03 5639 1212 (24 hours). It is also possible to
  make appointments for all three hospitals via
  WhatsApp (24 hours) 019 277 6316.

Penang
- **Island Hospital Penang**
  04 228 8222 (general), 04 226 8527 (emergency)
- **Gleneagles Medical Centre Penang**
  04 227 6111 (general), 04 220 2108 (emergency)

- **KPJ Penang Specialist Hospital**
  04 548 6688 (general), 04 548 6799 (emergency)
- **Pantai Hospital Penang**
  04 643 8888 (general), 04 643 8799
  (emergency/ambulance)

Johor
- **KPJ Johor Specialist Hospital**
  07 225 3000 (general), 07 225 3199 (emergency)
- **Gleneagles Medini Hospital**
  07 560 1000 (general). It is also possible to make
  appointments via WhatsApp on 017 847 1000
  during office hours. 07 560 1111 (emergency)

MONEY
Banking
The leading domestic banks are Maybank and CIMB. Both
have extensive branch networks extending into small towns,
but foreign banks provide better international services. During
the week, banks usually open from around 9am until 4pm,
but some open slightly earlier and close a little later. Hours
may change on Fridays.

Credit cards (Visa and Mastercard) are accepted more or
less everywhere except, perhaps, in more remote locations.
All cards are PIN-enabled. American Express and Diners are
not common.

Bank Negara provides useful information on consumer
banking as well as warnings about the latest financial scams.
www.bnm.gov.my

- **CIMB**
  www.cimb.com.my

- **HSBC Bank Malaysia**
  www.hsbc.com.my
- **Maybank**
  https://www.maybank2u.com.my
- **Public Bank**
  https://www.pbebank.com
- **Standard Chartered Bank**
  https://www.sc.com/my/

CASH

ATMs are most commonly found in bank branches and in shopping centres. Local banks have a more extensive network extending into smaller towns. Many banks are encouraging cashless payment through PayWave and other initiatives.

INSURANCE

From protecting your family, to your car and the contents of your home, insurance is easy to find in Malaysia. Many banks sell insurance products, which are usually guaranteed by Bank Negara, the central bank. It also provides useful guides to buying insurance in Malaysia. www.bnm.gov.my

TAXES

The tax department website explains the Malaysian taxation system and provides downloadable forms. Most people file their taxes online. www.hasil.gov.my

SHOPPING

The main shopping districts in KL are in Bukit Bintang (the stretch from Lot 10 to the Pavilion Shopping Centre), KLCC (the eponymous shopping centre plus Avenue K, which is opposite and the newly opened Four Seasons next door).

Bukit Bintang and KLCC are joined by an underground and elevated walkway, which takes about 10 minutes depending on how quickly you walk.

In the suburbs, MidValley Megamall is hugely popular with Malaysians and packed at the weekends. The more luxurious shops (think Tod's, DKNY and Louis Vuitton are in The Gardens section while the high street brands like Zara, Mango and Top Shop are in the Megamall side. There are two cinemas, as well as restaurants, gyms and even a contemporary art gallery.

Bangsar Shopping Centre (Jalan Maarof) is popular with expatriates and more well-heeled locals who like to hang out at the cafés. Publika (near Mont Kiara and Sri Hartamas) is a neighbourhood mall known for its vast supermarket (complete with restaurants), monthly craft markets and creative vibe. It has a theatre and exhibition space, as well as some local art galleries among the obligatory cafés and restaurants.

In Penang, the main shopping malls are Gurney Plaza, Gurney Paragon and Queensbay Mall. The World Heritage site has traditional shops (signboard carvers, rattan weavers, joss stick makers) and a few contemporary craft shops.

SUPERMARKETS
- **TMC, Lucky Garden, Bangsar**
- **Jason's, Bangsar Shopping Centre**
- **Village Grocer, Bangsar Village**
- **BIG, branches in Publika, DC Mall, Jalan Batai**
- **Isetan, KLCC**
- **Cold Storage, KLCC**
- **Jaya Grocer, branches at Intermark and Kiara 163**

BOOKSHOPS

Kinokuniya in KLCC has a huge selection of fiction and non-fiction, books in Chinese and a specialist art and graphic books' department on a mezzanine along with a café. Local chains MPH and Times (Publika, Pavilion and elsewhere) offer a reasonable choice of children's books while Popular (major shopping centres) is known for Chinese-language books and textbooks.

A number of independent bookshops have opened around KL and Penang in recent years. Silverfish Books (Bangsar Village 2) was a pioneer and has its own publishing arm, while Tintabudi (Zhongshan Building, Kampung Attap) offers hard-to-find works on politics, history and philosophy and is right next door to a delightful hole-in-the-wall coffee shop. In Penang, Gerakbudaya is worth a visit for its selection of Asia-focussed literature and non-fiction. It also has a sister store, Hikayat, on Victoria Street.

EXPAT ASSOCIATIONS

- **Internations**
  A web-based network that helps people of all nationalities connect with new friends as they move around the world. It operates in 420 cities around the world including Kuala Lumpur where it organises regular social and cultural events.
  https://www.internations.org

- **Association of British Women in Malaysia**
  Based in Bangsar. The association helps expat women of any nationality settle in and make friends through coffee mornings, reading clubs and sports. It also maintains a list of organisations that need volunteers.

http://www.abwm.com.my
Tel: 03 2284 4407

- **Malaysia-Australia-New Zealand Association (MANZA)**
  A group for expatriates from Australia and New Zealand,
  but all are welcome to join.
  http://www.manza.org
  Tel: 03 2284 7145

- **American Association of Malaysia**
  A support group for Americans and their families living
  in Malaysia that also helps connect expats with local
  volunteer opportunities.
  https://www.americanassociationofmy.com
  Tel: 03 2142 0611

- **Canadian Association of Malaysia**
  The association for Canadians and anyone with an interest
  in Canada. CAM organises social events and gets involved
  in voluntary work.
  http://www.canadians-in-kl.com

- **Ibu Family Resource Group**
  A support group for new Mums, both local and expatriate,
  and those with young families run by volunteer women. Ibu
  hosts playgroups, workshops and family events.
  https://www.ibufamily.org

- **The Japan Club of Kuala Lumpur**
  http://www.jckl.org.my
  Tel: 03 2274 2274

- **St. David's Society**
  The society for Wales and all things Welsh. The society has been in operation for 60 years.
  https://www.facebook.com/StDavidsSocietyMalaysia/

- **The Royal Society of St. George**
  England's 'premier patriotic organisation' which was founded in the 19th century. Has branches in Kuala Lumpur and Sabah.
  http://www.rssg.org.uk

- **Selangor St. Andrew's Society**
  Established in Malaysia in 1887 making it one of the oldest expat societies in the country. Famous for Burns Night and the annual St. Andrew's Ball.
  http://www.ssas-online.com

- **St. Patrick's Society of Selangor**
  The society founded in honour of St. Patrick, the patron saint of Ireland, has been in operation since 1925 and organises an annual ball as well as many other social events throughout the year.
  http://www.stpatsoc.org

CLUBS

- **Royal Selangor Club aka 'The Spotted Dog'**
  The club was founded in 1884 and overlooks Dataran Merdeka in the old heart of Kuala Lumpur. Women and children are still not allowed in the bar. The club has a sports ground near Mont Kiara.
  www.rsc.org.my
  Tel: 03 2692 7166

- **Royal Lake Club**
  Founded in 1890 and located in the lush surroundings of the Lake Gardens between parliament and the city centre.
  www.royallakeclub.org.my
  Tel: 03 2698 7878

- **Royal Selangor Polo Club**
  Founded in 1902, the Royal Selangor Polo Club focusses on equestrian activities although it is not necessary to be a rider to join.
  www.theroyalselangorpoloclub.com

- **The Raintree Club of Kuala Lumpur**
  Near the Polo Club in Ampang Hilir, the Raintree Club was established in 1983.
  www.raintree.com.my
  Tel: 03 4257 9066

- **Bukit Kiara Equestrian and Country Resort**
  Overlooking Bukit Kiara, as well as offering an extensive riding club and school, Bukit Kiara offers a host of other sporting facilities including a swimming pool, sports arena and golf course. Berjaya Clubs also has operates a number of other sporting and golf clubs.
  www.berjayaclubs.com/kiara
  Tel: 03 2093 1222

SCHOOLS

Note: Many of these English-language curriculum schools provide specialised language support to speakers of English as an additional language.

- **Alice Smith School**
Founded in 1946 and one of the oldest British international schools in the region. The primary and secondary schools are on separate campuses.
www.alice-smith.edu.my
Tel: 03 2148 3674 (primary)
Tel: 03 9543 3688 (secondary)

- **Australian International School of Malaysia, Seri Kembangan**
An Australian education on a purpose-built campus for all ages up to university entrance.
www.aism.edu.my
Tel: 03 8949 5000

- **British International School of Kuala Lumpur, Petaling Jaya**
One of the newer schools catering to children aged from two to 18 years old.
www.nordangliaeducation.com/our-schools/malaysia/kuala-lumpur/british-international
Tel: 03 7727 7775

- **Lycée Française Kuala Lumpur**
A French education from early years to university foundation.
www.lfkl.edu.my
Tel: 03 6250 4415

- **Garden International School, Mont Kiara**
Founded in 1971 and provides a British curriculum education from early years up to Year 13. Garden is

the biggest private school in Malaysia with some 2,200 students.
www.gardenschool.edu.my
Tel: 03 6209 6888

- **International School of Kuala Lumpur**
  Established in 1965 and the pre-eminent American curriculum school in Malaysia, offering elementary, middle and high school education.
  www.iskl.edu.my
  Tel: 03 4813 5000

- **KDU International School**
  A British curriculum school on a purpose-built site in Kota Damansara. As well as iGCSEs and A-Levels, it also offers the International Baccalaureate
  international.srikdu.edu.my
  Tel: 03 6145 3888

- **Tenby Schools**
  Founded in Ipoh in 1960 by British expatriates, Tenby now operates a growing group of schools including competitively-priced British curriculum international schools in Ipoh, Penang, Setia Alam and Miri (Sarawak) that cater to children between the ages of 3 and 18.
  www.tenby.edu.my (phone numbers for each school can be found on the website)

BOARDING SCHOOLS
- **Kolej Tuanku Ja'afar, Seremban, Negri Sembilan**
  A British curriculum school across 80 acres of parkland near Seremban. The school, popularly known as KTJ,

offers boarding from the age of 11.
www.ktj.edu.my
Tel: 06 758 2561

- **Epsom College, Bandar Enstek, Negri Sembilan**
  The Malaysian campus of the UK independent school.
  Pupils can attend for the day or board.
  www.epsomcollege.edu.my
  Tel: 06 240 4188

- **Marlborough College, Iskandar Puteri, Johor**
  The Malaysian campus of the British independent school
  Marlborough College. The school caters to boys and girls
  aged from three to 18 with an option to board.
  www.marlboroughcollegemalaysia.org
  Tel: 07 560 2200

TRADE AND BUSINESS ASSOCIATIONS

- **British Malaysian Chamber of Commerce (BMCC)**
  The BMCC was established in 1963 to boost bilateral
  trade between Malaysia and the UK by providing
  business networking opportunities and trading support to
  companies in both countries.
  www.bmcc.org.my
  Tel: 03 2163 1784

- **American Malaysian Chamber of Commerce
  (Amcham)**
  Founded in 1978, Amcham is the voice of US business
  in Malaysia. It organises lunch and dinner talks, often
  with senior government officials, and regular briefings on
  business and economic policies.

www.amcham.org.my
- Tel: 03 2283 3407

- **EU-Malaysian Chamber of Commerce and Industry (EUMCCI)**
  The business association supporting European Union businesses in Malaysia. It organises regular lunch talks, conferences and social events designed to deepen understanding between Europe and Malaysia and deepen business ties.
  www.eumcci.com
  Tel: 03 2162 6298

- **Bankers Club Malaysia**
  The Bankers Club was founded in 1987 as a private club for senior business people, community leaders and their associates. It has private dining rooms but also offers a range of talks and other social events.
  www.bankersclub.com.my
  Tel: 03 2142 4166

EMBASSIES

- **EU in Malaysia**
  The delegation to the EU, headed by the EU Ambassador, is deeply engaged in Malaysia politically, economically and culturally. Its film festival is one of the year's cultural highlights.
  eeas.europa.eu/delegations/malaysia/area/contacts_en
  Tel: 03 2723 7373

- **British High Commission**

  The British High Commission has moved from its own building to an office tower off Jalan Ampang in the city centre. It provides some notary and documentary services as well as marriage letters should you be marrying a Malaysian.

  www.gov.uk/world/organisations/british-high-commission-kuala-lumpur

  Tel: 03 2170 2200

- **US Embassy**

  The US Embassy is located in its own building on Jalan Tun Razak. It provides a range of services to citizens, and Malaysians wanting to visit the US, and organises a range of cultural events.

  my.usembassy.gov

  Tel: 03 2168 5000

- **High Commission of Australia**

  Australia's High Commission in Malaysia is across from the Petronas Twin Towers on Jalan Yap Kwan Seng.

  https://malaysia.highcommission.gov.au

  Tel: 03 2146 5555

- **Embassy of Japan**

  Japan's Embassy is just off Jalan Tun Razak and is gradually being surrounded by high-rise condominiums. Japan also has a Consulate-General in Penang and a consular office in Kota Kinabalu.

  https://www.my.emb-japan.go.jp/itprtop_en/index.html

  Tel: 03 2177 2600

- **Embassy of the Republic of Korea**
  South Korea's embassy is on the road towards Ampang near the Gleneagles Hospital.
  http://overseas.mofa.go.kr/my-en/index.do
  Tel: 03 4251 2336

GENERAL COUNTRY INFORMATION

- **Government departments and useful information on permits etc.**
  The site is in Bahasa Malaysia, but some sections are in English.
  www.malaysia.gov.my

- **General tourist information for Malaysia**
  www.malaysia.travel/en/my (visitor site)
  www.tourism.gov.my (corporate site)
  HQ: 03 8891 8000
  Tourism info line 1 300 88 5050

Individual states also have their own tourism promotion offices.

- **Information on Penang**
  https://mypenang.gov.my
  Tel: 04 264 3456

- **Information on Sarawak**
  Sarawak Tourism Board
  Tel: 082 423 600
  www.sarawaktourism.com

- **Information on Sabah**
  Sabah Tourism Board
  www.sabahtourism.com
  Tel: 088 212 121

- **Information on Iskandar, Johor**
  http://iskandarmalaysia.com.my

CULTURE AND HERITAGE

- **Malaysian Culture Group**
  Set up in KL in 1983, the Malaysian Culture Group
  organises lectures, tours and workshops for members
  to learn about Malaysia, its history and its peoples.
  www.mcgkl.org

- **Badan Warisan Malaysia**
  Malaysia's leading heritage non-profit, Badan Warisan is
  based in a lovingly restored old Malay house in the city
  centre and organises regular talks, as well as lobbying
  the government to protect the country's heritage. It
  also operates a small museum, No. 8 Heeren Street, in
  Melaka; a restoration of an 18th century shophouse.
  www.badanwarisanmalaysia.org
  Tel: 03 2144 9273

- **Malaysian Philharmonic Orchestra**
  The MPO made its debut in 1998 and is based in the
  Twin Towers in a purpose-built auditorium. Each season
  the orchestra performs from the classical repertoire, and
  has played host to internationally acclaimed performers
  from Kiri Te Kanawa to Vladimir Ashkenazy.
  http://mpo.com.my
  Tel: 03 2331 7007 (ticket booking)

- **Islamic Arts Museum**

  Housed close to the National Mosque in Kuala Lumpur, the Islamic Arts Museum is the largest in Southeast Asia with an exquisite collection that focuses on the Asian region.

  http://www.iamm.org.my

  Tel: 03 2092 7070

- **Ilham Gallery**

  A privately-funded public art gallery in a Norman Foster-designed tower in the city centre, that is dedicated to supporting the understanding and enjoyment of Malaysian art. It also organises a programme of talks and children's workshops in conjunction with its exhibitions.

  www.ilhamgallery.com

PETS

- **SPCA Selangor**

  Founded in 1958, the SPCA is the country's leading animal welfare association (call their emergency line if you find an animal in distress). The shelter in Ampang Jaya is also the place to adopt a cat or dog.

  www.spca.org.my

Boarding

- **Doghouse Broga**

  Like a five-star resort for dogs in Negri Sembilan. You might want to stay yourself.

  https://www.doghousebroga.com

  Tel: +6-012 207 3071 (Meng/Stephanie)

- **Mamadog Pet Services**

  Grooming, cage-less boarding and even relocation for your 'furkids'.

  www.mamadog.com.my

  Tel: 03 9074 4753

- **Scallywags Boarding Cattery**

  Scallywags offers outdoor boarding in a tranquil garden environment. Book early for peak periods.

  http://www.scallywags-malaysia.com

  03 7877 1507

Most vets offer boarding for much cheaper rates than a kennels or cattery, but dogs and cats may be kept in the same area and confined to a small cage.

FURTHER READING

CLASSICS

The Malay Archipelago, Alfred Russel Wallace, 1869.
Written in the 19th century, an exploration of the area's flora, fauna and natural history.

The Golden Chersonese, Isabella Bird, 1883
A travelogue from an intrepid explorer. A fascinating insight into a time that has long gone.

The Malayan Trilogy, Anthony Burgess, 1956–1959
Set in post-war Malaya, Burgess' three books (Time for a Tiger, Enemy in the Blanket, Beds in the East) depict the dying days of Empire and the emergence of an independent country. Burgess taught at the Malay College Kuala Kangsar, and later in Kelantan becoming fluent in Malay.

NON-FICTION

Among the Believers, VS Naipal, 1981
After the Iranian Revolution, the winner of the Nobel Prize for Literature spent six months travelling through a number of Muslim countries including Malaysia where he met a young 'firebrand', Anwar Ibrahim.

A History of Malaysia, Barbara Watson Andaya and Leonard Y. Andaya, 1982
Arguably the definitive account of how Malaysia came to

be from two University of Hawaii professors. The book was first published in 1982 and a third edition in 2017.

A Malaysian Journey, Rehman Rashid, 1993

Malaysian journalist and writer Rehman Rashid wrote this bestselling love letter to Malaysia on his return to his homeland in the early 90s. In 2016, he followed it up with Peninsula, wondering aloud what had happened to his country.

Malaysia's Political Economy: Politics, Patronage and Profits, Jomo Kwame Sundaram and Edmund Terence Gomez, 1997

A forensic insight into how Malaysia, and particularly UMNO (the party that dominated Malaysia from independence until 2018) got rich. Gomez and Jomo were both professors at the University of Malaya when the book was published. Jomo was appointed to the new government's Council of Elders, an advisory body, in 2018.

Malaysian Maverick, Barry Wain, 2009

An exhaustively researched and highly readable profile of Mahathir written by the late former Wall Street Journal reporter Barry Wain. The book traces Mahathir's life and political career until his first retirement from politics in 2003.

Floating on a Malayan Breeze: Travels in Malaysia and Singapore, Sudir Thomas Vadaketh, 2012

A young Singaporean's bicycle trip around Malaysia is a journey into the history and culture not only of Malaysia but also of Singapore, and the two nations' sibling rivalry.

The Face: Strangers on a Pier, Tash Aw, 2015

A slim but far from slight exploration of modern Asia told through the lens of Aw's own family story of migration and adaptation.

Billion Dollar Whale, Bradley Hope and Tom Wright, 2018

Parties with A-listers, Cristal on tap, luxury super yachts, Manhattan penthouses and the best diamonds other people's money can buy. Billion Dollar Whale tells the story of a mild-mannered Malaysian financier called Jho Low and an audacious scheme to siphon billions of dollars from state fund, 1MDB. The scandal led to investigations in at least six countries and the fall of Malaysian prime minister Najib Razak. A truly rollicking read.

FICTION

The Harmony Silk Factory, Tash Aw, 2005

Aw set his first novel in Penang on the eve of the Japanese occupation. The book won the Whitbread First Novel Award in 2005 and was described as being "as elusive as it is exotic."

A Gift of Rain, Tan Twan Eng, 2007

The debut work from Penang-born, South Africa-based Tan Twan Eng was longlisted for the Man Booker Prize. Like Aw's book it is set in Penang at the outbreak of World War Two and tells the story of a young man—half Chinese and half British—who discovers the Japanese diplomat he thought a friend is not all he seems.

State of Emergency, Jeremy Tiang, 2017

The debut novel of New York-based Singaporean writer and lawyer Jeremy Tang tackles the left-wing movements in Malaysia and Singapore in the mid-20th century, the Communist insurgency and its impact on families and communities.

Once We Were There, Bernice Chauly, 2018

The first novel from Bernice Chauly, writer, poet and director of the annual George Town Literary Festival. The book is the first to be set in the tumultuous years that followed Anwar's dismissal and incarceration on charges of sodomy.

The Weight of Our Sky, Hanna Alkaf, 2019

The first novel from young adult author and former journalist Hanna Alkaf and set at the time of the May 1969 riots was a publishing sensation when it was released in 2019. While pitched at young people age 12 and over, the moving evocation of one of the most sensitive moments in Malaysian history attracted readers far beyond its target market.

ABOUT THE AUTHOR

Kate Mayberry was born in the United Kingdom and long dreamed of living and working overseas. After a brief flirtation with Russia, she moved to Southeast Asia in the early 1990s and never left. After a few years working as a journalist in Singapore, she moved to Kuala Lumpur in 1999 where she has continued to report on Malaysia and the wider Asia-Pacific (with the occasional foray into Sri Lanka).

INDEX

Titles in the **CultureShock!** series:

Argentina	France	Philippines
Australia	Germany	Portugal
Austria	Great Britain	Russia
Bahrain	Greece	San Francisco
Bali	Hawaii	Saudi Arabia
Beijing	Hong Kong	Scotland
Belgium	Hungary	Sri Lanka
Berlin	India	Shanghai
Bolivia	Ireland	Singapore
Borneo	Italy	South Africa
Bulgaria	Jakarta	Spain
Brazil	Japan	Sri Lanka
Cambodia	Korea	Sweden
Canada	Laos	Switzerland
Chicago	London	Syria
Chile	Malaysia	Taiwan
China	Mauritius	Thailand
Costa Rica	Morocco	Tokyo
Cuba	Munich	Travel Safe
Czech Republic	Myanmar	Turkey
Denmark	Netherlands	United Arab Emirates
Dubai	New Zealand	USA
Ecuador	Norway	Vancouver
Egypt	Pakistan	Venezuela
Finland	Paris	Vietnam

For more information about any of these titles, please contact the Publisher via email at: genref@sg.marshallcavendish.com or visit our website at: www.marshallcavendish.com/genref